The Risk of Compressed Modernity

In memory of
Ulrich Beck

The Risk of Compressed Modernity

Chang Kyung-Sup

polity

Copyright © Chang Kyung-Sup 2025

The right of Chang Kyung-Sup to be identified as Author of this Work has been asserted in accordance with the UK Copyright, Designs and Patents Act 1988.

First published in 2025 by Polity Press

Polity Press
65 Bridge Street
Cambridge CB2 1UR, UK

Polity Press
111 River Street
Hoboken, NJ 07030, USA

All rights reserved. Except for the quotation of short passages for the purpose of criticism and review, no part of this publication may be reproduced, stored in a retrieval system or transmitted, in any form or by any means, electronic, mechanical, photocopying, recording or otherwise, without the prior permission of the publisher.

ISBN-13: 978-1-5095-6048-6 (hardback)
ISBN-13: 978-1-5095-6049-3 (paperback)

A catalogue record for this book is available from the British Library.

Library of Congress Control Number: 2024948788

Typeset in 10.5 on 12 pt Sabon
by Cheshire Typesetting Ltd, Cuddington, Cheshire
Printed and bound in Great Britain by CPI Group (UK) Ltd, Croydon

The publisher has used its best endeavors to ensure that the URLs for external websites referred to in this book are correct and active at the time of going to press. However, the publisher has no responsibility for the websites and can make no guarantee that a site will remain live or that the content is or will remain appropriate.

Every effort has been made to trace all copyright holders, but if any have been overlooked the publisher will be pleased to include any necessary credits in any subsequent reprint or edition.

For further information on Polity, visit our website:
politybooks.com

CONTENTS

Preface	vi
Introduction: Compressed Modernity and Its Structural Risks	1

Part I Democracy, Capitalism, Social Class

1 Borrowed Democracy, State-Projective Politics, and Institutional Functional Conflations	23
2 Normal Corruption: Utilitarian Institutional Dualities and Technocratized Authoritarian (In)justice	45
3 Class Contradictions of State Capitalist Industrialism: The "*Chaebol* Republic"	64
4 The Proletarian Predicament of Developmental Compression: Social Conditions of Flexibly Complex Capitalism	88

Part II Culture, Family, Life Risk

5 Reflexive Postcoloniality: Intellectual and Cultural Contradictions of Compressed Modernity	109
6 Compressed Modernity, Gender, and Obfuscated Family Crisis: Individualization without Individualism	125
7 Complex Risk Society: Risk Components of Compressed Modernity	145

Part III Prospect

8 A Beckian Metamorphosis?	161

Notes	172
References	195
Index	209

PREFACE

On a July evening in 2014, I had a lengthy chat with Ulrich Beck at an outdoor café of Seoul National University's guesthouse. We were discussing, among other issues, how correctly or erroneously Ulrich's theoretical ideas and analytical judgments were understood and utilized by South Koreans and other enthusiastic subscribers to his visionary scholarship. Ironically, not entirely without Ulrich's perhaps unintended responsibility, his thesis on reflexive modernization had frequently been accommodated as a praxis protocol, which would supposedly help to overcome various structural problems of South Korea as a "risk society." To many South Korean scholars and concerned citizens, their nation's recurrent manifestation of an endemic subjection to highly diverse and intense instances of social, cultural, industrial, financial, ecological, and even physical insecurities and impairments, along with all its globally envious developmental indicators, leads them eagerly, yet hurriedly, to recite Ulrich's concept or theory of risk society. Unfortunately, reflexive modernization's structural – though, according to Ulrich, "unintended" – responsibility for the universalized generation of risk society had yet to be systematically deciphered in proper theoretical terms and analytical judgments.

Ulrich did not entirely disagree with Anthony Giddens in accepting modernity's reflexive quality as a decisive impetus for key civilizational and societal transformations, but he simultaneously – or evolutionarily – felt that the same quality is crucially and increasingly liable for the widely and diversely distressing risks of modern society and its people, whether at the local, the national, the regional (continental), or the global level. Ulrich's realization, or even revelation, is already useful in understanding logically the dilemma of South Korea, among many other successfully developed or transformed societies (particularly in East Asia), in incurring socioeconomic sufferings and ecological jeopardies no less dramatic than its developmental and other achievements. Nonetheless, in this book, I go further in helping to complete his passionately insightful scholarship by theorizing and analyzing the risk structure of compressed modernity, mainly in the undisputably exemplary context of South Korea.

Such collegial meaning attached to this book also derives from Ulrich's sudden passing away, just several months after our gathering in Seoul. In mid December in the same year, he sent me an almost final draft of his new (and last) book, *The Metamorphosis of the World*, to ask for my comments, especially about various observations he made on China and East Asia. Since this was just two weeks before his shockingly unexpected death, I could not offer any useful inputs. (Polity Press, Ulrich's publisher, did manage to publish the book in 2016.) Actually, we had a plan for another gathering in Munich in late January 2015 in order to coauthor the entry of "methodological cosmopolitanism" for *The Wiley Blackwell Encyclopedia of Social Theory*, a multi-volume publication I was coediting with Bryan S. Turner and others. Relatedly, we had been mutually suggesting we should write together a book on the same topic. The concerned entry was taken over by Daniel Levy, who is among Ulrich's best-informed collaborators on the topic, but the discussed book has not yet been written, either by myself or by Ulrich's other collaborators. For the same encyclopedia, nevertheless, I ended up writing the entry of "reflexive modernization," in part by recollecting our conversation in the previous summer about a widespread (mis)use of "reflexivity" as a normative orientation. On the other hand, I much belatedly reply to Ulrich's request by concluding the current book with a chapter on "A Beckian Metamorphosis?", which discusses theoretical and empirical possibilities of compressed modernity's various risks in triggering a crucial metamorphosis in South Korea, or other similarly situated societies.

Aside from Ulrich Beck, I should thank all other colleagues and institutions that have supported me in carrying out research and writing on compressed modernity since the mid 1990s. Since most of them have already been acknowledged in my previous book, *The Logic of Compressed Modernity* (2022), let me hereby express special gratitude to those who have offered particularly indispensable assistance and encouragement for the current book. Above all, I am very grateful to those who have shared insightful thoughts and revealing findings on various occasions together with Ulrich Beck in particular,

PREFACE

Elisabeth Beck-Gernsheim, Edgar Grande, Han Sang-Jin, Hong Chan-Sook, Chou Kuei-Tien, as well as many members of Ulrich Beck's ERC (European Research Council) grant research team on "Methodological Cosmopolitanism – In the Laboratory of Climate Change."

More recently, I have greatly benefited from constructive and supportive interactions with Hubert Knoblauch, Mostafa Rezrazi, Benjamin Joinau, Christoph Michael, Erik Mobrand, Bryan S. Turner, Chua Beng Huat, D. Hugh Whittaker, Takehiko Kariya, Emiko Ochiai, Chang Woong Jo, An Chenghao, Park Woo, Yoon Jongseok, Kim Dokyun, Young Jun Choi, Bingqin Li, Wai-wan Vivien Chan, Stephane Heim, Michael Kennedy, Zhang Yi, Liu Dong, Xu Ming, C. P. Chandrasekhar, Jayati Ghosh, Jomo Sundaram, Yunxiang Yan, Pietro Masina, Kwon Seok-Man, Lee Jeong Man, Cho Youngdal, Kwon Hyeong-ki, Chey Jeanyung, Lee Hyeon Jung, Park Seung-Gwan, Seol Dong-Hoon, Shin HaeRan, Ku In-Hoe, Kim Hye-Lan, Kim Suyoung, Ryu Hong-Lim, Kim Eui-Young, Shin Wook-Hee, Ryu Keun-Kwan, Kim Eun-Mee, Kim Taekyoon, Lee Joonkoo, Lee Keun, Kim Se-Kyun, Sonn Hochul, Shin Kwang-Yeong, You Jong-Il, Kang Nae-hui, Lee Seung-Yoon, Cho Joo-hyun, Jang Jin-bum, Kim Chul-Kyoo, Chin Seung-Kwon, Kim Heung-Joo, Yoon In-Jin, Kim Hoki, Kim Dong-No, Park Jeong-Mi, Tae-Ung Baik, Seungsook Moon, Gary Steel, and numerous other colleagues. I am also greatly indebted to all faculty members in the Department of Sociology at Seoul National University for their considerate support and encouragement over the many years needed for this work. I am similarly thankful to many graduate students for assisting and stimulating me in various related activities, including Robert Easthope, Xu Xuehua, Yoon Byunghun, Kang Dagyeom, Kim Hee-Yeon, and Brian Kim.

I feel enormously lucky to get this book published by Polity Press, along with *The Logic of Compressed Modernity* (2022), under its director, John B. Thompson's enthusiastic support. Lindsey Wimpenny, Susan Beer, Judith Barrett, and Evie Deavall at Polity have very thoughtfully guided me about various logistic and editorial matters. Polity's design team once again offered me quite an impressive book cover, even exciting myself.

Some parts of Chapters 3, 4, 5, 6, 7 incorporate revised and/or updated substances from my earlier works: respectively, "*Chaebol*: The Logic of Familial Capitalism" in *South Korea under Compressed Modernity: Familial Political Economy in Transition* (Routledge, 2010); "The Disheveling between Male Working Life Course and Family Life Cycle" in *The End of Tomorrow? Familial Liberalism*

viii

PREFACE

and Social Reproduction Crisis (in Korean; Jipmoondang, 2018); "Knowledge, Culture, and Compressed Modernity: Reflexive Post-coloniality in South Korea" (in Chinese), *China Scholarship*, vol. 21 (2025); "The Stranded Individualizer under Compressed Modernity: South Korean Women in Individualization without Individualism" in the *British Journal of Sociology*, vol. 61 (2010); "Risk Components of Compressed Modernity: South Korea as Complex Risk Society" in *Korea Journal*, vol. 38 (1998) and "Risk Citizenship in Complex Risk Society" in *Transformative Citizenship in South Korea: Politics of Transformative Contributory Rights* (Palgrave Macmillan, 2022). Special thanks are due to Choi Sun-Young, Song Min-Young, and Xu Xuehua for superb research assistance and collaboration in these works.

Preparation of the current work has been supported by the Institute of Social Sciences, Seoul National University (SNU ISS Book Series 09). Hanmaeum International Medical Foundation has kindly helped to cover part of the publishing expenses of this book. I have also benefited from the generous SNU Distinguished Professorship of Seoul National University, enabling me to concentrate on research and writing for this book. Needless to say, all shortcomings in the book are entirely mine.

INTRODUCTION

Compressed Modernity and Its Structural Risks

1 The Theme and Purpose

The compressed realization of developmental, institutional, social, and cultural goals in many postcolonial nations has simultaneously been a historical process of structurally rendering their peoples and societies to confront particular difficulties, contradictions, and jeopardies that accrue to the contexts, conditions, and manners of such compressions. South Korea, despite its globally renowned performances in industrial development, political democratization, and sociocultural advances, has not been exempted from such hard historical and structural realities of compressed modernity, which is defined as:

> Compressed modernity is a civilizational condition in which economic, political, social, and/or cultural changes occur in an extremely condensed manner with respect to both time and space, and in which the dynamic coexistence of mutually disparate historical and social elements leads to the construction and reconstruction of a highly complex and fluid social system. Compressed modernity can be manifested at various levels of human existence – that is, personhood, family, secondary organizations, urban spaces, societal units (including civil society, nation, etc.), and, not least important, the global society. At each of these levels, compressed modernity necessitates people's lives to be managed intensely, intricately, and flexibly in order to remain normally integrated with the rest of society. Compressed modernity is thereby subjected to a mutual escalation effect among such different levels.
>
> (Chang, K. 2017a)

None of South Korea's achievements in compressed modernity can be clearly categorized as success, if not failure. If any, they have bravely or effectively incorporated economic, technoscientic, social

INTRODUCTION

institutional, cultural, and ecological risks as the basic conditions of developmental and other compressions. This is evident in that endemic political crises, frequent financial and industrial predicaments, widespread labor displacements, worsening intellectual and cultural confusions, and even radical symptoms of demographic meltdown have accompanied South Korea's globally distinct march in national development and modernization.

The current book aims to present an integrative critical account of South Korea's compressed modernity, focusing on various manifestant and latent risks accompanying its distinct risk-based developmental and other transformations, and also appraises its common structural conditions, shared with many other supposedly "successful" postcolonial nations. It thereby purports to universally configure compressed modernity's generalizable risk properties. This book has been prepared as a companion book to the author's previous book, *The Logic of Compressed Modernity* (2022, Polity Press; also published in Korean, Chinese, French). The two books will complete the author's lengthy effort at establishing an original theoretical-cum-analytic paradigm in studying postcolonial societies' social and developmental ascendance and its structural costs, with special attention to the exemplary South Korean case. Like *The Logic of Compressed Modernity*, this work builds upon critical scholarship on South Korea (and many other similarly situated postcolonial nations) as a sociological field and on compressed modernity as a theoretical framework. Its approach is critical both in the academic and social intellectual senses. Its critical scientific contributions to the comparative modernities debate, institutional and cultural sociology, political economy of development and social policy, and so forth, will also serve useful social intellectual functions in freshly rethinking and reforming various unforeseen predicaments of compressed modernity and development.

In an earlier article (published in a special issue of the *British Journal of Sociology*, 2010, edited by Ulrich Beck and Edgar Grande), I explained compressed modernity as *internalized reflexive cosmopolitization* in order to point out a modern and/or late-modern society's compressive exposure to and incorporation of spatially (civilizationally) and temporally (historically) boundless influences and resources of knowledge, technology, information, culture, ideology, capital, political power, and so forth. Accordingly, compressed modernity on the one hand assumes a historically and regionally universalistic nature and, on the other hand, incurs literally endemic social, ideational, institutional, financial, ecological, and other risks,

COMPRESSED MODERNITY AND ITS STRUCTURAL RISKS

whether or not each concerned society finds or judges itself to be successful in its reflexively or reflectively conceived goals of transformation. (See the next section for distinguishing between "reflective" and "reflexive.") Those societies in which collective transformative proactivism is distinctly intense and effective, and thus compressed modernity appears distinct by all standards, may be duly expected to generate and manifest particularly diverse and complex risks. To name a few in the late-modern context, South Korea, China, and the like have impressed the world with uncoincidentally parallel symptoms of encouraging developments and disturbing risks.[1]

This book has been written to systematically elucidate such risks of compressed modernity, mostly in the concrete sociohistorical context of South Korea, a country on which most of my earlier writings on compressed modernity have focused. As a related outcome, it will offer various sociological and historical implications of compressed modernity for the Beckian world of risk society (Beck 1992, 1999, 2011a), thereby helping to complement Beck's unfinished intellectual evolvement in exhaustively comprehending risk society and its metamorphosis, from the national to the European (or world regional) to the global level, and from the modern to the late modern, to the now late late-modern stages. This possibility will offer a critical step forward for theoretically and analytically bridging between "reflexive modernization" and compressed modernity.

This study on various risks of compressed modernity in the South Korean context, as well as under the broad postcolonial and cosmopolitan conditions, methodologically adopts the strategies of analytic induction and triangulation. While deductive explanations may be derived from the conventional history and social sciences to deal with separate elements of various components of compressed modernity and its risks, the structural relationship or order among these components can be addressed only by relying on *analytic induction* with regard to historical realities. This analytic strategy

> employs in a self-conscious and disciplined way the same strategies we see used in everyday life and in sophisticated historical explanation. Yet it has a more explicitly analytic orientation. It begins with thoroughly reflected analytic concerns and then seeks to move from the understanding of one or a few cases to potentially generalizable theoretical insights capable of explaining the problematic features of each case . . .
> (Rueschemeyer et al. 1992: 36–37)

Relatedly, it may often be very economic to flexibly reanalyze empirical results produced from those studies which happen to deal

3

INTRODUCTION

with subjects associated with compressed modernity and its risks, albeit, from possibly different theoretical or empirical interests. As to data collection, the strategy of *triangulation* is adopted, in order to complementarily use various quantitative, qualitative, archival, and secondary data as they are logically placed and integrated in the analytical narrative of each chapter.

2 Modernity as Risk(s): Historico-Social Realities and Theoretical Problematics

In theoretical and intellectual terms, (classic) modernity as risk was most emphatically elucidated by Max Weber, a Prussian scholar-intellectual and statesman, whose fundamental legacy has been manifested in numerous "neo-Weberian" schools of critical social theory. His analysis of social rationalization as embodied in bureaucratic principles and organizations incisively pointed out the "iron cage" of rationally processed and controlled social life, in which the so-called "means–end reversal" – that is, the procedural formalities–substantive purposes reversal – is routinely normalized (Weber 1948, 1968). Perhaps, not coincidentally, a distinct group of German intellectuals and academics (including Theodor Adorno, Herbert Marcuse, and Jurgen Habermas) have influentially elaborated on Weber's prescience in order to reveal and warn modern society's variously regressive tendencies in suffocating, not liberating, citizens and communities under the rigidly authoritative, or even authoritarian, systems of social control and administrative governance.[2]

In more recent decades, Emile Durkheim's critical concern on modernity has increasingly been reiterated and elaborated on, amid the widespread decline or degeneration of civil society across Western societies, not to mention postcolonial societies elsewhere. Durkheim's thesis on the organic solidarity, or intangibly contractual interdependence among autonomous socioeconomic subjects in the modern era, does not imply that such social order is automatically constructed if individuals (and private firms) are left to themselves to pursue random inclinations and interests (Durkheim 1933, 1972, 1979). In fact, it was Durkheim who most crucially underlined the indispensably concrete significance of the non-contractual basis – or the communally conceived and reproduced sociocultural foundation – of the liberal socioeconomic order. Durkheim went further on, to demarcate and categorize various human and social risks accompanying any absence, deficit, and/or destruction of such normative basis of liberal modernity, as exemplified in his investigations on suicide, anomie, and so forth (Durkheim 1972, 1979).

In contrast to Weber's and Durkheim's theoretical and historical foci on the institutional nature and/or systemic property of modern social order and governance, Karl Marx paid key attention to the historically manifestant structural relations between social classes that are differentially endowed with production resources or placed in mutually conflictual positions in the production system (Marx and Engels 1970, 1978). In Marx's view, the capitalist system and its social classes are not just risk-prone, but crisis-destined. He even prescribed that increasingly monopolistic capitalists and their political patrons in the state should be revolutionarily removed, if a society's maximum production potentials are to be realized and harnessed for unconditional communal welfare. Marx's earnest followers have been found no less crucially in the real world of state politics and social revolution than in the intellectual and academic domains. For this reason, political Marxism's risks, both in its pioneer nation, Russia, and in its adopter (or adoptee?) nations under state socialism or social democracy, have been epistemologically obfuscated and polemically conflated with capitalist modernity's risks to date. In a sense, capitalism as historical realities and political Marxism(s) have ideologically necessitated and structurally interpenetrated one another to such extents as are virtually impossible to differentiate clearly in their practical influences.

While arguments and warnings on modernity's structural risks (and crises) by classic sociological authorities were presented mostly in the early modern European context, such criticisms seem to have found much more drastic evidences in those societies that are colonially subdued and exploited by modern European forces. Authoritarian bureaucratic rule, socioeconomic order lacking a normative basis, and unilateral capitalist exploitation were all the more conspicuously witnessed and experienced by those societies, and peoples suddenly colonized by modernity's initial constituent nations. Thereby arose innumerable intellectuals, academics, and activists who would identify themselves or be identified as neo-Weberians, neo-Durkheimians, and neo-Marxists, in conjunction with dire historical realities of colonized territories, societies, and peoples.[3]

Such phenomena would not disappear, even when most of colonized subjects came to be liberated in particular after the Second World War, which was won mainly by the United States, a new hegemonic power equipped with the so-called "liberal internationalism" (Jahn 2013). Each postcolonial nation's situational exigencies of hurriedly

INTRODUCTION

institutionalizing the modern nation-state and socioeconomic order, and transformatively developing the national economy, necessitated accepting or reconceiving its former colonial exploiters and their Western allies as indispensable teachers and potential patrons for social and economic modernization, or for the much propagandic "catch-up" (Chang, K. 2022a, ch. 4). In this context, even without directly coercive influences exercised by Western nations, postcolonial societies and peoples began to *reflexively* align or simulate their public governance, social order, economic system, educational structure, and many other key affairs of modernity, in accordance with Western models, advices, and/or insistences.[4] The practical forces and effects of such Western elements had supposedly been evidenced paradoxically through their earlier colonial subjugation and exploitation under the West. Relatedly, many postcolonial nations' political, economic, and sociocultural elites have been blamed for colluding with their Western counterparts, to the sacrifice of grassroots citizens' interests, and for their assertion or utilization of risk-generative public governance (bureaucratic authoritarianism), socioeconomic rule (top-down impo-sition of market relations), and class bias (sociopolitically entrenched predatory capital).[5] Postcolonial reflexive modernity's risks have been all the more drastic and rampant, as flatly attested to by the extreme rarity of sustainably successful postcolonial nations in moderniza-tion and development. Furthermore, even exceptional success cases of modernization and development have not been exempted from similar and further tendencies of risk-generative public governance, socioeconomic rule, and class bias. In many instances, in fact, their supposedly successful modernization and development have resulted from even more intensively, and intentionally, risk-generative forms and practices in the administrative, socioeconomic, and class structural spheres. This has been particularly evident in those East Asian nations, including both capitalist and post-socialist ones, which have ushered in the so-called "Asian era" since the late twentieth century, albeit with the endemic sociopolitical, industrial and financial, and ecologi-cal risks and disasters inflicting on, and demoralizing, their respective citizenries. Aggressive technocratic authoritarianism, extensive incor-poration of communal spaces and social relations into the orbit of the market economy, state-allied capital's unrestrained domination over society, labor, and nature are, on the one hand, considered to have enabled and accelerated modernization and development with incomparable degrees of rapidity and scope and, on the other hand, to be symptomatic of nearly all capitalist and post-socialist nations in the region.[6] It should additionally be pointed out that these nations' ultimate or imminent catch-up with the West has rendered them to confront various worrisome tendencies of Beckian late-modern risk society (details of which are explained below), in manners as much compressed as their development and modernization.

3 Late Modernity as Risk(s): Ulrich Beck

While Ulrich Beck's risk society thesis has spearheaded the critical international debate on late modernity in risk terms, his intellectual comrades, such as Anthony Giddens, Scott Lash, and Zygmunt Bauman, all have converged on late modernity's structural instabilities, contradictions, and costs. Besides, a wide group of sociological, historical, and political economic critics on national and/or global neoliberalism have analytically and/or philosophically criticized the late-modern world's inherent political, social, economic, and ecological risks and jeopardies – namely, Raymond Williams (1989); David Harvey (1980); Colin Crouch (2004); Göran Therborn (2020); Bryan S. Turner (2016); Ben Fine (2012); and so forth. On the other hand, the latest realities outside the Western world, whether or not development and modernization have been meaningfully progressing, have triggered new lines of critical thinking on (extra-Western) modernity's risks – including postcolonialism and dependency theory (in economic and cultural relations) in particular. As the latter group's arguments and implications are in part understood in conjunction with the earlier discussion on classic sociology's potential relevance for postcolonial societies, let me here focus on Ulrich Beck's problematics of reflexive modernization and risk society, which broadly accommodate other sociological critiques on late modernity (or high modernity, liquid modernity, etc.) and frequently refer to neoliberalism's liabilities for accelerating and intensifying risk society on the global, regional (continental), as well as national scales.

Reflexive modernization is a theory of late-modern social change, led by Ulrich Beck in association with Anthony Giddens, Scott Lash, etc. (Beck, Giddens, Lash 1994). It is one of the self-critical sociological reactions to both murky social realities in the late twentieth century and alternative influential academic discourses on them – namely, postmodernism (e.g. Lyotard 1984) and postcoloniaism (e.g. Ashcroft Griffiths, and Tiffin 2002). Postmodernism forcefully argues that modernity has exhausted or abused its progressive potential, if any, only to spawn deleterious conditions and tendencies for humanity and its civilization and ecological basis; whereas postcolonialism

INTRODUCTION

cogently reveals that postcolonial modernization and development have been far from a genuinely liberating process due to the chronic (re)manifestation of colonial and neocolonial patterns of social relations and cognitive practices in the supposedly liberated Third World. In both perspectives, the civilizational evolutionary premise of modernity has been fundamentally falsified in history, so that social, cultural, and historical sciences also need to abandon their obsession with modernity. Reflexive modernization theory does not deny such distressful historical realities of *actual* modernity, but emphasizes that they still constitute part and parcel of the grand historical process of modernization. How this is the case can be understood by systematically scrutinizing the *reflexive* structure and dynamic of modernity.

Reflexivity is a defining characteristic of modern society (and people), which produces a built-in dynamic of cognitively and politically bounded social change. As Ulrich Beck and his associates deplore, "The 'reflexivity' in 'reflexive modernization' is often misunderstood" as if it were "simply a redundant way of emphasizing the referential quality that is a constitutive part of modernity" (Beck, Bonss, and Lau 2003: 1). Such referential quality of modernity has been lucidly explained by Anthony Giddens (1990). In terminologically specifying reflexivity, Beck adopts Scott Lash's distinction between "reflective" and "reflexive." According to Lash (2001: ix), "To reflect is somehow to subsume the object under the subject of knowledge. Reflection presumes apodictic knowledge and certainty . . . Beck's work from the very start has presupposed a critique of such objectivist knowledge." What instead draws Beck's special analytical attention is the *intentionality* of knowledge in second modernity. In Beck's view, Lash (2001: x) interprets, "The problem here, although it is at the same time its saving grace, is that what is intended leads to the most extraordinary unintendedness, to side-effects, to unintended consequences." In short, "Reflexive he argues has more to do with reflex than reflection. Reflexes are indeterminate" (Lash 2001: ix). Reflexivity thus shackles people and their society to a complex structure of *known unknowns*. Reflexive modernization is a form of social change driven by judgments and actions that are supposedly scientific or rational, but in practice are comprised of reflexes (entangled with or contaminated by given knowledge, image, technology, wealth, power, desire, etc.), and therefore destined to engender a risk-ridden state of affairs in society.

It should be emphasized that late-modern individuals, groups, and organizations do not self-consciously (and cannot) choose to be reflexive, instead of being reflective. In what Beck considers the second

8

modern stage of modernity, on the one hand, the radical proliferation of knowledge and, as its determinants and consequences, of social relations, institutional requisites, material interests, power structures, and religious/cultural identities ironically incapacitates the reflective potential of individuals, groups, and organizations. They (are forced to) *choose compulsively* from among the floods of choices presented to them in the name of rationality. On the other hand, there have been abrupt realignments and enlargements of boundaries of human existence and institutional operation that simultaneously cause drastic amplification of the already proliferated pool of knowledge and its social coordinates, and heavily intensify ontological indeterminacies and uncertainties concerning people and society. Reflexive modernization is a combined process of society's nuclear fission and fusion, by which social change is characterized by extreme-intensity implosions, explosions, ruptures, and fusions in society. In this process, under humanity's exposure to unprecedented amounts and varieties of knowledge, image, technology, wealth, power, and pleasure, many of (first or classic) modernity's basic social institutions, relations, norms, and identities come under rethinking, rebuttal, and/or rearrangement. State, labor market, industry, family and intimacy, sexuality, death and life, nation(alism), class identity, and life course, among others, become "liquid" in boundary and effect (cf. Bauman 2000).

In Beck's later work, reflexive modernization is often equated with "reflexive cosmopolitization" (Beck 2011a, 2011b). Beck frequently adopts my interpretation of this process (Chang, K. 2010: 444–445) as (1) involving "global free trade and financialization, corporate deterritorialization and transnationalized production, globalized labor use and class struggle, globalized policy consultation and formulation, informatization and cyberspace, globally orchestrated bioscientific manipulation of life forms (to include human bodies gradually), borderless ecological and epidemiological hazards, transnational demographic realignments (i.e. migration of labor, spouses, children), cosmopolitanized arts and entertainments, and, not least critically, globally financed and managed regional wars" and (2) manifesting that "[t]here are no permanent systematic hierarchies, sequences, or selectivities by which different groups of nations – whether at different levels of development, in different regions or of different races – are exposed to these new civilizational forces in mutually exclusive ways" because "[t]hey are globally reflexive – that is, compulsively occurring through 'the autonomized dynamism of (second) modernization' across national borders." Reflexive cosmopolitization is a sort of Beckian globalization, leading to a "world risk society" (Beck 1999).[7]

INTRODUCTION

4 Compressed Modernity and Its Structural Risks

As detailed in my earlier work (Chang, K. 2022a), compressed modernity is a critical theory of postcolonial social change, aspiring to join and learn from the main self-critical intellectual reactions since the late twentieth century as to complex and murky social realities in the late-modern world, including postmodernism (Lyotard 1984, etc.), postcolonialism (Chakrabarty 1992; Ashcroft, Griffiths, and Tiffin 2002, etc.), reflexive modernization (Beck, Giddens, and Lash 1994, etc.), multiple modernities (Eisenstadt 2000, etc.), and so forth. In the mostly state-driven modernization process of liberated nations in the post-World-War-II period, their postcoloniality is frequently expressed in terms of reflexively simulative experimentation with Western modernity in institutional, technological, and even ideational spheres. A sort of *reflexive postcoloniality* has prevailed in these nations amid the painful collective recollection of their social displacement and exploitation under the overpowering colonial interests and influences of the (earlier-modernized) Western nations and the practical judgment on their seemingly unavoidable accommodation and utilization of the formerly colonialist and presently world-dominant West's modernity. Accordingly, their compressed modernity is an aspirational historico-political project, whether it is actually realized or not.

Compressed modernity as an aspirational project of reflexively postcolonial nations tends to overly emphasize Western modernity's instrumental utilities, particularly under the state-centered purpose of catching up with the West, and thereby discourages, prohibits, or even punishes critical opinions and objects, whether by influential intellectuals or ordinary citizens, about its structural and/or contextual discrepancies. These tendencies inevitably lead to the following problems:

(1) If compressed modernity is reflexively achieved, these societies cannot but incur all inherent risks of Western modernity that are aptly elucidated by Ulrich Beck, and others. In fact, as analyzed in Chapter 7 of this book, their subjection to such risks is compressed in proportion to the velocity and width of the reflexively attained compressed modernity.

(2) Their frequently hasty accommodation and clumsy utilization of Western institutions, organizations, technologies, knowledges, and ideas, inevitably engender *a novice's risks and harms*,

which are often societally disastrous. Given each postcolonial indigenous society's instability and complexity, it is usually, yet ironically, the hurriedly formed authoritarian state that attempts to establish a West-reflexive liberal order, spawning an endemically antinomic liberalism and its problematic side-effects, with the generalized instabilities and distortions of democracy being perhaps the most crucial pitfall.

(3) Western historical and social sciences have endeavored to elucidate various transformative, structural, and sociocultural conditions and processes of Western modernity's construction and reproduction. Then, its instant simulative incorporation by a postcolonial society, without having the correspondent conditions and processes, cannot be expected at all to meaningfully generate various desired and necessitated outcomes for its people. Within the Western contexts – as argued by Durkheim, Weber, Marx, and others – modern social orders, such as organic contractual social relations, rationalized bureaucratic governance, and capitalist class rule, all necessitated complicated historico-social conditions and processes (as briefly explained above). When social orders and systems are more declared than constructed or established in a postcolonial society, it then has to *reverse-realize* their (West-correspondent?) historico-social conditions. This paradoxical task's chronic difficulties, if not impossibilities, keep afflicting postcolonial modernity's supposed social constituencies (that is, subaltern yet sovereign citizens). If the concerned society has a meaningfully long history as an integrated civilizational and/or political entity, such reverse-realization of Western modernity's historico-social conditions would logically require a social revolution for uprooting or replacing indigenous sociopolitical orders, relations, and ideologies incompatible with, or obstructive to, Western modernity. In history, such mechanically West-reflexive social revolution is rarely achievable, whereas a sort of innovative or (re)inventive modernity (as exemplified by the Maoist mass-line revolution in China) has been conceived and accomplished in various parts of the world.

(4) The generalized reflexive openness of most postcolonial liberal societies to various aspects of Western modernity, though constrained by religious and/or political intransigence, is often translated into arbitrary dualities between formal but conditional modern values, principles, institutions, etc., and effective yet arbitrary real-world practices (that are in turn variably formalized according to each postcolonial society's political

INTRODUCTION

and/or civilizational rebirth, indigenization, and degeneration). Thereby arise endemically puzzling risks from the institutional, legal, ideational, and social relational inconsistencies, contradictions, confrontations, and deceptions between West-reflexive modernity and its local counterpart constituencies.

(5) The historical reality of many civilizationally rich and socio-economically stable (non-Western) nations' abrupt subjection to Western colonial (and neocolonial) domination does not necessarily imply that their traditional order and culture did not deserve sustenance in the modern era, or that such order and culture lacked potentialities for autonomously engendering contemporarily compatible and rational modernities. It is not just Orientalist and/or colonialist/neocolonialist Westerners but also West-dependent procolonialist/proneocolonialist local elites that have often unconditionally refuted and suppressed indigenous traditions and practices in various spheres of each concerned society. The most crucial risk or opportunity cost here consists in the fatally unrepairable loss of its historically and socially organic potentials for developing alternative modernities that would possibly better liberate and salvage both national and cosmopolitan citizenries, than what Ulrich Beck critically analyzed as risk society modernity.

Many of the above-explained risks of compressed modernity as an aspirational project of reflexively postcolonial societies will be analyzed and explained in the subsequent chapters of the current book. For readers' convenience, let me briefly summarize each of them in the next section.

5 Subjects

This book attempts to offer an integrative critical account of South Korea's compressed modernity, focusing on its unique structural nature of risk-interwoven developmental and other transformations, and a broad appraisal of its common structural conditions, shared with many other supposedly "successful" postcolonial nations, thereby universally configuring compressed modernity's generalizable risk properties. The main substances of the book are summarized as below by each chapter.

As explained in Chapter 1, "Borrowed Democracy, State-Projective Politics, and Institutional Functional Conflations," South Korea's postcolonial political departure as a full representative democratic system was based upon a sort of reflexive institutional declaration in conjunction with its subjection to American influences. Paradoxically, this seemingly celebratory political process was predicated upon a violent suppression, instead of a serious bolstering, of civil society. This crucially reflected the strategic international politico-military necessity for firmly establishing a hegemonic status of liberal (reads conservative) pro-American sociopolitical forces in the immediate post-liberation period. Formal democracy's social representation has thereafter been replaced by a sort of statist self-representation. In order to be qualified for formal representation in the national and local political arenas, citizens, classes, and communities have had to prove their compliance with various ideological and political criteria set by the self-imposing conservative state. Despite their arduous sociopolitical struggle for (re)democratization against a series of military and civilian autocracies, South Korean citizens, on the one hand, have realized that democracy is not necessarily a genuine institution for representing citizens' autonomous values, interests, and demands in a bottom-up manner, and, on the other hand, have been accustomed to being mobilized, directed, and even regimented by the authoritative (and often authoritarian) state in pursuing various supposedly national goals superimposed in a top-down manner. A sort of *state-projective politics* has routinely prevailed in the everyday operation of political institutions and administrative organs (of a supposedly representative polity), which, in turn, have been strategically assisted by legal, journalistic, and academic collaborators with widespread political ambitions. The chronically nullified or neutralized authority of the parliament has been detested, not only by opposition politicians and parties, but also by conscious citizens and intellectuals, many of whom would devote themselves in organizing social movements and organizations as complementary, if not substitutive, political instruments for society's self-representation into the work of the state. With their multi-divisional structure and multi-functional activism, they have oftentimes made up for the failure of the parliament and formal political parties in meaningfully representing citizens, classes, and communities in the state's public services. News media have seriously taken such social movements and organizations as if they were influential quasi-political parties, especially when the political opinions, sentiments, and interests of ordinary citizens need to be monitored and reflected in news coverage. Many newspapers and broadcasts, in turn, have quite frequently appointed themselves as in-effect political parties in covering virtually all kinds and areas of news with strong

INTRODUCTION

political and/or ideological insistences that often reflect their own, frequently partisan, political interests and orientations.

It is shown in Chapter 2, "Normal Corruption: Utilitarian Institutional Dualities and Technocratized Authoritarian (In)justice," that South Korea's liberal systemic modernity has been pervasively and chronically contaminated (and distorted) by the virtually normalized structures and practices of corruption shared among the mainstream actors and organizations in economic production and social services. In most postcolonial societies, modernization began as a *reflexive* process, in that their initial critical self-appraisal was usually focused upon their perceived weaknesses and deficiencies vis-à-vis Western forces that had ruled and exploited them. In South Korea and elsewhere, postcolonial/neocolonial reflexive modernization has usually taken on an institutionalist nature, in that most related efforts have been centered upon institutional emulation or replication of the politico-legal, economic, and social systems of "advanced nations" (*seonjinguk*). Reflexive institutional(ist) modernization is, in a sense, modernization by institutional isomorphism, whether through parliamentary legislations, government decrees, professional organizational statutes, civilian communal proclamations, or even dictatorial orders. It should crucially be indicated that reflexively adopted Western institutions in political, economic, and social affairs do not necessarily enable them to solve the impending material and organizational exigencies in most of the postcolonial societies populated by exploited and deprived grassroots citizens, and devoid of stable and sound conditions of economic production and social provision. In fact, the simulated or emulated Western social institutions – such as market economy, democracy, and social citizenship – are the long historical outcome of the concerned Western societies' arduous efforts, struggles, and achievements in encountering and solving wide-ranging and incessantly varied material and organizational exigencies, conflated with politico-military, racial, and ecological challenges. In other words, most of postcolonial South Korea's immediate, and even long-term, material exigencies of economic production and social provision have had to be acquired through various self-taught/learned measures, causing or necessitating very flexible coordination, compromise, distortion, or even nullification of West-reflexive formal institutions in public governance and socioeconomic life. In the long run, as it has turned out, South Korea has ended up establishing an effectively functioning, yet sociopolitically vulnerable and chronically unlawful, system of industrial capitalism and social provisioning that effect its liberal order's endemic legitimation crisis. A general systemic order of *normal corruption* has thereby prevailed under the pervasively utilitarian institutional dualities between the West-reflexively adopted liberal institutions and the practically devised methods and improvised orders for pragmatic and expedient problem-solving, often beyond legal boundaries or principles. The state's judicial organs – prosecution in particular – have not functioned simply to incriminate such systemic corruption but to reflect carefully practical national and/or social utilities by flexibly ignoring or pardoning its legal problems, whereas news media have tried to deliver their own verdicts on both sides of corruption – that is, unlawful practices in problem-solving and arbitrary (non-)adjudication on them. As the state's political leadership, whether autocratic or democratic, has had to juggle with such complicated practical and (il)legal necessities, South Korea's liberal systemic order has incurred built-in irregularities and instabilities, regardless of its success in practical problem-solving in economic production, social provision, and other necessities.

As explained in Chapter 3, "Class Contradictions of State Capitalist Industrialism: The "*Chaebol* Republic," the so-called *chaebol* system, the South Korean version of familially controlled capitalism represents one of the most inventive components of South Korean modernity. The principal ingenuity of the *chaebol* has consisted in its internal structure of control over complexly interconnected firms under which a head and his/her family rule dozens of firms operating in different industries without holding legally sufficient shares. To the extent that their industrial undertakings have been instrumental to state-led economic development, the *chaebol* system (of exaggerated control over not clearly owned firms) seems to have accelerated South Korea's compressed march to economic modernity. However, to the extent that the managerial decisions and practices of *chaebol*-affiliated firms have often been irrationally and/or illegitimately dictated for the sake of each conglomerate head's exclusive interests, the same system seems to have engendered a distorted and unjust economic order by which the economic rights and potentials of other concerned actors are systematically sacrificed. The dramatic restoration of South Korea's democracy in the late 1980s has spawned an ironic long-term consequence of empowering the *chaebol*, as a sort of illiberal bourgeoisie, in their relations with the government and civil society. While the government itself has been subjected to serious democratization since 1987, its former tools for authoritarian developmental rule – i.e. the *chaebol*, judiciary organs, and major newspapers – have staunchly resisted progressive political and economic reforms. (This trend has been crucially enmeshed with the utilitarian institutional dualities

INTRODUCTION

and relatedly deformed justice explained in Chapter 2.) In fact, in this process of defying progressive democratization, the illiberally liberal *chaebol* have been able to form a new line of coalition with dominant conservative elements in mainstream newspapers, courts, and economic ministries, as well as military-originated/associated conservative political factions. In this context, regulating and/or reforming the *chaebol* has become as much a political project as an economic policy. Given the preponderantly illiberal influences of the *chaebol* across nearly all elite sections, the deepening of South Korea's liberal democracy, which managed to rehabilitate democratic procedures for political competition only very lately, is now critically conditioned upon the politico-legal rectification of the *chaebol*, as well as democratic reforms in the court, prosecutorial authority, media, etc.

Chapter 4, "The Proletarian Predicament of Developmental Compression: Social Conditions of Flexibly Complex Capitalism," by analyzing South Korean men's (and women's) working life courses, shows an ironic reality that most of the nation's working population have undergone chronic vulnerabilities and instabilities in job status, not only under the recent incidents of the national financial crisis and the concomitant neoliberal economic restructuring, but also during the initial phase of rapid capitalist industrialization and the latest phase of sustained industrial re(up)structuring into the most advanced sectors. The so-called lifetime employment system was unrealizable and often undermined in South Korea's success in a miracle-paced industrialization. That is, the actual working life course of South Korean men should be viewed first in the context of unprecedentedly rapid capitalist industrialization (and deindustrialization) because their society continually saw radical structural changes to its industries. A series of breath-taking shifts have taken place – from agriculture to labor-intensive industries to capital-intensive industries to ICT and advanced service industries. The fact that these changes all have occurred within a few decades, the length of an individual's occupational life, suggests that most workers have inevitably encountered chronic job instabilities. Moreover, the rapid economic concentration into a handful of gigantic export conglomerates (i.e. the *chaebol*) have not necessarily represented enhancement in employment and occupation; instead, in comparison with Germany and Japan, it has often accelerated technological and labor force outsourcing, limiting the demand for long-term skilled labor. The national financial crisis on the eve of the new millennium critically intensified domestic labor displacement as South Korean industries instantaneously transnationalized their production platform across Asia on top of radical domestic labor reshuffling. As an accompanying result, South Koreans' (already heavy) concentration in self-employment (mostly in petty tertiary sectors) has become incomparably high after decades of miracle-paced industrialization. Unlike the popular characterization of the East Asian labor regimes, lifetime employment has been an exceptional privilege for a tiny minority of the South Korean working population, due to its radical success, not failure, in industrial progression and globalization. The dominance of the uniquely illiberal bourgeoisie (*chaebol*), coupled with the pervasively transitory proletariat, has led to the deformed class relations or structure, both in the economic order and representative politics that deviates from the normally expected sociopolitical basis of liberal modernity.

As argued in Chapter 5, "Reflexive Postcoloniality: Intellectual and Cultural Contradictions of Compressed Modernity," the vague manifestation and largely unclear effect of Asian culture and philosophy in modern societal transformations do not necessarily imply that Asian societies and citizens have instead incorporated Western culture and philosophy earnestly for such transformations. The ideology of *dongdoseogi* (Eastern spirit, Western machine) seems to have at least justified a broad tendency of instrumentalism, under which the utilization of Western knowledge, technology, goods, and social institutions intentionally omits, or conveniently bypasses, the deep understanding and accommodation of the essential cultural and philosophical foundations of such matters in the Western context. In reality, West-reflexive instrumentalist modernization in South Korea and elsewhere has induced the concerned nations to balk on their own traditional culture and philosophy in the public domain. (At the private level, nonetheless, the universal neo-Confucianization in family norms and relations, paradoxically under the formal abolition of the Confucian gentry status, helped to widely and crucially complement the public waning of the traditional sociocultural order.) Thereby arose a historical process of *aphilosophical* modernization and development, in which the nationalist goal of catching up with the West became a surrogate philosophy in itself, and the technocratic rules and means have kept replacing or overriding the moral concerns and civilizational considerations of civil society, whether West-centered or indigenous. In an ironic consequence of the broad disembedding (or even nullification) of culture and philosophy from the institutional and material order, South Korean society and people have been exposed to nearly unconstrained varieties of culture – however, in routinely reifying settings and formats. *The remarkable*

INTRODUCTION

diversity and plurality of cultural experiences have ironically been conditioned upon the practical irrelevance of culture and philosophy in the institutional and material world. At the social level, culture and philosophy have routinely been bypassed as purely superstructural objects, so that their diversity and plurality would not disturb the dominant sociopolitical and political economic order. While family-level neo-Confucian norms and rituals have widely been upheld, they have not been societally extrapolated into any consistent cultural or ideological order across society.

As explained in Chapter 6, "Compressed Modernity, Gender, and Obfuscated Family Crisis: Individualization without Individualization," South Korean families have functioned as a very effective receptacle for the nation's highly compressed conditions of modernity and late modernity. It is as much due to the success of South Korean families as an engine of compressed modernity as due to their failure that they have become functionally overloaded and socially risk-ridden. Such familial burdens and risks have been particularly onerous to South Korean women because of the fundamentally gender-based structure of family relations and duties, which has in part been recycled from the (neo-)Confucian past, and in part manufactured under industrial capitalism. Under these complicated conditions, South Korean women have had to dramatically restructure their family relations and duties, as well as their individual life choices. Furthermore, under the most recent condition of what Ulrich Beck dubbed second modernity, other institutions of modernity, such as the state, industrial economy, firms, unions, schools, and welfare programs, have become increasingly ineffective in helping to alleviate such (gender-based) familial burdens and dilemmas. As a result, South Korean women have experienced dramatic changes in marriage patterns, fertility, family relations, and so forth. South Korean women's individualization has thereby taken place primarily as a matter of practicality rather than ideational change. A brief analysis of the situations in the neighboring societies of Japan and Taiwan reinforces the conclusion that individualization without individualism, particularly among women, is a region-wide phenomenon in East Asia.

As detailed in Chapter 7, "Complex Risk Society: Risk Components of Compressed Modernity," South Korea's sensational national financial crisis in the late 1990s was preceded by a series of tragic, hard-to-believe accidents in the early to mid 1990s – most scandalously, for instance, the collapse of Seongsu Grand Bridge over Han River and of Sampoong Department Store in downtown Seoul,

18

killing so many citizens respectively. Additional shocking calamities such as severe underground gas explosions, huge oil spills from stranded supertankers, and train overturns, all on unprecedentedly big scales and within a very short period, aggravated South Koreans' fear that their life was under the constant threat of fatal accidents of one kind or another. Aside from such gigantic accidents, South Koreans kept feeling enormous stress in everyday life from traffic and industrial accidents at levels of "backward countries," rapidly increasing pollution-related hazards, widespread food risks, and so forth. Thus, they came to exchange a highly telling joke, "What matters is the quality of death, not the quality of life." In this context, German sociologist Ulrich Beck's argument on "risk society" was readily embraced by South Korean scholars and media. Beck's proposition that high risk is a built-in feature of Western modernity sounded no less plausible in South Korea's West-oriented modernization. The South Korean dilemma, however, is that the chronic safety crisis has involved much more than what might be regarded as the risk consequences of South Korea's rapid achievement of Western modernity. That is, the types of accidents and hazards inflicting South Koreans include, in addition, those largely overcome by Western societies through their social development *and* those situationally particular to South Korean society. Among the latter, the explosive pace of industrial growth and expansion and concomitant social change have required South Koreans to cope with risks that tend to proportionally increase along socioeconomic compressions and repeated inexperience in ceaselessly changing activities and organizations. Furthermore, the politicized priority of developmental compression has often induced or justified crucially anomalous, illicit, and/or unclear socioeconomic practices, thereby amplifying ordinary industrial and other risks. In this sense, South Korea is not simply a risk society similar to Western societies but a *complex risk society* experiencing accidents and hazards common to advanced industrial societies and undeveloped societies respectively, plus those unique to South Korea. The compressed nature of South Korean modernity is intricately linked to variegated risk dimensions of its developmental miracle. In spite of South Korea's entry into the apparently post-developmental phase in the twenty-first century, its multifarious risk structure has not been meaningfully alleviated, but, in fact, frequently been complicated or aggravated by neoliberal socioeconomic policies and practices for coping with economic downturns and instabilities, inducing risk (in)justice to chronically challenge the socioeconomic integrity of South Korean democracy.

INTRODUCTION

In lieu of this book's conclusion, Chapter 8, "A Beckian Metamorphosis?," reexamines if the diverse societal risks embedded in or enmeshed with South Korea's compressed modernity, as analyzed in the current book's previous chapters, have structural potentials for what is suggested by Ulrich Beck in his last book, *The Metamorphosis of the World* (2016), as "emancipatory catastrophism" and will enable it to proceed to post-(compressed) modern stages of fundamentally meaningful social progress – that is, a Beckian civilizational and/or systemic metamorphosis. More specifically, given South Korea's globally conspicuous dynamism in sociopolitical, industrial, techno-scientific, and cultural affairs – with all quite recent national or societal crises in the concerned areas – should we carefully reexamine if all the contradictions and risks of compressed modernity analyzed earlier in this book are emancipatorily catastrophic?

Part I

Democracy, Capitalism, Social Class

— 1 —

BORROWED DEMOCRACY, STATE-PROJECTIVE POLITICS, AND INSTITUTIONAL FUNCTIONAL CONFLATIONS

1.1 Introduction: Democracy as Risk?

South Korea's repeatedly catastrophic political situations under the vaguely and/or confusingly "conservative" state leaders from the mid twentieth century into the twenty-first century – namely, Rhee Syng-Man, Park Chung-Hee, Chun Doo-Hwan, Kim Young-Sam, Lee Myung-Bak, Park Geun-Hye, and Yoon Suk-Yeol – reflect that democracy as a liberal institutional(ist) modernity has endemically been disrupted by those statist political power groups who *work under the sun, but aim at the dark side*.[1] The Republic of Korea was set up by adopting the liberal democratic republic system as an (internationally) reflexive knowledge, but it instantaneously began to be degenerated by the (residually feudal and colonially and neocolonially collaborative) ancient regime elites' power cartel into a statist ruling instrument well before the meaningful beginning of its social rooting. Such political tendency is still ongoing after several decades.

The extreme and pervasive overexpansion of governmental administrative power under the particularly despotic reigns of Rhee Syng-Man, Park Chung-Hee, and Chun Doo-Hwan endemically obstructed and nullified the parliament's authority and capacity in democratic social representation. Formal party politics, rather than functioning as a bottom-up social representation process, was degenerated into a deceptive top-down process of projecting interregional rivalry and bigotry and other manipulative sociopolitical agendas, for the purpose of engineered statist domination.[2] That is, South Korea's modern politics has been *much more state-projective than society-representative*.

Power-thirsty media appointed themselves, or were willingly co-opted for various auxiliary functions in such state-projective politics. Many academic disciplines, schools, and scholars – often dogmatically committing themselves to West-reflexive policy goals and prescriptions, while unproblematically neglecting or skipping relevant and rigorous reality checks – have not abstained from unconditionally supporting and praising politically and technocratically pre-set public agendas and policy measures. State prosecutors, as authoritarian judicial technocrats, on the one hand closely collaborated with various public and military intelligence organs and, on the other hand, were mobilized and reorganized for the formal and informal tasks of routinely screening, practically blackmailing, and conveniently criminalizing (or pardoning) various civilian subjects (in particular, intellectuals, activists, labor leaders, journalists, opposition politicians, business elites, and so forth) besides key administrative, judicial, and military officers.

In return for their sufficiently satisfactory functions, collaborations, and contributions in assisting and operating the statist, or illiberal, power system, numerous technocrats, journalists, scholars, and even prosecutors were routinely and practically appointed into the parliament (through politically engineered or manipulated elections) or executive administrative positions in the government and para-governmental organs. This trend – as combined with the seriously frail sociocultural rooting of journalism, university, and law as liberal civil society institutions – led to these institutions' nearly normalized subjection to abuse and distortion of the genuine institutional purposes and functions by such state-collusive figures and cliques.

The currently opposition-positioned party (The Democratic Party) and its politicians have grown as the main counter force to the statist conservative political power. They have nonetheless adhered to the deceptive and collusive political institutional exclusion of various (more germanely progressive) grassroots sociopolitical organizations and movements from mainstream formal politics. Such political exclusion has been most decisively consolidated and reproduced through the (conservative–liberal) collusive *political constituentization* of a staggering majority of voters (political citizens) as regional rivalry subjects. This hard reality has come to inhibit the post-1987 (re)democratization process from becoming a fundamental historical basis for South Korean democracy's firmly rational social rooting. Furthermore, the three presidential governments of the main liberalist party since 1998 (or in the post-financial crisis period) failed in effectively diagnosing and handling unprecedented socioeconomic disruptions, displacements, and inequalities in the neoliberal or post-developmental era, thereby allowing Lee Myung-Bak, Park Geun-Hye, and Yoon Suk-Yeol to take over presidency, whether rather easily or unexpectedly.

The 2016–2017 candlelight uprising – or the "candlelight revolution" in the views of its enthusiastic citizen participants (and that of Moon Jae-In, as its opportune or opportunistic usurper) – clearly attested to the grave fact that the core material front of realpolitik in South Korean society consists in the confrontation between statism (or state-directed liberalism) and civilism (?) (*civil liberalism*, not civilianism), rather than between political left and right, or between the seemingly confrontational regions of Southwest (Honam) and Southeast (Youngnam). The same was the case even in the candlelight protest in 2018 against the Lee Myung-Bak government. In recent years, such political civilism is increasingly fueled and sustained by *liberal individualism*, as opposed to nationalism or other collectivist ideologies.

All social contradictions of South Korean politics in the twenty-first century cannot be meaningfully understood and resolved by formal (presidential and parliamentary) elections alone, but are critically contingent upon whether and how to design and execute *reinstitutionalization* of society's civilist demands and desires. This historical project, in turn, necessitates a grand reinvention of South Korean democracy, including the fundamental reconstruction of mainstream political parties (undisputably including The Democratic Party, not to mention the currently ruling conservative party, i.e. People Power Party), which would be possible only under civil society's effective and permanent participation, supervision, and struggle, on top of the formal institutional and legal measures by the state and political parties and elites in that direction.

1.2 The Generalized Instabilities of Postcolonial Democracies

The Republic of Korea was launched in 1948 as a *full democracy* in its institutional form and legal foundation. Korea's liberation from Japanese colonialism took place rather abruptly on Japan's defeat by the U.S. in the Pacific War, instead of being a direct outcome of the Koreans' own effective national(ist) struggle against colonial capitalist exploitation and military suppression. Likewise, the launching of a democratic political system in postcolonial Korea was not a direct result of its people's revolutionary struggle for national political rebirth.[3] A liberal democracy, mainly modeled after the political system of the United States, was *declared* as South Korea's political system in a manner of institutional replication or borrowing – a sort of *institutional cuttage*, as explained in my earlier work (Chang, K. 2022a). The country's political history thereafter continued to display the chronic sociopolitical vulnerabilities and legal–institutional instabilities of a hurriedly replicated system of democratic governance. South Korea's cuttage-based formal democracy would not easily, not to mention automatically, mature into a full tree-like condition, even after several decades of its operation. Nor would South Korean citizens' democratic political rights be firmly materialized in tandem with the summarily declared constitutional stipulations, making constitutional amendments uttered almost everyday by frustrated citizens and politicians alike.

As discussed in my earlier book, *The Logic of Compressed Modernity* ("Chapter 4. Internal Multiple Modernities"), the widespread and chronic deficit in the social materiality of transnationally borrowed or adopted institutions in postcolonial/neocolonial reflexive modernization has remained, in numerous public and civilian spheres, at a stage or state of what can be characterized as *cuttage modernity*. Shallowly planted branch-like social and legal institutions could not have effectually functioned for a long while, whereas their immediate (ab)use in complicated postcolonial realities has often hindered a stable growth into a stably rooted tree-like condition. (In this sense, institutional cuttage should be differentiated from the hitherto widely adopted analogy of institutional transplantation, which implies the plant's root also being inserted in the designated soil.) This predicament has been most manifestly and painfully revealed by the turbulent fluctuations of South Korean democracy (Choi, J. 2002). Besides such stultification of political institutional modernity, the immature operability or malfunctioning of cuttage-level institutions has frequently induced or allowed other types of institutions to be (ab)used, or practically repurposed, as surrogates. This widely and chronically observed phenomenon may be describable as *institutional functional conflations*. If certain organizational inertia and/or structural interests are consolidated by such surrogate institutions, they tend constantly to jeopardize and complicate the normal growth and functioning of the supposedly proper institutions in charge and, no less problematically, distort their own original institutional purposes and functions. For instance, the intense and endemic politicization of the military and media have decisively obstructed the robust formation and stable growth of normal political parties, while retarding or derailing their own institutional advances in the respective domains of modernity.

There has not been any established social scientific theory or confirmed historical example of liberal democracy's suitability for cuttage-based institutionalization. Nevertheless, as persuasively argued by Badie in his *The Imported State* (2000), the post-World-War-II world became predominantly democratic in its political institutional configuration mainly through postcolonial nations' institutional importation of their former colonial rulers' political systems.[4] In many liberated nations, indigenous communities, peoples, and politico-intellectual elites did fight their way into political independence. But such historical achievements were rarely founded upon autonomously revolutionary or innovative programs for postcolonial political governance. Not infrequently, those groups and/or figures accredited with decisive contributions to liberation – usually dubbed "revolution" – frequently attempted to modify or reformulate the initially launched political systems in the hope of monopolizing political power indefinitely. Their projects of *political institutional indigenization* have mostly been degenerated into personalized, paternalistic, racist, and/or plutocratic abuses of ordinary citizens' political and civil rights. Such tendency, in turn, leads to frequent international conflicts, as the concerned political leaders or regimes try to control local discontents and protests by manipulating or (re)inventing external threats (Colgan and Weeks 2015).

In South Korea, its first president, Rhee Syng-Man, was trying hard to manipulate politics for the sake of a possible permanent rule, but had to find himself ousted by a student-led uprising in 1960, after nearly twelve years in power. His civilian democratic successor, Yoon Bo-Sun, was allowed only a year in national presidency, as a military coup in 1961, led by Park Chung-Hee, forced the Republic to accept the stoppage and distortion of democratic procedures for his self-imposed autocratic rule, which would last until his assassination in 1979. Furthermore, another period of military political rule ensued under Chun Doo-Hwan, who orchestrated a coup for brutally quelling sociopolitical demands for (re)democratization and unlawfully enthroned himself into national presidency. The staunch criticism and resistance by students, intellectuals, industrial workers, and middle-class urbanites forced Chun to agree to the recovery of genuine democratic procedures after his controversial seven-year national presidency, but he was still able to see his two (democratically elected) presidential successors, Roh Tae-Woo and Kim Young-Sam, produced from the dominant conservative bloc that he had helped to form.

It was Kim Young-Sam's devastating blunder in economic policy, causing an unprecedented national financial crisis in 1997, that enabled

Kim Dae-Jung, a candidate from the seemingly permanent opposition party, to be elected into national presidency. Kim Dae-Jung and his successor, Roh Moo-Hyun, broadly from the same political bloc, had to confront wide discontents from almost all social classes, due to the severe socioeconomic distresses accompanying the radical neoliberal reforms required as IMF's conditionalities for a financial bailout of the nation (Chang, K. 2019). Such popular resentments functioned to induce South Koreans to turn consecutively to two conservative (neo)developmentalist candidates for national presidency, Lee Myung-Bak and Park Geun-Hye. These symbolic heirs of the Park Chung-Hee era were not able to satisfy socioeconomically desperate citizens, whereas their political foul plays and corruption scandals ignited nationwide political protests, famously dubbed "candlelight protest" (*chotbulsiwi*) and "candlelight uprising" (*chotbulhangjaeng*). In particular, the several-month-long candlelight uprising in 2016–2017 actually led to Park Geun-Hye's impeachment, which enabled Moon Jae-In, Roh Moo-Hyun's close friend and political ally, to charge easily into national presidency in 2017, heading "the government of the candlelight revolution."[5]

Throughout the complicated and often violent political transitions explained above, ordinary South Korean citizens have been led to develop a broadly pessimistic, or even cynical view on the social value of democracy. They have come to realize that the breaking of democratic principles should be criticized and punished, but such judgment against undemocratic elites falls short of constituting a firm and clear social foundation of democracy as the supreme political institution of the nation. In a Durkheimian perspective, democracy in South Korea as the central national political institution seems to have chronically lacked its non-institutional, or sociocultural, basis (see Introduction in this book).

This is far from a surprising situation. Upon liberation from Japanese colonialism, (liberal) democracy was politico-intellectually replicated on to South Korea by the American military occupation authority and its rightwing Korean collaborators (Cumings 1981). Ironically, this was preceded by a violent process of assaulting civilians and their communities, amid a random suspicion of their actual or possible allegiance to socialist influences. *Institutional democratization in the newly established republic was an inherently undemocratic process*, even claiming hundreds of thousands of civilian lives during the brutal armed attacks on them across South Korea.[6] It was not civil society but the self-imposing state that defined the historico-social necessity of "free" democracy in the South Korean context and reflexively

28

designed its institutional structure mostly in line with the American system (Chang, K. 2022a, ch. 4). Thereby arose an anti-social (or counter-liberal) liberal polity, whose definition of "freedom" implied citizens' unfree subjection to the successive Cold War dictatorships.

From its very beginning, formal democracy was elitist, and even aristocratic, in that certain sociopolitically and economically entrenched groups began to monopolize political positions and activities. Such aristocratic departure of South Korean democracy was to a crucial extent consolidated by the instant formation of a core opposition bloc (and a political party, named Hangukminjudang) mainly by politically conservative and socioeconomically entrenched elites. Those political parties named "~ Democratic Party" (~minjudang) ever since have reflected or inherited this political bloc. In this respect, the military's political takeover consisted more in the annulment and/ or distortion of the formally declared democratic procedures than in the destruction of the social foundations of democracy. As an unintended consequence, both Rhee Syng-Man's (civilian) disguised autocracy and Park Chung-Hee's military dictatorship seem to have helped establish and strengthen the social underpinnings of democracy, by awakening South Korean citizens – students and intellectuals in particular – to the crucial sociopolitical exigency of fighting against the illegitimately self-serving political forces.[7] Increasing numbers of citizens – including many who had been subjected to the state's atrocious violation of even basic human rights for sociopolitically criticizing or resisting the tyrannical state – came to realize that protecting themselves from state-driven violence and corruption was in their essential interest.[8]

Such awakening culminated in 1987, the year of sociopolitical democratization from below (vis-à-vis the top-down institutional democratization in 1948). The attempt of the so-called "new military junta" (singunbu) to extend its extremely oppressive rule was instantly accompanied by society-wide insurrections for demanding an immediate recovery of democratic political procedures, which had been suspended and distorted since 1961, under a series of military-based political forces. Under the new military junta's rule, led by Chun Doo-Hwan since 1980, South Koreans' sociopolitical frustration came to its extremity, due to ceaseless instances of exceedingly violent suppression of basic civil, political, and even human rights. The intensity of such popular frustration was directly reflected in the dramatic vigor and potency of the anti-junta struggles by nearly all social classes and regions that, in what is proudly dubbed "the June uprising," ultimately forced Chun to withdraw from his earlier avowal to practically extend the junta's political rule and agree to adopting a genuinely democratic constitution (Yoon, S. 1997).

Unfortunately, the democratic restoration in 1987 did not necessarily put a clear end to South Koreans' wide and chronic political frustrations. Most of the democratically elected presidents and their administrations since 1987 have been subjected to quite intense popular disapproval and even condemnation. This trend is not necessarily an outcome of any commonly poor performance of each administration in its policy programs. (Key members of some previous administrations are very unhappy about having been criticized and discredited to similar extents to those other administrations with apparently worse performance.) Both grassroots citizens and expert intellectuals have felt that the nation's "democracy after democratization" (Choi, J. 2002) has been fundamentally flawed in functioning in a genuinely democratic manner and delivering meaningfully democratic social services. A series of social scientists and political intellectuals has begun to denote the sociopolitical processes and outcomes of the 1987 democratic uprising as "the 1987 system" (*1987–nyeon cheje*) in order systematically to analyze its limited and/or deformed characteristics, under the formality of democratic political institutions.

The supposed flaws of the 1987 system, in the current analysis, cannot be properly comprehended without (re)scrutinizing what may be dubbed *the 1948 system*, by which ordinary South Koreans were offered radically democratic forms of institutions and rights for the time, however, without meaningful (bottom-up) access to sociopolitical channels and organizations for democratic representation and appointment. This popular political dilemma was in no sense fundamentally overcome by the 1987 uprising and subsequent political reforms. South Koreans have even ended up democratically electing, and then being deceived by, two heirs of the Park Chung-Hee dictatorship – Lee Myung-Bak, an (in)famous industrialist in the Park era, and Park Geun-Hye, Park's daughter – who would use their supreme political power mainly in pursuing quite controversial and substantially illegal purposes, reflecting their own scandalous interests, and ultimately getting imprisoned after another societal political uprising in 2016–2017.

South Koreans' repeated popular political uprisings, despite their global headline-making intensity and potency, have fallen short of making their arduously won "representative democracy" (*daeuimin-jujuui*) represent themselves meaningfully and systematically. While chronically accustomed to such systemic failure of the supposedly representative polity, many of them – in particular, those with the so-called "Park Chung-Hee nostalgia" (Lim, K. 2009; Hong, S. 2015) – have personally underscored each state leader's genuine devotion and wisdom as a key political criterion, while downplaying the fundamental normative difference between democracy and dictatorship. It is no surprise that such citizens are concentrated in the senior age groups, but they have recently found quite unexpected political allies(-in-effect) among rapidly increasing conservative youth, who feel alienated or ignored by the mainstream liberalist party and a few administrations it formed.[9]

1.3 The Practical Conditions of Democratic Politics: Society-Representative Democracy vs. State-Projective Democracy (and Autocracy)

In a fundamental historical paradox, postcolonial South Korea's political modernization project of instituting a liberal representative democracy was preceded by an atrocious politico-military campaign, by the allied forces of the American military occupation authority and its local collaborators in administrative and political domains, for uprooting actual and potential socialist influences in society and dispersing ordinary citizens' sociopolitical allegiance to them (Cumings 1981). The launching of a representative democratic system was predicated upon a violent restructuring of society, according to strategic politico-military necessities, for firmly establishing a hegemonic status of the liberal (reads conservative) pro-American socipolitical forces (including numerous former colonial collaborators under Japan).[10] To a crucial extent, thereafter, formal democracy's social representation has consisted in – or been substituted by – a sort of *statist self-representation*. In order to be qualified for formal representation in the national and local political arenas, citizens, classes, and communities have had to prove their compliance with various ideological and political criteria set by the conservative rightwing state.[11]

Despite their arduous sociopolitical struggle for (re)democratization against a series of military and civilian autocracies, South Korean citizens, on the one hand, have realized that democracy is not necessarily a genuine institution for representing citizens' autonomous values, interests, and demands in a bottom-up manner, and, on the other hand, have been accustomed to being mobilized, directed, and even regimented by the authoritative (and often authoritarian) state in pursuing various supposedly national goals superimposed in a top-down manner (Mobrand 2019). A sort of *state-projective politics* has prevailed in the everyday operation of political institutions and administrative organs (of a supposedly liberal representative polity), which in turn have been strategically assisted by legal, journalistic, and academic collaborators with widespread political ambitions (see also Chapter 2 of this book). Furthermore, under the military's take-over of state leadership between the early 1960s and the mid 1980s, state projectivism in politics was outright normalized. While the parliament as the representative democracy's key political institution usually remained idle and low-keyed, except during election times, the authoritarian military state tried to reach out into far corners of society, in order to project (or represent) itself ideologically, and impose and legitimate its policy agendas (centered in socioeconomic development issues).[12]

The two interrelated key national agendas of (state capitalist) national economic development and (anti-communist) national security were deemed to fully justify the state's comprehensive and authoritative precedence over civilian interests and values. These super-agendas were given a sort of *existential priority* in the inter-national politico-military context.[13] To the military as a profession in charge of inter-state armed defense and conflict, the ideology of *bugukgangbyeong* (rich nation, strong army) was taken as a sacred code above and for South Koreans' civil society in the national(ist) framework. Internationally, the South Korean military state's such collectivist approach to national development and security was not refuted or contradicted, either by the other postcolonial states, or by the hegemonic liberal West. In fact, the United States even helped to establish and develop certain branches of social sciences in this line – namely, development economics, international politics, and so forth (Kim, J. 2015).[14] The theories, concepts, methods, and policy suggestions from such branches of Western academic knowledge were eagerly and conveniently appropriated in the execution of state-projective politics in South Korea (and elsewhere).[15] The military's formal retreat from politics since the early 1990s would not clearly change this situation, as was dramatically shown when Kim Young-Sam's self-proclaimed *munminjeongbu* (civilian government) drove the nation into a sudden financial insolvency, after several years of a suicidal (neo)developmental drive (Chang, K. 1999, 2019).

While economic development and military security were irrefutable national(ist) agendas, their actual implementation was not socially integrative. In fact, the anti-social authoritarian military state began to reorganize society politically, so that certain classes, generations, and regions would become core constituencies of the increasingly exclusionary politics of national development and security, and would permanently support the statist rule, out of a sort of state-clientele consciousness. This mode of politics, which may be conceptualized as *statist political constituentization of society*, would not necessarily be overcome or even circumvented by the arguably democratic factions that have managed to establish themselves as mainstream political forces and intermittently dominate the parliament and/or take over national presidency.[16] The very lengthy military rule and its lingering sociopolitical aftermaths, well into the twenty-first century, have left South Korean citizenry as a rigidly and fiercely divided social entity according to regional rivalry (or bigotry) and ideological rift. Many of the political outcomes of parliamentary and executive elections, both at the national and the local levels, have been determined according to individual voters' regional belongings and generations (as proxy of ideological lines).

In a sense, both of the two supposedly mainstream political parties, whether broadly succeeding the junta or politically opposing it, have benefited from such tendencies because their shared dominance in formal politics has been automatically ensured by the state-severed structure of society and population. These two parties, albeit under the continually changing names and leaders, have collaborated with each other strategically in maintaining the political (election) system designed to ensure the winner-takes-all status of each party among their respectively hegemonic regions and generations (Chang, K. 2022b, ch. 3). By consequence, a sort of divide-and-rule politics has been collusively maintained between political heirs and challengers of the military's statist dictatorship. South Koreans' state-mediated mutual hostilities and bigotries between different regions and generations will not be cured until their democracy becomes genuinely representative of society – a catch-22 situation indeed.

The lengthy and even recurrent state-projective politics has kept inducing its elites to monopolize or manipulate the public interpretation and evaluation of such illiberal rule. In a crucial episode, the Park Geun-Hye government preferred its direct control of public-school textbooks in history, much like during her father's autocratic reign.[17] Her wish got severely complicated as some supposedly favorable academics ended up preparing textbook drafts that justified not only her and her father's leaderships but also an entire series of authoritarian statist orders, including even Japan's colonial rule. *The state's control of public-school textbooks, particularly in history, is very much symbolic of state-projectivist politics.* Park Guen-Hye's time fundamentally differed from her father's in that South Korea's highly educated citizenry were not in favor of an obvious possibility that their children would end up learning arbitrarily distorted or biased history.

The state's attempt at controlling people's access to knowledge (and, ultimately, people's knowledge itself) has spanned far beyond history textbooks. Public censorship of books, cinemas, and songs was too frequent and widespread during the military rule between the early 1960s and the mid 1980s. In particular, those books in social sciences and humanities that supposedly deny the exclusive legitimacy and utility of "free" democracy and capitalism or justify the "enemy" thoughts and systems (of Marxism and leftist nationalism) were not to be read or even possessed under the National Security Law (*Gukgaboanbeop*). Even in the twenty-first century, those public domains under organized ideological allegiance to the military era (for instance, military, police, prison, and so forth) maintain internal decrees or policies for banning certain arbitrarily discredited books to their members or inmates.[18]

It is undeniable that, in spite of such serious sociopolitical side-effects, most South Koreans ended up becoming significant beneficiaries of the nation's economic miracle and sustained physical (military) security. In a paradox, this was reflected well into the twenty-first century amid the so-called "Park Chung-Hee nostalgia," in the wake of the nation's total financial crisis in the late 1990s (Lim, K. 2009; Hong, S. 2015). However, the radical neoliberal restructuring of the South Korean economy since the crisis – in particular, its aggressive and unrestrained corporate transnationalization in production and wholesale labor market reshuffling – forced the nation into a post-developmental era in which, according to Roh Moo-Hyun, the president succeeding Kim Dae-Jung's post-crisis socioeconomic management, "Power has been transferred to the market" (*Hankyoreh*, 16 May 2005).

When Park Geun-Hye ran for (and won) national presidency in 2012, as a beneficiary of the supposed Park Chung-Hee nostalgia, she needed to seriously make up for the neoliberalized national economy's pitfalls of un(der)employment and bipolarity, with propagandic lip services to the welfare state and economic justice. Once in presidency, in reality, she was able to protect her power only by relying on similar functionaries in the state's physical control of society to those used by her father – namely, public security prosecutors (*gongangeomsa*), police (both lawful and functionally illicit), intelligence agencies, and even army generals. Even the ruling political party under her tutelage was dominated by politically ambitious and opportunistic figures from these domains of public physical coercion such as prosecution, police, and intelligence. The mainstream "conservative" party was then commanded not by any clear or coherent policy line of socioeconomic conservatism but by the obsessive desire of an exclusive group of political opportunists to monopolize state power. As an ultimate legacy of state-projective dictatorial politics, an empty conservatism now haunts South Korean citizens and self-identified conservative politicians alike.

State projective politics has continued well into the supposedly democratic era since the late twentieth century and into the twenty-first century. Impulsive statist projects combined with repressed social demands and criticisms have repeatedly led to anachronic wasteful "public bads" (cf. Beck and Grande 2010). The self-proudly "civilian" president, Kim Young-Sam's post-military national presidency between 1993–1998 was marred by the unprecedented national economic crisis, popularly called "the IMF crisis," caused by his clumsy mimicry of the Park Chung-Hee-style developmentalist drive, complicated with national financial regulatory blunders and global financial capital's predations. Lee Myung-Back, another Park Chung-Hee mimicker capitalizing on his construction industrialist career during the late Park era, was elected into national presidency in 2007 by seducing neoliberally precariatized South Koreans into a supposedly renewed developmental state era (Chang, K. 2022a, ch. 4); whereas he only rampantly destroyed environments under the so-called "four grand rivers-saving project," which was a deceitful camouflage of the popularly protested, and thus formally relinquished, project of the Korean Grand Canal System (Hanbandodaeunha). Park Geun-Hye, Park Chung-Hee's daughter, also ushered herself into national presidency in 2012, primarily as Park's symbolic successor, claiming that South Korea's advanced industrial economy is mainly the outcome of her father's political (economic) leadership; but she (and her secret cronies) only aggravated the nation's economic systemic distortion by extorting Samsung and other business conglomerates in exchange for various regulatory favoritisms, and ultimately was impeached for the first time in the national political history. Through these frustrating political episodes, South Korea's supposedly restored democracy has kept being crucially spoiled, both in its procedural and substantive qualities.

As another lingering dilemma of state-projective politics in the formally democratic era, South Korea has remained a sort of *theater state by consequence*, in which each state leader's particular negativities are projectively amplified onto the public screen of national politics, thereby repeatedly disconcerting South Koreans as political citizens.[19] Perhaps the worst recent episode was Park Geun-Hye's impeachment in 2017, after the revelation of her habitual absenteeism in national executive duties and frequent dependence on scandalous secret cronies, both in official state affairs and stealthy transactions with business, which enraged her citizens into nationwide protests by millions over a few months. Ironically, such public political frustrations, as combined with the above-mentioned substantive and procedural mutilations to democratic governance, tend to strongly fuel South Koreans' electoral motivation in urgently removing the crucially detrimental political figures and factions from state office by votes. South Koreans' impressively high participation in national presidential and parliamentary elections, for all their repeated disappointment and anger at state work, may be understood substantially in this regard (*Yonhapnews*, 7 April 2024).

1.4 State-Projective Politics and Regularized Institutional Functional Conflations

State-projective politics has necessitated and effected a series of institutional functional distortions, conversions, and substitutions. Above all, the government, as almost exclusively accountable to the supreme executive power of the president, has virtually monopolized the law-making process, leaving the parliament (and political parties) devoid of a meaningful political efficacy. For instance, according to the bill information system of the National Assembly (https://likms.assembly .go.kr/bill/main.do), the government's direct legislative proposals used to outnumber those by (members of) the National Assembly in the early phase of the restored democracy (i.e. the 13th and 14th terms of the National Assembly), whereas the latter began rapidly to increase from the 2000s – to such an extent that the National Assembly is being ridiculed as *ipbeopgongjang* (legislative factory; *Kukinews*, 25 April 2024) – with the former remaining mostly unchanged. In recent years, the government prefers to reframe (launder?) most of its actual legislative proposals as assembly member proposals, due to various regulatory requirements and hurdles to governmental legislative proposals. The likelihood of actual enactment has always been higher for the former, and that of the latter has declined drastically in the recent terms of the National Assembly. When most of the supposed lawmakers' – or law-passers' (?) – public service consisted in automatically passing government ministry-drafted laws, technocratic superimposition of state agendas has thereby replaced political consultation with citizens and communities. This mode of politics occasionally turns impractical when parliamentary elections result in a majority position by opposition politicians, dubbed *yeosoyadae* (the ruling party's minority status and the opposition party's (or parties') majority status in the parliament). In such situations, whenever possible, the president's office tried to manipulate the political landscape by coopting and/or threatening certain opposition politicians and/or parties for individual changes in party affiliation or even inter-party mergers, and thereby managed to restore a parliamentary majority platform for top-down technocratic rule.[20]

The chronically nullified or neutralized authority of the parliament has been detested, not only by opposition politicians and parties, but also by conscious citizens and intellectuals, many of whom would devote themselves to organizing social movements and NGOs as complementary, if not substitutive, political instruments for society's self-representation in the work of the state (Kim, D. 2013). The sociopolitical prominence of a sort of comprehensive NGOs such as Chamyeoyeondae (PSPD, or People's Solidarity for Participatory Democracy) and Gyeongsilyeon (CCEJ, or The Citizens' Coalition for Economic Justice) can be understood against this political context or culture. With their multi-divisional structure and multi-functional activism under strong scientific intellectualism, they have oftentimes made up for the failure of the parliament and formal political parties in meaningfully representing citizens, classes and communities in the state's public service (Yang, G. 2000). Many news media have generally taken such NGOs as if they were influential quasi-political parties, especially when the political opinions, sentiments, and interests of ordinary citizens need to be seriously monitored and reflected in news coverage. Most of the general public, whether individually in support of these comprehensively activist NGOs or not, have not been opposed to being customarily represented as such in news media. However, those conservative media that have colluded in decades of state-projective politics have frequently derided such intellectually driven NGOs' activities as "citizen movements without citizens," and criticized many NGO activists' direct participation in formal politics (Kim, H. 2006).

Many newspapers and television channels, in turn, have quite frequently appointed themselves as *in-effect political parties* in covering virtually all kinds and areas of news with strong political and/or ideological perspectives (An, S. 2021).[21] They have even kept allocating big parts of news coverage to suggesting and demanding certain policies and actions from the state and other public entities.[22] They often carry special series of politically suggestive reports as formal expression of their political position and ideological line. In this way, South Korean journalism has fundamentally compromised its definitional attribute as press. News media's generously frequent coverage of comprehensive NGOs' views and contentions, to a significant extent, reflects their own political motivations. Given these uniquely politicized NGOs and news media, the frequent recruitment of renowned NGO activists and journalists by major political parties is nothing surprising. Many of them have been functioning prominently in formal politics, however, without necessarily rectifying state-projectivist politics. Accordingly, grave public and intellectual concerns have been expressed about the possible negative impacts on civil activism and journalism under the customary career transfers of too many civil society activists and journalists.[23]

Instant political careers have also been coveted, through more individualized endeavors, by other professionals, academics, and, as suggested in the previous section, various functionaries of public physical coercion. The political as well as administrative utility of academics, particularly in social sciences, has been systematically embedded in the (West-)reflexive nature of state-projective politics under the grand rubrics (or goals) of industrialization and modernization that would hopefully enable South Korea to join the world rank of "advanced nations" (*seonjinguk*) within the shortest time possible.[24] Amid the inconsistency, complexity, and obscurity of conservatism as a sociopolitical ideology in South Korea, *seonjinhwa* (that is, emulating and, ultimately, joining the (Western) advanced nations) has been upheld as the nation's goal among many moderate conservatives with high educational and/or public career backgrounds.[25] Much of state-projectivism has been practiced on the basis of the state's hoped and planned guidance to a West-emulative (or West-simulative) path of national progress on all fronts. West-trained academics have been seen and used as a sort of *transnational knowledge medium* both in politico-administrative services to which they have been invited and in academic institutions in which they have taught students (Kim, J. 2015). Academics' acceptance (or desire) of prestigious political and/or governmental appointments, even without their own creative or innovative ideas, has been nothing to blame in this regard. However, as too many of them have been practically moonlighting between universities and political camps, while damaging their main academic duties in research and teaching, they have been derogatorily called "polifessors" by critical media and students (Chang, K. 2022a, ch. 4) Besides, their frequent use of media exposure for additionally strengthening individual political utility has led many of them to be called "telefessors."

During the latter part of his lengthy dictatorship, Park Chung-Hee became more and more dependent upon the loyalty and cruelty of functionaries in public physical coercion (against increasingly defiant intellectuals, workers, and opposition politicians). This situation quickly increased political career opportunities for many shrewd figures in charge of "public security" (*gongan*) as prosecutor, police, intelligence agency, military, and even presidential security service (Han, S. 2017).[26] (Officials in the key governmental and military intelligence organs were even endowed with prosecutorial authority.) In fact, their political careers did not necessarily require a formal transfer to political parties or other administrative organs because they were already entrusted with a crucial part of autocratic executive power.[27] Furthermore, their prosecutorial-cum-political power became absolutized under the frequent interference and threat by the presidential office as to the autonomy and authority of the court.[28] As indicated in the previous section, the national presidency of Park Chung-Hee's daughter, Park Geun-Hye, was maintained in a strikingly similar manner, with most of her executive power practically exercised by a few former and current "public security" prosecutors (*gongangeomsa*).[29] She even helped former prosecutors to occupy dominant positions in the then ruling conservative party, currently named People Power Party. Its earlier head (as of January 2020), Hwang Gyo-An, was her minister of law and then prime minister, appointed mainly thanks to his acceptable service as a public security prosecutor. The technically (as well as judicially) required sociopolitical neutrality of these officials in punitive services was theoretically contradictory to their potential as (society-representative) politicians, but practically convenient in remaining accountable only to the supreme source of their derivative power (i.e. the presidential office). Their minimum qualification as a functionary of state-projective politics was to faithfully accept the nation's exigencies of (state-led) capitalist development and (anti-communist) national security, even at a practical sacrifice of the rule of law (or all citizens' equality before the law).

The widespread political aspiration of varieties of professionals has been structurally linked to the state-driven/framed process of developing or promoting the supposedly civil society institutions if seen in the liberal West's historical experiences – high education, journalism, law, medicine, and even culture (Chang, K. 2022a, ch. 4). There is an administrative propensity to call each of them "industry" so that the developmentalist state can comfortably engage in, or meddle with, their operation and possible development. More fundamentally, the modernizationist state has dealt with each of these professions from the perspective of a grand (inter)national institutionalizer. In no surprise, the chronic and rampant politico-bureaucratic interferences have been detested by most members of such professions, who at least theoretically interpret their jobs as civil society callings (Baik, J. 2001). However, the same situation has also induced or enabled many opportunistic members, particularly in high organizational positions, to seek political opportunities on the basis of their state-friendly performances. In particular, so many university presidents have been appointed into prestigious political and/or governmental ranks, whereas most of the heads of the legally enfranchising professional associations in law, medicine, education, etc. have also been offered attractive political or administrative positions with the supposedly related functions.[30] They have thereby dampened a historical possibility that the predicament of state-projective politics can be meaningfully alleviated under the concerted efforts of civil society institutions. Apart from frequently wasteful practical consequences of their political and administrative participation, such opportunistic abuse of main civil society institutions by the (ir)responsible leaders tends to fundamentally distort civil society's civilizational value status merely for the sake of individual positional rent-seeking.

It is against this worrisome tendency that many critical rank-and-file members of these professions have proactively allied to organize themselves into alternative or "democratic" professional associations for genuinely representing civil society and ordinary citizens in the correspondent professional spheres (i.e. law, medicine, education, etc.). They include Minbyeon (Lawyers for a Democratic Society; https://www.minbyun.or.kr/), Ineuihyup (Association of Physicians for Humanism; https://www.humanmed.org/?module=Html&action =SiteComp&sSubNo=1), Mingyohyeop (The National Council of Professors and Researchers for Democratic and Equal Society; https:// professornet.cafe24.com/eng/), Mineonryeon (Citizens' Coalition for Democratic Media; https://www.ccdm.or.kr/), and so forth (also see next chapter). These bottom-up associations tend to take on the nature of both professional and grassroots civil organizations in line with their members' common ethos as a sort of *citizen professionals*. Their civil society-centered liberal values and purposes, as distinguished from some members' nationalism and socialism as individual orientation, have often been obscured by the fabricated claims and criticisms about their ideological agitativeness by the statist conservative forces in the state, the so-called mainstream media, as well as the respective professions (Cho, H. 2000).[31]

1.5 Conclusion and Discussion

South Korea's restored democracy, whether indicative of the military's retreat from its physically coercive rule in 1987 or a non-military or civilian politician's election into national presidency (self-declared as *munminjeongbu*, or civilian government) in 1992, has repeatedly been disrupted, corrupted, or contested in various crucial aspects and manners. The dramatic institutional restoration of formal democratic rules and procedures fell far short of constituting a revolutionarily expectable state of political and social affairs. Consequently, many aspects and traits of the pre-democratic (or state-authoritarian) era have engendered lingering side-effects well into the twenty-first century.

Above all, each confusingly or variegatedly conservative president, after their respectively democratic election into state leadership, has ended up seriously hurting or shockingly disappointing the entire national citizenry through a sort of top-down state-projective (as opposed to society-representative) politics. The self-proclaimed proudly democratic Kim Young-Sam's ambitious mimicry of the Park Chung-Hee-style developmentalism during his national presidency (1992–1997) would soon drive the entire national economy into a wholesale financial insolvency, from which South Korea was bailed out only by accepting the "IMF conditionalities" of radical labor reshuffling, financial austerity and restructuring, capital account liberalization, and so forth (Chang, K. 2019). Such controversial neoliberal remedies would, in turn, transform the nation's economic system and social structure in an irreversibly fundamental manner. The *togeon* (civil engineering) heroism of Lee Myunb-Bak (an ex-CEO of Hyundai Construction Inc., the nation's largest construction company) during his national presidency (2007–2012) resulted in a nationwide ecological calamity by his deceitful state project of *sadaegang salrigi* (saving the four largest rivers), mainly composed of straightening and deepening the major rivers and constructing innumerable river dams for containing (or, more correctly, blocking) water – all being construction industry projects without any clearly eco-friendly utility (*Yonhapnews*, 30 April 2023). This was a euphemistic renaming of Lee's original plan to construct the grand canal networks across South Korea, which had to be given up under the nationwide critical popular protests. Aside from this policy havoc, Lee would be convicted of political deception and financial embezzlement, incurring quite lengthy imprisonment later on. Park Geun-Hye, who would become the nation's first impeached president in 2017 shortly before her original presidency's expiration, was immersed in a sort of quasi-royal self-isolation, occasionally reminding South Korean citizens, including industrial conglomerate (*chaebol*) heads who now control preponderant shares of national wealth, of her father's developmental leadership and accomplishment without which the nation's current prosperity and stability would supposedly be unthinkable (*Kyunghyang Daily*, 26 December 2012). In the meantime, her secret cronies were instead exercising state-executive power, virtually on Park's behalf, in collecting bribes from some *chaebol* and, if necessary, influencing the government organs and functionaries to illicitly support the involved *chaebol* – ultimately ushering Park into impeachment and imprisonment.

In contrast to these unfortunately finished conservative presidents, the three liberal presidents – Kim Dae-Jung, Roh Moo-Hyun, and Moon Jae-In – spent most of their respective presidencies in managerially coping with various immediate calamities and catastrophies in national socioeconomic conditions.[32] In this way, they would remain relatively acceptable, if not hugely appreciable, to ordinary citizens, who, in turn, would choose the next president or government mainly according to individually beneficial election pledges whether from conservative, liberal, or progressive candidates or parties. Such opportunistic stance of most voters would induce themselves to be forgetfully enticed to potentially corruptive and divisive benefits without serious regard to the nation's collective progress and welfare. South Korea's "democracy after democratization" (Choi, J. 2006) has thereby kept being degenerated into a sort of institutionalized justification mechanism for collective socioeconomic corruption.

The democratically elected conservative presidents' political over-action and mischief did not necessarily imply that they were in fully effective control of state power apparatuses as well as social classes and organizations. In fact, under the military junta's autocratic rule, various technocratic, judicial/prosecutorial, and other public apparatuses of authoritarian political rule were heavily strengthened and expanded. Democracy's formal institutional recovery did not automatically induce such state apparatuses to be reformed for their socially rational and accountable operation. In particular, economic policy technocrats, prosecutors, and various other public officials had been tightly cartelized through their incumbent state authorities, intimate network with ex-official cliques in industry and politics, and respective sectoral clients' interests and payback bribes (Chang, K. 2019). In a grave paradox, *democratization enabled such public-cum-private cartels to be freed of the military-turned absolutist state leaders' strict command.* They thereafter did not have to fear the state executive power's often whimsical yet permanent control of their positional and organizational fate, but now only needed to skillfully collaborate with each constitutionally short-duration president and his/her political camp formed hurriedly and narrowly during each presidential election. In another paradox, given that the nation's economic (and social) order is decisively shaped by the far-flung shares and influences of such cartels, the actual impact of a certain president's (and/or his/her inner circle's) often personally driven irrational or wasteful blunder in public policy could be somehow limited or contained, however, if under no critical international or global economic and politico-military threats or uncertainties.

South Korea's frequently dualized politico-technocratic rule between a sort of *theatre presidency* and the societally organized interests of technocratic cartels in the supposedly democratic era has entrusted news media with extraordinary influences and privileges that, unfortunately, tend to be usurped by politically opportunistic journalists and media industry moguls (Park and Chang 2001). The five-year one-term-only *theatre presidency*, in the absence of broadly and robustly established political agendas and policy goals, indispensably necessitates mass media's collaboration or collusion in heavily propagandic politics, which would be attainable only in exchange for significant political opportunities and/or financial benefits of various sorts.[33] Conversely, if such collusive, and often illicit, exchanges are denied by the state leadership, some mainstream (conservative) media would stage fierce political attacks.[34] In this openly corrupt practice of journalism, media owners and journalists turn mutually parasitic and thus self-degenerative, thereby sacrificing both public interests and media's professional authority.

In fact, the political parties, from which successful (or unsuccessful) presidential and parliamentary candidates have been nominated, have had to cope with similar sociopolitical shortcomings and dilemmas and thus desperately seek news media's favorable or, at least, fair or neutral stance to them. Furthermore, as the two mainstream political parties (under the constantly changing names) have found it extremely convenient and practical to keep corruptly or falsely *constituentizing* voter citizens as sociopolitical blocs of interregional rivalry (or, perhaps more correctly, bigotry) and of inter-gender and intergenerational distrust, every political election has been severely manipulated and distorted by major news media, as a way of political collusion and exchange, or even as a strategy of political self-aggrandizing. In this context, news media have become a crucial culprit in the politically inducted, reproduced, and aggravated conflictual divisions in civil society across regions, genders, generations, as well as classes.

Besides, the socially controversial and politico-legally vulnerable nature of cartelized technocratic interests both within officialdom and in conjunction with private client interests or privatized (privately refashioned?) public interests routinely requires mass media's close collaboration in terms of praising, justifying, and/or not disclosing the concerned affairs, interests, and connections (Park and Chang 2001) This becomes especially hazardous to public welfare and justice as the chronic irregularities and distortions in the state's enforcement of law and administration can be intentionally overlooked or bypassed by media. Particularly problematic are innumerable state prosecutors' collusive participation in the cartelized (political) economic order, whether currently in office, serving as ex-officer lawyers, or repositioned as politicians (Choe, K. 2018). Conversely, prosecutors and journalists are frequently found in closely collusive relationships, whether as illicitly collaborating professionals, hidden business partners, or allied current politicians.

South Korea's democratic era has somehow managed to sustain formal democratic procedures (namely, political elections, public appointments and policy decisions, legal changes and enforcements, etc.), however, at the path-dependent structural costs of the frequent regeneration of state-projective politics and the technocratic–judicial–journalist triadic collusion in manipulatively controlling behind the curtain the preponderant shares of national public interests and assets. This is the exact reason why disturbed grassroots citizens, exploited laborers, enraged intellectuals, devoted social activists and advocates, and even socially concerned religious preachers have had to take to the streets in hundreds of thousands, or sometimes in millions, in the quasi-revolutionary candlelight protests or uprisings, condemning and forcing to evict collusively corrupt ruling elites. This is in spite of their regular exercise of political voter citizenship, or because of the repeatedly disappointing results of such formal political participation.

— 2 —

NORMAL CORRUPTION

Utilitarian Institutional Dualities and
Technocratized Authoritarian (In)justice

2.1 Introduction:
Compressed Modernity and Systematized Corruption

South Korea is replete with extreme rates, proportions, and digits indicating its intensities, particularities, and complexities in the conditions and changes of nearly all spheres of national order, social structure, and personal life. The nation's highest political, industrial, and social echelons are not excluded from such indicators. Above all, as partly indicated in Chapter 1, South Korea's seemingly robust formal democracy (recovered since 1987) has been marred by the scandalous subjection of many of its successive top executives (presidents) to post-presidency imprisonment (i.e. Lee Myung-Bak, Park Geun-Hye, Yoon Suk-Yeol, as well as Roh Tae-Woo, a democratically elected president with a politically controversial military career), politico-legally driven suicide (Roh Moo-Hyun), and shameful impeachment (Park Geun-Hye and Yoon Suk-Yeol) – perhaps the modern developed world's highest proportion of such disgraced former presidents.

Not unrelatedly, South Korea's miracle-paced industrialization and economic growth have been accompanied by the criminal indictment and imprisonment of most of the former or current heads (called *chongsu*, meaning general heads, or group presidents) of the largest industrial conglomerates (*chaebol*) – including Samsung, Hyundai, SK, etc. Their crimes include bribing the national presidents and/or their top ministers and specialized administrators for seeking unlawful state-executive favoritism, embezzling the illegally extracted secret funds (*bijageum*) from affiliated or subsidiary individual firms for various legally problematic purposes, diverting the due interest and profits of similar firms through various transactions of products, services, assets, and debts for illegally or unfairly benefiting themselves and/or their family members, and so forth. Again, this may amount to the developed world's highest proportion of prison-term incriminated top industrial elites. In addition, no less pervasively, so many virtual entrepreneurs in business-like public social services – particularly in private schools, ranging from the primary to the tertiary level – have been indicted, imprisoned, and sometimes institutionally evicted because of diverse crimes broadly similar to those of incriminated *chaebol* heads (Hong, D. 2006; Kim, I. 2022). Indeed, many of them have simultaneously established and managed profit-sector enterprises, which are arranged to enter complicated relationships and transactions with non-profit social service institutions practically owned and controlled by the same figures or families.

Another quite curious political trend, mainly in the twenty-first century, lies with a preponderant proportion of former state prosecutors as key politicians (namely, congressmen and party leaders) of the repeatedly ruling rightwing party. In fact, South Koreans ended up electing a former prosecutor(-in-chief) into national presidency in 2022, who has thereafter been widely criticized for his scandalously heavy political and administrative dependence on former and current prosecutors – causing *geomchalgonghwaguk* (prosecutorial republic), *geomsadokjae* (prosecutors' dictatorship), and so forth. As combined and interrelated results, South Korea is incomparably distinguished in the high proportions of (former and current) prosecutors among top conservative politicians, top presidential executive staff, and, paradoxically, top politico-administrative convicts (incriminated along with their supreme bosses (i.e. national presidents), and so forth.[1] As a not entirely unrelated trend, South Korean politics has been decisively influenced by journalists and employer media – in particular, the dominant conservative newspapers – and heavily staffed by former journalists, many of whom used to practice their journalism profession in the ostensibly and even corruptively political manners and thereby entered virtual political collusion with major political parties and their leaders (Kim, S. 2017; Park, S. 2017).

How can we understand these unique features of South Korea's supposedly democratic politics and advanced industrial economy (besides largely effective social governance)? Certain crucial parts of the answer may be detected from the substances of the previous chapter (Chapter 1). This chapter will offer an integrative structural answer on them, by conceptualizing, theorizing, and analyzing the concerned political, economic, social, and not least importantly, legal spheres under compressed modernity, in terms of a general order of *normal corruption* built upon the pervasive utilitarian institutional dualities in such spheres and the technocratized authoritarian practices in delivering (in)justice. South Korea's proud advancement to the global rank of advanced nations – seemingly confirmed by its membership in the OECD (Organization for Economic Cooperation and Development) ratified in 1996 – supposedly reflected not only its accomplishment of rapid economic development and social affluence but also its robust institutional modernization in the market economy, the rule of law, political democracy, etc. These two lines of national achievements have been idealized and celebrated in public discourses, but their mutual relationship has produced heated academic debates. Many of those institutionalist or heterodox scholars critical of the mainstream liberal explanations on socioeconomic development consider South Korea to be a prototype of effective statist mercantilism in the postcolonial world. Such accounts tend to justify the military's authoritarian rule associated with aggressive yet flexible technocratic intervention in industrial build-up and, though less explicit, key social services. An aspect of this order is pervasive public corruption. A general systemic order of *normal corruption* has thereby prevailed under the pervasive utilitarian institutional dualities between the West-reflexively adopted liberal institutions and the practically devised methods and improvised orders for pragmatic and expedient problem-solving, often beyond legal boundaries or principles.[2] The inertia of normal corruption in the developmental stage is a key constraint to the effective operation of democracy which has come about alongside development.

2.2 Antinomic Liberal Modernity: Utilitarian Institutional Dualities in Industrial Production and Social Service

In a majority of postcolonial societies, modernization began as a *reflexive* process (Giddens 1990; Beck, Bonss, and Lau 2003; Chang, K. 1999) in that their initial critical self-appraisal was usually focused upon their weaknesses and deficiencies vis-à-vis Western forces that had ruled and exploited them, hence leading to an open decision to emulate the West in institutional modernity, economic system, and so on.[3] While the thesis of reflexive modernization was originally presented as an account of late-modern social change in Western societies, a more explicitly corresponding process had taken place as a postcolonial world order, enabling the West to be honorably repositioned from an invader-exploiter to a civilizational model. In South Korea and elsewhere, postcolonial/neocolonial reflexive modernization usually took on an institutionalist nature in that most of the related efforts were centered upon institutional emulation or replication of the politico-legal, economic, and social systems of "advanced nations" (*seonjinguk*). Reflexive institutional(ist) modernization was, in a sense, modernization by isomorphic institutional declaration, whether through parliamentary legislations, government decrees, professional organizational statutes, civilian communal proclamations, or even dictatorial orders.

It should be crucially indicated that reflexively adopted Western institutions in political, economic, and social affairs did not necessarily enable people to solve the impending material and organizational exigencies in most of the postcolonial societies populated by exploited and deprived grassroots citizens, devoid of stable and sound conditions of economic production and social provision and stripped of social constituentization in public governance. In fact, the simulated or emulated Western social institutions – in particular, industrial market economy, rigorous democracy, and comprehensive social citizenship – were the long historical outcome of the concerned Western societies' arduous efforts, struggles, and achievements in encountering and solving wide-ranged and incessantly varied material and organizational exigencies conflated with politico-military, racial, and ecological challenges.[4] Conversely, most of postcolonial South Korea's immediate, and even long-term, material exigencies of economic production and social provision had to be acquired through various self-taught or improvised measures, causing very flexible coordination, compromise, distortion, and/or even nullification of West-reflexive formal institutions in public governance and socioeconomic life. In the long run, as it has turned out, South Korea has ended up establishing an effectively functioning, yet sociopolitically vulnerable and chronically unlawful, system of industrial capitalism and social provisioning that effect its liberal order's endemic legitimation crisis.

Above all, South Korea's now globally competitive industrial capitalism has been organizationally framed (or arrested) by the so-called *chaebol* system – a family/kin-nested structure of corporate conglomeration, involving almost normalized practices of unlawful management control and profit embezzlement through affiliated firms' stealthy transactions and collusions.[5] As such business conglomerates' industrial undertakings have supposedly been instrumental to state-led economic development, the *chaebol* system may have accelerated South Korea's condensive advancement to economic modernity (Amsden 1989). At the same time, however, as the managerial

48

decisions and practices of *chaebol*-affiliated firms have been irrationally and/or illegitimately dictated for the sake of the respective ruling figures' or families' exclusive interests, the same system may also have caused a distorted and unjust economic order by which various rights and potentials of other economic and social actors are systematically sacrificed (Kang, M. 1996; Chang, K. 2010a). Such complicated effects and consequences tend to make the *chaebol* system a highly contested social, political, legal, as well as economic terrain, replete with intricate collusions and severe confrontations among the main subjects of South Korea's industrial capitalism. As Chapter 3 in this book systematically addresses the *chaebol* issue, the current chapter will mainly elaborate on major social services (including education, health, and care in particular), which have crucially shaped both all citizens' social interests and life conditions and the nation's political and legal governance, as below.

As in most Western societies, welfare protection of dependent and/ or handicapped persons, medical services, and education, among other human and social services, have been defined as non-profit sectors in South Korea. However, the everyday institutional practice of the concerned organizations and their relationship with the state chronically confuse the public as if they were commercial business domains. Such tendency is not necessarily due to South Korea's subjection to American libertarian influence in the concerned sectors. In fact, even the U.S. has maintained the basic non-profit principles in education, medicine, and care, so that South Korea's reflexive institutional isomorphism in these sectors necessitated utilitarian institutional dualities, as earlier indicated. Let me brief on each service's practical nature in the South Korean context as below.

In education, most of the private universities have survived financially – in fact, used to prosper for so many years – mainly on the basis of privately paid tuition, the level of which has continuously been among the world's most expensive; whereas the financial contribution of the governing foundations has usually remained minimal or negligible, except during the initial founding stage (Kim, I. 2022).[6] In fact, South Koreans' internationally unparalleled "education zeal," as materialized into their global top rank in the population's proportion of tertiary education completion, has been infrastructurally enabled by those aggressive entrepreneurs in education(-as-business) who have capitalized on the government's *de facto* policy of allowing – or, more correctly, not inspecting and punishing – their practical profit-seeking through a wide range of legally and socially problematic practices (besides reaping the extremely high-priced tuitions), in return for their initial entrustment (by consequence, business investment) of sizable assets in education(-as-public service) (Hong, D. 2006).[7] As a very widely revealed and indicted practice, nearly countless school foundations have been implicated in dishonest internal trades with construction companies that are controlled, directly or through family members, by the foundation heads – in particular, government-subsidized construction projects for educational facilities being contracted out for heavily bloated prices.[8] A similar rule governs various types of public medical and welfare services under a sort of improvised welfare pluralism, as below (Chang, K. 2019).

Hospitals are legally defined as non-profit entities for social service, but most of them, except university medical school-affiliated ones, have been set up and managed by entrepreneurial figures including business-oriented physicians. Hospitals, despite their legal status in social service, have practically been allowed to refuse medical service to those who are unable to pay, and prices for medical service have been high enough to enable most physicians, whether hospital-hired or in individual practice, to join the far upper-income class. Individual practitioners in medicine can operate without serious regulatory constraints on their practical business interests. (Individual medical practice has been a *de facto* profit sector, assuming the nature of self-employment.) The Korean Medical Association, representing all registered physicians' socioeconomic interests, has adamantly and successfully opposed the social demand and government attempt to increase the annual supply of new physicians by the expanded national student quotas of all university medical schools, thereby protracting South Korea's second worst ratio between physicians (including doctors of indigenous Korean medicine) and national population among the all OECD countries. and leaving so many localities devoid of dependable access to timely medical care.[9] This shortage in medical service has been particularly serious in such essential areas as surgery (cardiothoracic surgery in particular), internal medicine, obstetrics/gynecology, and pediatrics, which are conversely regarded as *gipibunya* (avoided specialization areas) by medical students.[10] Its purpose is simple and clear – to minimize (market-based) competition among medical care providers and thereby sustain sufficient profitability in medicine. This effort not only betrays general citizens as daily recipients of medical service, but has recently contradicted the main interest of those large hospitals confronted with worsening difficulties in hiring sufficient physicians needed to satisfy affluent South Koreans' bloated demand for high-level medical service. Not unrelatedly, everyday practices in medical service have been marred by wide irregularities, the most serious or rather absurd of which consists in the almost normalized use of nurses and nursing assistants in various legally defined functions and duties of physicians, including doctor-substitutive surgery, prescription under a doctor's name, ward rounding in a doctor's gown, and so forth.[11] So many nurses and nursing assistants have ended up being legally punished for such *unconsented* roles of "ghost doctors." Another widespread, or practically generalized, corruption is the so-called "rebate" payments from pharmaceutical and medical equipment companies to physicians and hospitals, which frequently amount to sizable portions of physician incomes and hospital revenues. Some hospitals have tried to save expenditure by simply asking their employee physicians to regard this stealthy income as part of their regular salary.[12]

Numerous privately established non-profit care institutions for orphans, deprived elderly, the handicapped, and other needy persons have operated mainly on the basis of government subsidies, charitable donations, and so forth. During the pre-democratic era, many of them even exploited inmates' labor for commercial production and construction and abused them physically, mentally, and/or spiritually.[13] One of the most notorious examples was Hyeongjebokjiwon (the name meaning "brotherly welfare institution"), an ad hoc institution for accommodating *burangja* (floating persons) during the *Singunbu* (New Military) era of the 1980s.[14] This incident traumatized South Korean society, not just for its cruelties to innocent citizens, but also by the fact that such a shocking episode had taken place for so long in the middle of a multi-million city (Busan), with so many accountable officials, as well as next-door neighbors, remaining neglectful and indifferent. In this regard, the City of Busan had to make a public apology, given by its mayor: "Those incarcerations, violence, intimidation, forced labor, and so forth perpetrated to innocent citizens from 1975 to 1987 in Hyeongjebokjiwon in Busan were terrible human rights violations that should have never existed . . . The City of Busan is responsible for failing to protect the citizens' human rights by neglecting then its duty for managing and supervising welfare facilities. As mayor representing the City of Busan, I sincerely apologize, though too late, to all citizens and, above all, to the concerned victims and their families" (*Beminor*, 17 September 2018; https://www.beminor.com/news/articleView.html?idxno=12601).

In a recent corruption incident of a miscellaneous yet widespread nature, numerous privately founded kindergartens (operating with public funds allocated in proportion to the size of accommodated children and government-subsidized tuition revenues) were found to have misused such revenues for private needs and purposes of the "owners" of them, including luxury brand bags, karaoke bars, and so forth (*Yonhapnews*, 17 October 2018; https://www.yna.co .kr/view/AKR20181017135500057). While such deviances had widely been known to regulatory government organs, they used to share with kindergarten operators an interpretation that privately founded kindergartens are private properties whose public use (for children) should be compensated in one way or another by government subsidies, parental expenses, etc. (Kim and Hwang 2019). That is, the publicly allocated operating funds used to be virtually seen as private income from a sort of small business. The same trend has prevailed, albeit at much larger scales, among innumerable long-term care centers for chronically ill or handicapped elderly that operate with care expenses paid mainly from the National Long-Term Care (LTC) Insurance for the Elderly, and partially by financially able children, if any, of the accommodated elderly. The government's special investigation in 2018 of 836 elderly care centers (about 4% of all such centers in the nation) revealed that 775 units, or 92.7 percent of them, had deceptively exaggerated their care work and/or personnel for overcharging the LTC Insurance, embezzled public subsidies and institutional budgets, and/or committed various other wrongdoings (*Hankyoreh*, 3 June 2019). Most of them are still *in business*, whether under the same governing bodies or their kin network. This implies that a staggering majority of these elderly care centers have operated by cheating the public without worrying too much about serious regulatory sanctions or legal punishments.

In frequent instances, as a highly interesting development, the supposedly non-profit foundations for these social services organizationally resemble the *chaebol*-controlled industrial/commercial enterprises in terms of familial control of management (and *de facto* ownership).[15] Besides, and not coincidentally, the governing families often control a complex mix of social service foundations and industrial/commercial enterprises simultaneously, so that the rampant illicit internal trades between their non-profit social service institutions and foundations and for-profit business enterprises have functioned as a core mechanism for the phenomenal growth of their private wealth.[16] The state's (non-)regulation of these social service entities has virtually ensured their profitability through a liberal pricing policy permitting fully profitable prices for the concerned services and a wide legal leniency to various illegitimate or illegal practices for amassing private wealth.[17]

In recent decades, the government has openly taken the notion or position of *industrial policy* for developing and/or restructuring these social services into globally competitive and profitable sectors. Among others, the possibility of commercial medical service by specially licensed hospitals, for foreign visitors at the beginning, has ignited a huge societal controversy (Lee, P. 2015). On the other hand, numerous South Korean universities have already turned into quasi-commercial entities in openly accepting rapidly increasing numbers of high tuition-paying foreign students, in particular from other Asian countries, who have critically helped to make up for the continuously worsening demographic shrinkage of domestic Korean students (*Maeil Business Newspaper*, 10 July 2017; https://www.mk.co.kr/news/soci ety/10781192).[18] These trends imply that transnational human flows in social globalization such as foreign students and "medical tourists" are accommodated, or expected, as convenient inputs in facilitating the business-oriented transformation of the formally non-profit social services.[19]

All in all, South Korea's liberal system-modernity has been pervasively and chronically contaminated (and distorted) by the virtually normalized structures and practices of corruption shared among the mainstream actors and organizations in economic production and social provision under the state's technocratic and legal patronage. Mutually entangled corruption has prevailed between main organizations of industrial production and social services on the one hand and politico-administrative and legal power on the other hand. South Korea has achieved quite remarkable levels of sustained industrial development, material and cultural affluence, and social stability under (despite or due to?) such normalized corruption of the economic, social, as well as state institutions. No matter whether any functional fits exist between South Korea's national economic and social goals and normally corrupt mainstream institutions, the nation and its citizens have inevitably been inflicted by the fundamental legal, sociopolitical, and even civilizational dilemma of having to ordinarily witness and endure the legally (and sociopolitically and philosophically) problematic structures and practices of such mainstream entities in the economy and society. When (and as) most citizens, not to mention elites, have compromised their lives with them as inescapable social elements for the sake of immediate individualized socioeconomic benefit and security, the corruption order becomes a societal phenomenon. What about the state's judiciary apparatuses (the court and the prosecution service) and society's intellectual apparatuses (such as news media, etc.)? Does the seemingly permanent corruption of the dominant economic, social, and political institutions attest to a possibility of collusive corruption – or incapacity – by judiciary and journalist elites?

2.3 Mutually Embedded Corruption and Technocratized Authoritarian (In)justice

The expression "too big to jail" typically refers to failures to prosecute big corporations such as Wall Street banks. However, the same expression has mostly been used for failures to prosecute the founding families of *chaebol*, large business groups controlled by founder families in South Korea. The failure to hold these founder families accountable for crimes of embezzlement or breach of fiduciary duty undermines the rule of law and the corporation system, which are foundations of the market economy ... Korea's judiciary system has been notorious for its lenient rulings toward *chaebol* founder families, regardless of the type or nature of the crime, known as "three–five rule": a three-year prison sentence whose execution is suspended for five years and then exempted if no further violations occur during the suspended period ... The lenient rulings toward *chaebol* affiliates can be confirmed in a broader set of data. Choi and his colleagues (2016: 85–104) found that no manager or controlling shareholder from member firms of a large business group has ever been sent to prison without probation in the sample of 28 individuals charged with embezzlement or breach of fiduciary duty of publicly traded firms in Korea between 2004 and 2008. By contrast, nineteen out of fifty managers from the other publicly traded firms charged with the same crimes were sentenced to imprisonment in the same time period ... These lenient rulings are not because of the practical challenges involved in finding evidence of the crime. Even in cases where the evidence is clear and irrefutable, the court typically argues that the founder families of the *chaebol* are considered to be so valuable to the economy that it may serve public interest not to hold them accountable for their crimes. When the string of suspended sentences drew strong criticism for the application of separate legal standards to the rich, the Supreme Court's Sentencing Commission changed its guidelines, mandating strict minimum statutory punishment on significant embezzlement or breach of trust. However, in practice, these guidelines were not well observed by judges.

(Park, S. 2020)

The National Movement Headquarter for Reform and Corruption Expulsion in Private Schools, The Korean Teachers and Educational Workers Union, and other educational and civil organizations in a press conference ... indicated "The Ministry of Education comptroller is in general charge of inspecting about 450 educational institutions, including offices of education, universities, national hospitals, etc." and criticized "Comptroller Kim, as the officer-in-charge and the chair of the inspection process appraisal committee, has so far adjudicated more than ninety percent of inspection cases to 'warning', i.e. no further question in practice." According to the results of their analysis of the White Book of The Private School Reform Committee of the Ministry of Education, the Ministry in the recent ten years has discovered 3,106 cases of private school corruption but accused or requested investigation of only 205 cases (6.6%). More than ninety percent of those involved in corruption have been subjected only to warning or caution. They pointed out "a civil servant must take accusation once a crime in office is detected," but Comptroller Kim did not do so even about embezzlement at work, violation of the private school act, and other matters that must naturally be subjected to accusation and investigation request.

(Yonhapnews, 26 March 2020)

The above realities point not only to the widespread practices of corruption by South Korea's major industrial conglomerates and private providers of the supposedly non-profit social services such as public education, etc., but also to the virtually regularized dereliction of duty by public organs and officials in charge of institutional regulation and judicial control over them. The latter situation may well derive from some individually corrupt attitude and atmosphere of such organs and officers, but their apparent delinquencies or neglects in office may also reflect a *systemic order of mutually embedded corruption* under utilitarian institutional dualities in economic management and social service provision. The seemingly turbulent yet robust structure of South Korea's supposedly utilitarian institutional dualism in industrial governance and social service provision has been established and reproduced through a sort of *corruption-mediated governed interdependence* between such devious and/or illicit organizations in business and society and the authoritarian state's technocratic and (technocratized) prosecutorial and judicial organs.[20]

From the former to the latter, more specifically, the following three key elements are served (Chang, J. 2010; Oh, S. 2019, 2020): (1) the generalized patterns of loyalty and complicity to highly centralized state authorities; (2) the efficient and practical problem-solving under the utilitarian technocratic criteria, often through institutional informalities and irregularities; (3) financial and/or occupational kickbacks to the state's (executive, administrative, and judiciary) organs and officials in return for specific favoritism and/or routinized patronage.[21] From the latter to the former, the following three key elements are served: (1) the supposedly strategic preferential allocation of politically and/or administratively mobilized national resources and social opportunities as industrial, financial, and social policy; (2) political, administrative, and legal protection and/or exemption with respect to generalized and repetitious violations of public laws, government regulations, and even socially just norms; (3) the cooptation and suppression of those regions, communities, industries, classes, and citizens, whose interests and rights are systematically and/or ordinarily sacrificed in the economic, social, and political spheres controlled by the hegemonic order of utilitarian institutional dualism (Chang, J. 2010; Oh, S. 2019; Oh, S. 2020). The above-explained collusive interdependencies between the internally entangled state agencies and private subjects of industry and social service inevitably imply that the systematically generalized corruption order implicates not only opportunistically corrupt entrepreneurs and their administrative and political patrons, but also the state's prosecutorial and judiciary organs in charge of delivering punitive justice to such actors of corruption. That is, under the orchestration of the executive state power (invested in national presidency), major government organs and technocrats, prosecutorial and judiciary offices, and the president's political party (*jipgwonyeodang*) and its core members are systematically yet informally coalesced into an internally fused institutional entity.[22]

The most problematic institutional aspect of this hegemonic governance system is, of course, the pervasive compromise, breaking, and even practical annulment of (the rule of) law under the routinized tacit participation of prosecutors (and sometimes judges), which indispensably necessitates their intimate cooperation and collusion with key political and administrative elites (as well as congenial relationship with potentially punishable subjects in business and social service). Particularly during the military's authoritarian rule, prosecutors were entrusted with wide discretionary authority in nearly all affairs and processes of criminal adjudication, which was derived from their close communication and collaboration with the state's executive office (the Blue House).[23] Prosecutors, with their subordinate crime inspectors, used to supervise, command, and sometimes replace police in crime inspection and practically nullify or substitute the court by (ab)using their monopoly power in crime indictment. Most criminals or suspects, including those involved in the above-explained utilitarian corruption, could not but feel that their judicial fate was almost exclusively in the hands of prosecutors, who, in turn, would be under the tight influence or command of the state's executive office. In such unconstrained politico-judicial capacity, many prosecutors tended to feel that their judicial authority was insuperable and frequently tried to practically liquidate the court's due authority by aggressively or cunningly manipulating their indictment capacity (Choe, K. 2018).[24]

In order to supervise this hegemonic governance system, the state's executive office used to rely on multiple state agencies of (vaguely defined) intelligence, including (1) explicit intelligence agencies such as KCIA (Korean Central Intelligence Agency; currently, National Intelligence Service), military intelligence service (Defense Security Command), police intelligence department, etc., and (2) in-effect intelligence agencies, such as government-dispatched prosecutors, national audit authority, national tax authority, national banking supervision authority, etc. Interestingly, after South Korea's formal (re)democratization, these agencies have been described in media as "power institutions" (*gwonlyeokgigwan*), and, not coincidentally, their heads have been appointed from the president's most intimate figures. These intelligence agencies have kept their "no secret" surveillance function over the state's own organs and offices, over its collaborative or collusive partners in business and social service, over its political victims and critics in social spaces (universities in particular), and, perhaps most problematically, over news media and journalists. Journalists ended up inventing a derisive term, *gwanseongija* (state-appointed reporter), to point to various state-dispatched intelligence agents hovering even in newspaper offices.[25]

The internal collusive fusion of the state apparatuses in administration and prosecution (and the frequent sidelining of the parliament and the court) has induced South Korean media and citizenry – and sometimes opposition politicians – to describe the executive state authority as "emperor presidency" (*jewangjeok daetongryeongje*). Under this circumstance, South Korea's journalism has come to assume a sort of second division (quasi-)state power, which complements, or even replaces, the formal judiciary (and parliamentary) authorities. (News media's substitutive and/or complicit assertion of political representative functions under South Korea's state-projective politics has been explained earlier in Chapter 1 of this book.) Newspapers and news broadcasts have ordinarily watched and investigated prosecutorial organs (and police), besides criminals or suspects, under the assumption of the former's potential manipulation or even concealment of criminal affairs, in conjunction with political influences, in particular, from the state's executive office (Park and Chang 2001). Emperorlike presidents, whether from the conservative or liberal factions, have had to reckon seriously with (legally private and sociopolitically independent) news media's such derivative sociopolitical, and in-effect prosecutorial, influences. Innumerable journalists and major conservative newspapers have tried to capitalize opportunistically on such sociopolitical and legal conditions by shrewdly showing off their potential utilities and/or threats to political elites (as well as politically and/or administratively dependent industrial and social elites), in particular, about chronically politicized high-level criminal cases (Park and Chang 2001).[26]

The above-explained collusive governance involving, on the one hand, main players in industry and social service and, on the other hand, administrative, prosecutorial/judiciary, and even journalistic institutions, tend to induce South Korea's entrenched private interests and classes to routinely and circumspectly engage in both nominally legal and widespread unlawful attempts at bribing state executive, administrative and judicial elites and journalists, in order practically to privatize the rule of law and manipulate public information and opinion. A popular term has been coined in depicting the concerned practices and relationships, namely, *janghaksaeng* (scholarship awardee). In particular, the nation's largest conglomerate, Samsung Group, has repetitiously been revealed to be secretly enlisting judiciary as well as administrative officials (and ex-officials), major conservative media, and even some socially influential academics and activists.[27] Besides, there are a wide array of nominally legal and/or public arrangements designed for similar effects – a most conspicuous example being each major conglomerate's launching of *eonlonjaedan* (journalism foundation), which functions to finance journalists' overseas graduate study and various other exclusive perks. Samsung and Hyundai even run their own or intimately connected conservative newspapers.

2.4 Democratic Political Ambivalence and Civil–Liberalist Reform Movements

In South Korea's systemic order of normal corruption, complex political, social, and academic controversies and doubts have inevitably abounded, on the one hand, about whether the nearly generalized institutional, legal, and, ultimately, political irregularities are justifiable with respect to the basic ideological premise of the nation's liberal polity and, on the other hand, about whether the same irregularities have been – and continue to be – actually effective in delivering the nation's practical economic and social necessities. Reactions and answers to such concerns have crucially fluctuated in accordance with the nation's overall economic and sociopolitical conditions – namely, economic development and democratization. These two conditions kept interactively changing, decisively culminating in South Korea's dramatic democratization (or democratic restoration) amid its sustained economic ascendance in the late 1980s. It was by then apparent that the nation had successfully established itself as an economically and socially prosperous entity, no matter whether or how much its utilitarian institutional dualities and accompanying order of normal corruption had contributed to such achievement. Logically, the supposed utility of institutional dualism and normalized corruption may have become more and more questionable. In fact, if they have actually helped to solve practical necessities and thereby relieved the current necessity of depending on them, such order could turn increasingly anti-systemic and dysfunctional. This will be particularly problematic if the inherent inequalities and disparities of a liberal economy are arbitrarily intensified due to the state's *no-more-utilitarian* financial support and regulatory and legal patronage for the entrenched rich industrial and social subjects. More crucially, the same order, at least in principle, may not be sociopolitically compatible with the arduously recovered (formal) democratic polity (and, needless to say, the rule of law).

Has such sociopolitical incompatibility of corruption-mediated institutional dualism been seriously problematized and reformed by the democratically elected state leaders and representatives? Have South Korean citizens, including critical intellectuals and activists, successfully or at least visibly demanded such changes? Irrespective of how much aggressive or pervasive civilian actors' legally problematic practices in industrial production and social service have been, it is beyond dispute that South Korea has managed its modern history in an extremely state-authoritarian manner, however, without a legitimately stable framework of political representation – above all, the systematically and legitimately functioning political parties. In the very onset of formal democracy (in 1948), the military's usurpation of state power (in 1961 and 1980), and the socially accomplished reinstatement of normal democratic procedures (in 1960 and 1987), South Korea's mainstream political parties have existed and functioned in fundamentally self-serving manners with most of their political votes politically engineered through *de facto* bribing of various fluid social constituencies by societally irrational or wasteful pledges and gifts (frequently including cash payments to voters).

Unfortunately, even the apparently more liberal Democratic Party of Korea, under its continually modified names, has failed to make sustained meaningful differences in firmly establishing a genuinely representative political platform, whether for justifiable class interests or effective policy models. It has benefited from the nation's notorious interregional rivalry (or bigotry) politics, which is a sort of socially divisive populism, as opportunistically as its conservative opponent party (currently, People Power) (Chang, K. 2022b, ch. 3).[28] Due to their fundamentally defective nature in democratic political representation, both of South Korea's two preponderantly dominant parties have comprised serious entities of normal corruption themselves, regardless of arguable differences between them in administrative performance (or failure). In the eyes of defiant social critics, they do not meaningfully differ as practically unreluctant hostages to the entrenched industrial and social interests under the systemic order of normal corruption.

While South Korea's utilitarian institutional dualities in industry and social service and technocratized authoritarian (in)justice governing them have critically lost their contextual validities, the self-assertively democratic political factions, whether socially liberal or conservatively statist, have failed to meaningfully reform such outmoded order, and thus necessitated civil society's proactive reform movements, which are highly unique and complex in nature. By and large, besides general citizens' mass protests and critical opinions, there are several lines of civil society-driven liberalist reform movements as follows: (1) functionally comprehensive citizen movements and organizations that promote socioeconomic reforms and legal justice, indispensably along with watchdog functions over prosecutorial, judiciary as well as regulatory administrative organs – above all, People's Solidarity for Participatory Democracy (Chamyeoyeondae; www.peoplepower21.org) and Citizens' Coalition for Economic Justice (Gyeongsilyeon;www.ccej.or.kr); (2) functionally specialized citizen movements and organizations targeted at *sabeopgamsi* (judicial oversight), *sabeopgaehyeok* (judicial reform), and so forth; (3) major profession reform movements within and without (as described in the previous chapter), most of which are oriented at overseeing, criticizing, and resisting state-collusively centralized ruling forces within and across the supposedly liberal professions (as civil society's infrastructural institutions) and take on the nature of both professional and grassroots civil organizations in line with their members' common ethos as a sort of *citizen professional* – including, above all, Lawyers for a Democratic Society (Minbyeon; https://www.minbyun.or.kr/) and Citizens' Coaltion for Democratic Media (Mineonlyeon; https://www.ccdm.or.kr/); (4) major profession reform movements in social services (education, medicine, welfare, etc.) – including National Council of Professors and Researchers for Democratic and Equal Society (Mingyohyeop; https://professornet.cafe24.com/), Association of Physicians for Humanism (Ineuihyup; https://www.humanmed.org/), Citizens' Alliance for Welfare (Wooribokjisiminyeonhap; http://m.wooriwelfare.org/), etc.); (5) (progressive) trade unions, (activist) political parties, and other grassroots, if not peripheral, social organizations of activists and rank-and-file members, often combining the traits and/or statuses of occupational, sectoral, professional, intellectual, and civic organizations – including, among others, Korean Confederation of Trade Unions (Minjunochong; https://nodong.org/), Korean Teachers and Education Workers Union (Jeongyojo; https://www.eduhope.net/), National Union of Media Workers (Eonlonnojo; https://media.nodong.org/), various activist political parties (such as Justice Party, Basic Income Party, Green Party, Progressive Party, etc.), and so forth. All these civil, professional, industrial, social, and political subjects of South Korea's nominally liberal social order and state system find themselves structurally interdependent in rectifying and overcoming the arguably hegemonic yet chronically unjustifiable ruling order of normal corruption. Their nation's integrity as a genuine liberal democratic system necessitates a sort of allied social struggle, if not united front, by various basic constituents of civil, professional, proletarian, industrial, political, and intellectual functions and purposes against the structurally collusive ruling cartels among their upper counterparts in the industrial, social, political, administrative, judicial, and journalist establishments.

Perhaps the historico-social necessity of such united struggles of unidentifiably diverse grassroots subjects was most dramatically manifested in the "candlelight uprising" in the winter of 2016–2017, by which Park Geun-Hye, Park Chung-Hee's daughter, was virtually ousted from presidency by repeated multi-million subaltern protests, which pressurized even most of conservative as well as liberal politicians to agree to the parliament's impeachment act, as noted in the previous chapter. The subsequently elected Moon Jae-In government declared itself as the "candlelight revolution government" and, very appropriately, carried out various progressively corrective reforms in social, economic, educational, environmental, and many other affairs. Accordingly, Moon briefly enjoyed remarkable political approval across society, however, only to pass state leadership over to a political regime that is most contradictory or dysfunctional in rectifying the use-by date-expired system of utilitarian normal corruption. In a sense, civil society's strategic attempt to utilize the Moon government as a sociopolitical Trojan horse for effectively integrative social, economic, environmental, political, and legal reforms resulted in a disturbing failure, due to the political limits and logistic mistakes of this vaguely or confusingly democratic regime.

2.5 Conclusion: Normal Corruption, Government–Business–Law Collusion, and South Korean Democracy

A general systemic order of *normal corruption* has prevailed in South Korea under the pervasively utilitarian institutional dualities between the West-reflexively adopted liberal institutions and the practically devised methods and improvised orders for pragmatic and expedient problem-solving, often nullifying legal boundaries or principles. South Korea has achieved quite remarkable levels of sustained industrial development and material and cultural affluence, with such normalized corruption of the main economic and social institutions. No matter whether any functional fits exist between national socioeconomic goals and normally corrupt mainstream institutions, the nation and its ordinary citizens have inevitably been inflicted by the fundamental legal, political, and even civilizational dilemma of having to ordinarily witness and endure the legally (and politically and philosophically) problematic structures and practices of such mainstream entities. As most ordinary citizens, besides elites, compromised their lives with them as inescapable social elements for individualized socioeconomic benefit and security, the corruption order became a general societal phenomenon.

What about the state's judiciary apparatuses (the court and the prosecution service) and society's intellectual apparatuses (such as news media, etc.)? Does the seemingly perpetual corruption of the dominant economic and social institutions attest to a possibility of judiciary and journalist elites' collusive corruption? The state judicial organs – prosecution in particular – have not functioned simply to incriminate such systemic corruption but to carefully incorporate practical national and/or social utilities by flexibly ignoring or pardoning its legal problems. Not unrelatedly, news media – conservative newspapers in particular – have tried to deliver their own verdicts on both sides of corruption, namely, unlawful practices in problem-solving and arbitrary (non-)adjudication on them. As each state leadership, whether autocratic or democratic, has had to juggle with such complicated practical and (il)legal considerations, the nation's liberal systemic order has kept confronting built-in irregularities and instabilities, regardless of its immediate or sustained success in practical problem-solving for economic production and social service provision.

All rank-and-file civil, legal, professional, industrial, social, and political subjects in the nation's nominally liberal social order and state system have found themselves structurally interdependent and allied in rectifying and overcoming the hegemonic yet chronically unjustifiable ruling order of normal corruption. South Korea's integrity as a genuine liberal democratic system necessitates a sort of allied social struggle, if not united front, by various basic constituents of civil, professional, proletarian, political, and intellectual functions and purposes against the structurally collusive ruling cartels among their upper counterparts in the industrial, social, political, administrative, judicial, and journalist establishments. The further the economy and society develop, the more urgent such necessity for allied social struggles becomes.

— 3 —

CLASS CONTRADICTIONS OF STATE CAPITALIST INDUSTRIALISM

The "*Chaebol* Republic"

3.1 Introduction: State Capitalist Development and the *Chaebol*

The condensed nature of South Korea's capitalist development has been amply incorporated in the historical and organizational characteristics of the *chaebol*.[1] The *chaebol* system – the South Korean version of familial capitalism – represents one of the most inventive components of South Korean modernity. As of the 1960s, the South Korean economy was practically devoid of a viable industrial capitalist class, so that "the developmental state" under Park Chung-Hee had to launch a class-making project (Kim, E. 1997). While a handful of the existing industrial entrepreneurs, most of whom Park disliked for political reasons, were co-opted out of practical consideration, the South Korean bourgeoisie by and large had to be invented anew in a condensed manner (Kang, M. 1996). However, this political background to the *chaebol*'s rise should not lead to a hasty speculation that these business groups thrived mostly on politically generated opportunities and benefits. As instantly self-established individual entrepreneurs in a war-torn society, most conglomerate heads were not endowed with sizable amounts of capital. But they have evolved their way into a conglomerate system, by which their capital deficiency does not prevent them from expanding into whatever new industries South Korea finds competitiveness in.

The *chaebol*'s principal ingenuity has consisted in its internal structure of control over complexly interconnected firms, under which a conglomerate head and his/her family rule dozens of firms operating in different industries, without holding legally sufficient shares. To the extent that their industrial undertakings have been instrumental to state-led economic development, the *chaebol* system (of exaggerated control over not clearly owned firms) seems to have accelerated South Korea's compressed march to economic modernity. However, to the extent that the managerial decisions and practices of *chaebol*-affiliated firms have been illegitimately dictated for the sake of the head's exclusive interests, the *chaebol* system seems to have engendered a distorted and unjust economic order, by which the economic rights and potentials of other economic actors are systematically sacrificed. Furthermore, given the fact that the *chaebol* used to function as a strategic partner or tool of the developmental state for national economic development, the economic operations of *chaebol*-affiliated firms are structurally interwoven with the political stake of the developmentalist government, the public economic interests ensuing from their special access to national socioeconomic resources, various interests and rights of their workers, the property rights of their ordinary shareholders, and the business interests of their potential competitors (Chang, K. 2010a; Kang, C. 1999). Such a complex set of social, political, and economic interests make the *chaebol* system a highly contested social, political, as well as economic terrain, replete with complex collusions and tense confrontations among the core subjects of South Korea's industrial capitalism.

As has been widely researched, reported, witnessed, and criticized, the dominant presence of the *chaebol* not only engenders practically normalized distortions in the market economic order and its regulatory and legal principles, but also induces widespread administrative, political, and even judiciary corruptions. As a combined outcome of these structural irregularities, the liberal systemic order has incurred fundamental legitimation crises in the economic, social, and politico-legal aspects. If seen in the class perspective, the *chaebol*, as South Korea's mainstream bourgeoisie, have been responsible for the complex and chronic distortions of the nation's liberal order, and thereby contradict (Western) liberal modernity's historico-societal foundation of bourgeois civility and autonomy. South Korea's liberal industrial modernity without liberal bourgeoisie – or, conversely, its state capitalist industrial modernity with the state-dependent (and increasingly state-parasitic) (il)liberal industrialist class – has necessitated nearly permanent fundamental contradictions, instabilities, and conflicts in the nation's social, politico-legal, as well as economic order.

Such systemic risks of the *chaebol* have been crucially conflated with South Korea's tumultuous transition to democracy, i.e. liberal political modernity. Its dramatic restoration of formal democracy under progressive intellectual and grassroots uprisings in the 1980s

DEMOCRACY, CAPITALISM, SOCIAL CLASS

was soon perceived as a critical threat to the entrenched collusive interests of the *chaebol* and their political, administrative, judiciary, and even academic patrons. Besides, in another manifestation of the nation's democratic evolution, the increasingly organized industrial labor's forceful resistance to the state–business collusive suppression of workers' just rights to material reward and welfare, as well as social freedom, had to be directly reckoned and managed by the industrialists because of the (procedurally) democratized state's gradual neutralization in labor relations. South Korea's dynamic democratization made the *chaebol* feel multifarious threats to their vested economic interests and politico-legal securities, so that they immediately, yet covertly and successfully, reached out for various state and social elites to organize a new line of political economic collusion (*jeonggyeongyuchak*), pivoting around their own initiatives and agendas, broadly and conveniently framed in neoliberal ideas. Quite curiously, many of the democratically oriented (and elected) elites and reform-minded social activists and intellectuals also subscribed, in consequence, to neoliberalism in their critical understanding and rectification of the *chaebol* system and its politico-administrative as well as economic hazards.

It was in this context that South Korea's embracing of neoliberalism took place so rapidly and widely, stunning its keen observers with lingering impressions about the (supposedly counter-liberal) developmental state's proactive pursuit of national(ist) capitalist industrialization. It was also in this context that the neoliberally driven national financial crisis in the late 1990s did not lead to a rethinking of neoliberalization but to a further intensified implementation of neoliberal policies, programs, and activisms. (Even the so-called "IMF conditionalities" for a financial bail-out of South Korea were so readily and eagerly accommodated.) The thereby reformed (or reborn?), yet still *chaebol*-centered, South Korean capitalism has unfortunately ended up, on the one hand, socioeconomically disenfranchising or precariatizing a preponderant proportion of its working population across nearly all generations and, on the other hand, radically being incorporated into global financial capital through its predatory (portfolio) takeover of economy-wide industrial ownership. South Korea's appallingly worsening inequalities in income and asset tend to be generated as conflated outcomes of (anti-labor) state capitalist industrialism, the *chaebol*'s organizational, legal, and financial irregularities, and global neoliberal interests, whose mutual distinctions are increasingly blurred.

3.2 The Political Birth, Developmental Transformation, and Corporate Expansion of the *Chaebol*

In the immediate post-liberation period, the sudden departure of Japanese colonial capitalism left the Korean economy devoid of a serviceable capitalist class possessing self-sufficient capital and autonomous entrepreneurship. Industrial assets left behind by the fleeing Japanese capitalists were claimed by the infantile South Korean state, but it was in no position to know how to utilize them efficiently for national economic restoration. Despite the independence of 1948, the state leadership could barely stand on its own feet, even in the political dimension. The Rhee Syng-Man government decided to distribute the left-behind Japanese industrial assets to private entrepreneurs, many of whom, in fact, were in kinship or social network with the political oligarchy in the government and the two-chamber parliament (Gong, J. 2000). This political connection pretty much predetermined, on the one hand, the preferential terms of distribution of the Japanese assets and, on the other hand, the clientelistic nature of state–business relationship that developed thereafter. Thereby was born a *political economic entrepreneurial class*, which would evolve into South Korea's globally famous (or infamous?) business conglomerates, called *chaebol*. In a highly ironical yet critical fashion, Japanese colonial capitalism – or, more precisely, the postcolonial context accompanying its military defeat – contributed to the formation of a South Korean bourgeoisie, which in turn would shape the basic nature of the country's capitalist political economy.

The question as to the supposed Japanese colonial origin of capitalist entrepreneurship in South Korea is a hotly debated topic in East Asian history and Korean studies.[2] While historical inferences in scholarship supporting this view are not discountable, a concrete empirical continuity and/or causation between the few Korean corporations existing during the colonial period and the mostly new mammoth conglomerates of the industrialization period, has yet to be established. As Amsden notices, most Korean entrepreneurs during the Japanese colonial era had to operate in a political economic environment fundamentally dissimilar from the post-independence political economy of development (Amsden 1989). The Japanese colonial state in Korea basically adopted a predatory position toward indigenous Korean entrepreneurs (unlike its supposedly developmental stance to expatriot Japanese entrepreneurs), so that they had to operate on a rather independent basis.[3] The post-independence South Korean state, especially in its developmental version, maintained a collusive relationship with private entrepreneurs, exchanging administrative patronage for entrepreneurial and political cooperation. Not much of the structural nature and behavioral pattern of the contemporary *chaebol* can be traced back to the colonial era. By contrast, the physical transfer of Japanese industrial assets to the South Korean government and then to its client entrepreneurs (many of whom became fresh new entrepreneurs, precisely thanks to such transfer of industrial assets) can be counted as one undisputable origin of South Korean industrial capitalism.

Despite its generous offering of Japanese industrial assets, Rhee Syng-Man's government could not deliver what would be much more crucial in the long run for its client business community. Lacking the technocratic and political capacity for establishing and activating a modern economy, the Rhee government merely expanded the preferential treatments for client entrepreneurs in terms of practically minus-interest loans, permits for monopolistic production and trade, and exclusive use of U.S. aid materials, and thereby intensified the rent-seeking nature of business (Kang, M. 1996). As the South Korean economy continued to suffer from instability and stagnancy in the 1950s, the corrupt aspect of business reliance on political favoritism far overshadowed any productive aspect. If the dictatorial nature of the Rhee government brought about a student-led political uprising in April 1960, its economic failure led to a military coup in May 1961. The former called for a sound liberal democracy, whereas the latter would embody mercantilist nationalism.

As an initial political initiative, Park Chung-Hee's military regime set out to purge those industrialists and politicians guilty of illegal amassing of wealth (*bujeongchukjae*). However, it soon recognized the indispensable role of industrialists for achieving strategic economic development. In return for active entrepreneurial responses to government programs for industrialization, the Park regime pardoned corruption-charged businessmen, and itself presented various policies and schemes for supporting private industries (Amsden 1989). In particular, the regime set in full motion an export drive, under which the export contributions of private enterprises would be highly acknowledged and heavily rewarded. Thereby arose industrial export tycoons among the *chaebol*. While the export-led industrialization made the national economy grow at unprecedented paces, such impressive national economic growth was far dwarfed by the phenomenal corporate growth and sectoral expansion of the *chaebol* (Kang, C. 1999). Park Chung Hee's self-assigned mission of "national revival" (*minjokjungheung*) was tantamount to "*chaebol* revival" as his developmental policy resulted in the explosive growth and expansion of the *chaebol*, at the structural expense of the interests of workers, peasants, and small/medium industrialists.

The *chaebol* have not always been triumphant. Neither government policymakers nor *chaebol* managers have been all-knowing in the rapidly changing domestic and international economic environments. Besides, political suppression of the interests of workers, peasants, and citizenry in general was not always feasible. Sometimes *chaebol* bosses and/or managers committed serious political mistakes leading to fatal administrative punishments. There have so far been three critical sources of the *chaebol*'s crisis – namely, "readjustment of insolvent enterprises" (*busilgieop jeongri*), democratization, and national financial collapse.

The readjustment of insolvent enterprises was carried out, in turn, during three periods – i.e. the late 1960s to the early 1970s, 1979–1980, and 1985–1988 (Kang, C. 1999: 95–112). In the late 1960s to the early 1970s, the government decided not to tolerate "foreign loan-based enterprises" (*chagwangieop*) that had idly sat on government-endorsed low-interest foreign loans (vis-à-vis domestic loans with much higher interest and high inflation) and ultimately became insolvent. Many such enterprises were sold off to or merged with other enterprises. In 1979–1980, many of the overinvested heavy and chemical industries (in part caused by the government's policy of promoting aggressive investment in heavy and chemical industries since 1973) had to be compulsorily reshuffled through divisions and mergers among the concerned enterprises. In 1985–1988, six rounds of readjustment were carried out to restructure the entire national economy.[4] Ironically, every instance of readjustment turned out to be boon to the *chaebol*, as they were provided with various extremely preferential terms for corporate overtaking or debt redemption.

The sudden political democratization since 1987 dealt a critical blow to the pro-business state policy concerning labor relations, welfare rights, etc. As the government increasingly restrained its coercive intervention in industrial fronts, united workers were able to challenge authoritarian business and to push for higher wages and better working conditions (Yoon, S. 1997). At this point, the government promised to initiate or enhance various social security programs, formally under the rubric of "the welfare state." This conciliatory position of the state, however, never altered its pro-business developmentalist doctrine (Choi, J. 2002). In the early 1990s, its social concession policy was reverted or redirected into a neoliberal policy mandating the deregulation of industrial and financial activities (mostly of the *chaebol*) and regimenting labor markets under the slogan of "new economy."

The national financial crisis of 1997–1998 was doomed to occur under the partially neoliberal and partially developmental policy of the Kim Young-Sam government. *Chaebol*-affiliated enterprises did their best to capitalize on financial deregulations as well as promotional industrial policies, so that industrial overinvestment and corporate overborrowing became rampant across the board (Lee, D. 2007; Kong, T. 2000). Since many of the hazardous corporate borrowings had been virtually underwritten by the government under the financially vulnerable *chaebol*'s virtual control of national economy, a sudden change of heart by international private investors and the International Monetary Fund (or, more precisely, the U.S. government) instantly caused a near-moratorium situation in South Korea. The IMF-backed economic rescue program involved a literal wholesale of otherwise competitive South Korean enterprises to foreign investors, a "public fund" (*gongjeokjageum*) solution for insolvent enterprises (i.e. banks renewing corporate loans, and the government bailing out banks that were near-insolvent due to insolvent corporate loans), as well as massive lay-offs under the rubric of "employment readjustment" (*goyongjojeong*) (Chang, K. 1999b). The radical restructuring of the South Korean economy was soon accompanied by revived economic growth and export expansion, but its structural vulnerability associated with the excessive concentration of the national economy in the *chaebol* worsened.

Despite the suddenly enlarged stock shares of foreign investors, the same *chaebol* (such as Samsung, Hyundai, LG, and SK) continued to dominate most industries – sometimes relying on economic nationalism to fend off possible foreign takeovers (Chang, K. 1999b). An irony of the post-crisis era is that the strong presence of foreign financial capital in terms of owning nearly half of major corporations' stock shares has necessitated South Korea's continuing reliance on the *chaebol*'s unique management control based on fictitious shares in mutually or circularly invested firms. In a nutshell, these conglomerates continue to rule the national economy in the twenty-first century through their control of horizontally and vertically interlinked mammoth firms that account for staggering proportions of GDP, stock values, and many other major indicators of South Korea's economic capacity.

3.3 The Organizational Logic of the *Chaebol*

The fact that the *chaebol* used to function as a strategic partner or tool of the developmental state for national economic development implies a unique social, political as well as economic position for *chaebol*-affiliated firms (CAFs hereafter).[5] While they are under the strong organizational control of a conglomerate head and his/her family, their economic operations are structurally interwoven with the following concerns: the political stake of the developmentalist government, the public economic interests ensuing from CAFs' absorption or utilization of national economic resources, the economic and political rights of CAFs' workers (whose welfare is frequently sacrificed for supposed developmental purposes), the property rights of CAFs' ordinary shareholders (whose ownership status rarely counts in conglomerate head-dictated management), and the business interests of CAFs' potential competitors in various *chaebol*-dominated economic sectors. This complex set of social, political, and economic interests make CAFs a highly contested social terrain, in which the conglomerate head's decisions and his/her managers' actions chronically contravene the claims of various stakeholders and easily provoke tense confrontations. Whereas such confrontations have been highlighted by frequent media coverages, abundant academic studies, and government supervisory reports, the institutional and social nature of the conglomerate head's domination of CAFs' ownership and management still awaits a comprehensive analytical framework. Only when a satisfactorily comprehensive and systemic analysis of the conglomerate head's domination of CAFs is undertaken can the sacrificed or foregone interests of other stakeholders be fully identified.

Three Operational Goals of Chaebol Firms

Individual firms belonging to the *chaebol* show unique patterns of corporate behavior, which often betray the interests of ordinary shareholders and effect breaches in regulations and laws for governing private economic activities. On a legal level, each firm is supposed to be accountable to its direct shareholders, but myriads of mutual/circular/pyramid stock ownership among CAFs defy any clear sense of the complete shareholding structure of each firm. One thing certain is that the artificial entity of conglomerate head, usually with an *ad hoc* title of "group president," assumes a ruling force over CAFs (whose status of affiliation itself is artificial) that operate as his/her strategic tool in the control of each concerned firm. Thanks to his/her *supposed* control of such CAFs, the conglomerate head does not have to disclose whether his/her individual shareholding is sufficient for the exclusive corporate control of each concerned firm. It is even possible for the conglomerate head to control an affiliated firm without owning a single share. Given this highly complex structure of corporate governance, CAFs usually manage their undertakings according to the following three unique operational goals (besides the universal goal of profit-making): (1) the growth of corporate size (usually sales volume); (2) the expansion of the conglomerate head's (or his/her family's) ownership and management control of the concerned CAFs; (3) the maximization of the conglomerate head's (or his/her family's) individual financial benefits involving various acts of rent-seeking with respect to CAFs. The latter two goals often betray the legitimate interests of ordinary shareholders. Even the first goal is often problematic as each CAF's corporate profit (and dividend) is sacrificed in favor of the growth and expansion of the concerned *chaebol*, which in turn serves various strategic interests of the conglomerate head.

First, CAFs, like any other firms in a capitalist economy, are thirsty for profit, but they often indulge in corporate size aggrandizement by expanding or entering seemingly loss-making operations. In the early years of state-led export promotion, such seemingly loss-making operations involved various export industries for which the concerned firms were publicly subsidized by the state with preferential loans, tax benefits, exclusive import licenses, under-priced raw materials, etc. (Amsden 1989). The gradual disappearance of such diverse forms of government-arranged subsidies did not fully discourage CAFs from aggrandizing their corporate sizes through loss-making operations. The size matters not only in many conventional senses (i.e. market share for monopoly or oligopoly influence, economy of scale in production and marketing, brand image, etc.), but also in a political economic sense. That is, each *chaebol*'s (as well as each CAF's) overall business volume and standing in the national economy often turn out to be critical determinants of its political economic status by which access to political leadership, associability with bureaucracy, and influence over media are determined (Kang, C. 1999). These leverages of the major *chaebol* result in exclusive public contracts and business licenses, preferential administrative treatment and protection, inside information on policy changes and new policies, etc. Many conglomerate heads receive presidential courtesy as only the nation's president seems to have the authority, albeit informal, to call them up to his office. More importantly, as related with the third operational goal of the CAFs, the chance for the conglomerate head's arbitrary, illegitimate or illegal managerial intrusion for the sake of his/her (or their family's) exclusive interests increases in proportion to each CAF's business volume and scope. Frequent instances of such intrusion include, among others, personal abuse of managerial prerogatives, embezzlement of corporate expenses, and illicit transfer of corporate assets (Kang, C. 1999). Not a single head of the largest *chaebol* conglomerates has been exceptional in such instances of corporate robbery, literally speaking. The national business leadership, organizationally housed in the Federation of Korean Industries (*Jeongyeongryeon*), used to be constituted almost entirely by "ex-con" conglomerate heads with various records of convicted economic crimes.

Second, while the head (along with his/her family) of each conglomerate usually owns a surprisingly small portion of CAF stocks, this does not necessarily indicate a vulnerable status as corporate ruler but rather attests to the maximum extension of corporate control (both in terms of ownership and management), given a certain amount of capital in his/her hands. One of the most significant attributes of a CAF's portfolio is to ensure the conglomerate head's current corporate control over themselves and sibling CAFs and, when necessary, to enable the head's expansion or his/her heir's inheritance of corporate control over existing and new business operations. The CAFs' unique practices such as the (earlier) preference for loans (policy loans, if available) over stock-based financing and the reciprocal/circular investment (stock ownership) and debt underwriting used to be engendered as each conglomerate head has attempted to expand his/her business operations without losing the control of corporate ownership and management. In fact, most of the crucial decisions on CAF portfolios appear to have been made in secret meetings in the conglomerate head's presidential office (*hoejangsil*), the legal status of which is not clearly established. The offices of the conglomerate heads are often disguised under such names as "the planning and coordination office" and "the headquarter for structural adjustment," whereas some use more frank names like "the secretarial office of the president" of the business group. Whatever their names are, CAFs are subject to managerial rule by a sort of *legal ghost* housed in these masterminding offices. Many decisions made in such offices serve the conglomerate head's interest at the expense of that of other shareholders of CAFs, and thus cause controversies and conflicts, in particular, at the year-end shareholder meetings. Naturally, the South Korean government keeps issuing orders to disband such extra-legal organizations, but no official would think they can replace the conglomerate head's *de facto* governance system with whatever *de jure* systems of corporate governance they may conjure up.

Third, the maximum extension of the conglomerate head's corporate control over CAFs then becomes the main basis for managerial decisions and practices that are designed to aggrandize the head's (and his/her family's) exclusive privileges and benefits. A sort of rent-seeking regime governs CAFs from outside – i.e. by the conglomerate head's office. Managers of CAFs, and sometimes conglomerate heads themselves, have often been blamed for and charged with such notorious practices as: (1) accumulation of secret funds (*bijageum*) for strategic managerial actions, which, however, are too often embezzled for the head's private interests, sometimes including his/her expenses for living, leisure, and even gambling; (2) abnormal expansion of the head's (or his/her family members') stock shares through irregularly issued convertible bonds or through outright preferential selling of company-owned shares: (3) unjust transactions with the head, his/her family members or other firms they own, involving products, parts, raw materials, and corporate assets; and (4) unreasonable support for other CAFs (which, by definition, is controlled by the same head) thorough investment and debt underwriting. The unjust perks generated through the stealthy practices ranging from (1) to (4) constitute a unique set of *internal rents* exclusively usurped by the conglomerate head. To such internal rents are added the ordinary remunerations of a manager's salary and individually allocated business activity expenses (*pangongbi*) and a shareholder's dividend. These ordinary and legitimate remunerations of the conglomerate head seem to have been minuscule as compared to the extraordinary material benefits that are basically rents realized through the abusive managerial actions unique to the *chaebol*.

External vs. Internal Rents

In accordance with the CAFs' operational goals explained above, a conglomerate head will do his/her best to utilize his actual capital in a way that allows a maximum expansion of corporate control. The more corporate control he/she wields, the more internal rents involving the entire conglomerate he/she can extract.[6] Endless convicted instances of conglomerate heads' managerial foul play and embezzlement indicate that internal rents accruing to conglomerate heads' exaggerated power of control over CAFs dwarf by far their legitimate financial entitlement to corporate profits (i.e. dividends). They can enjoy more of these rents even when their dividends, proportional to corporate profits, decrease. In fact, a conglomerate head's internal rents are often responsible for serious reductions in corporate earnings because the concerned firms allocate their resources and opportunities for the sake of the head's illegitimate personal benefits. In this context, the decision in 2006 by the Ministry of Justice to revise the Commercial Law for incriminating the "usurpation of corporate opportunities" by corporate officers (in practice, by conglomerate heads and their families) was immediately met with loud objections from the business community. In return, the Economic Reform Alliance – a specialized NGO with an impressive record of challenging unjust social and legal practices of the *chaebol* – presented concrete figures for an alleged usurpation of corporate opportunities by conglomerate heads and their families (*Pressian*, 24 November 2006). On the top of the list was Hyundai Motors Group, with 1.1 trillion won. This charge was legally substantiated, so that Chung Mong-Gu, head of the conglomerate, was sentenced to a prison term, along with a huge fine. Chung has not been alone in this regard. Most of the country's top *chaebol* have recently seen their commanders-in-chief wanted by the court on similar charges. Just a few years before, the head of SK conglomerate was imprisoned on charges of embezzlement, etc. Also, the head of the Samsung conglomerate was practically found guilty of illegally transferring corporate assets to his son, although the indictment was made to his managerial staff, who were, on paper, responsible for the concerned transactions.

It is often argued that the CAFs' irregular managerial practices listed above are not necessarily meant to attend the conglomerate heads' individual interests, but are designed to serve corporate interests in such a way as to allow smooth navigation through South Korea's complicated business environments. Interestingly, such navigation, when successful, is often expected to bring in *external rents*, which are usually provided by the state. In fact, many of the legal cases against CAFs' irregular managerial practices have incriminated government officials and politicians, as well as conglomerate heads and managers of CAFs. If any external rents are thereby realized, conglomerate heads tend to entrust themselves with exclusive entitlement to the rents, perhaps thinking that they deserve to be compensated for their risk, intelligence, and leadership. That is, CAFs' external rents often translate to the internal rents of conglomerate heads.

The economic and political nature of CAFs' external rents has been subjected to lively international academic debates (e.g. Amsden 1989; Evans 1995; Chang, H. 1994; Kang, C. 1999). South Korea's economic development has been upheld as a paradigmatic success story of a developmental state that used to devise and implement an industrial policy for promoting the country's *dynamic* participation in the world economy. This industrial policy betrayed the neoclassical conception of static international comparative advantages by fostering new manufacturing industries, whose international comparative advantages were *created* as a result of concerted efforts between the state and business. The will of the state was communicated to business mainly in terms of various material incentives, including preferential policy loans, tax reductions and exemptions, debt reductions and annulments, exclusive import permits, permission of domestic monopolies, export subsidies, concessive land, energy, and raw materials, and even pardoning of tax evasions and various other legal and administrative breaches. These preferential conditions for doing business in accordance with the government industrial policy came to constitute a rent-seeking political economy, from which numerous industrial tycoons emerged by skillfully reaping policy-linked rents on the basis of timely performances in exporting industrial goods. According to an estimation by Kang Chul-Kyu, the financial fortunes of these industrial tycoons may have been accounted for much more by windfall rents than by corporate profits per se.[7] Nevertheless, as Chang Ha-Joon notes, not all such rents seem to have been wasted unproductively, since the South Korean share of international export kept hiking dramatically (Chang, H. 1994).

Although the industrial policy of the South Korean government has not been designed specifically to serve the family-based ownership/ management of CAFs, each *chaebol* has responded to it in such a way as to reinforce its familial rule. As the industrial composition of strategic export promotion has kept shifting rapidly, each *chaebol* has tried to swiftly diversify its industrial operations, in an effort to continue rent-reaping. It does not mean that they would give up previously supported industries, in which their monopolistic or oligopolistic status in the domestic market still ensure stable profits under a protective policy regime. Each *chaebol* has ended up with a fleet-like structure of industrial operations, for which the familial network of corporate ownership and management functions as a critical organizational leverage against potential contenders for corporate control.

THE "*CHAEBOL* REPUBLIC"

Economies of Scale, Scope, and Hierarchy

Against widespread domestic and international criticism of the *chaebol*'s fleet-like (*seondansik*) management, Alice Amsden voices a supportive opinion focusing on its functionality as the following:

> Within a very short time, therefore, the business groups in Korea were multiproduct, yet still under family management, with salaried managers in command at the industry level and with a capability to enter new industries quickly ... Korean management appears to have accumulated experience in the areas of feasibility studies, task force formation, purchase of foreign technical assistance, training, equipment purchase, new plant design and construction, and operation start-up. This experience ... allowed the *chaebol* to be Korea's first movers in many industries.
>
> (Amsden 1989: 128)

> *An economy of scope arose in the form of the capability to diversify.* Entering new industries at minimum cost and at lightning speed raised the firm's ability to compete in many markets. With state subsidies and a diversified structure, the *chaebol* became willing and able to undertake risk.
>
> (Amsden 1989: 151)

In Amsden's appraisal, as far as rapid industrial restructuring and expansion have been indispensable for South Korea's sustained economic growth, the *chaebol*'s diversified yet efficiently coordinated business structure has worked to enhance their international competitiveness. Such emphasis on a potential economy of scope, however, does not deny the fact that the *chaebol*'s industrial diversification has been critically propped up by their rent-seeking motives. The economy of scope may have been as relevant in rent-seeking as in risk-taking.

Another type of economy arises in accordance with the *chaebol*'s unique organizational structure. The stratified structure of control in CAFs' ownership (and subsequently in their management) is predicated upon an *economy of hierarchy* in controlling as many and as large firms as possible with a limited amount of capital. The in-group hierarchy among CAFs and/or their top shareholders (i.e. the conglomerate head, his/her family, and other allies) partially or wholly involves a pyramid structure, whose number of hierarchical relationships and hierarchical levels, given a certain amount of capital, can be translated into proportional increases in the number and sizes of controlled CAFs. To this hierarchy is added complex

77

interrelationships among CAFs, accruing to mutual/circular investment, debt underwriting, etc.

A South Korean sociologist, Chang Duk-Jin incisively reveals:

> As such, the ruling shareholder's strategy of positioning himself/herself at the highest point of the vertical hierarchy realized in the relationships among blocks (of related firms) and at the highest point of the vertical hierarchy among the individual firms of the (highest) block – i.e. the strategy of occupying the highest point of the 'nested hierarchy' – is a strategy that enables the maximization of (corporate) control vis-à-vis his/her cash flows. It was revealed that this form was common to the 49 biggest *chaebol* as of 1989 ... What is to be noted here is that the status of the ruling shareholder needed to be able to control the entire group of firms does not derive from any one individual's capability for mobilizing funds but from the occupying of a certain position in the network structure (of corporate ownership).
>
> (Chang, D. 2002: 158)

This tendency has been intensified since the economic crisis of 1997–1998 as the *chaebol* have tried to "subdivide the existing nested hierarchies" and "minimize idle capacities" for corporate control (Chang, D. 2002: 159).

Nested hierarchy differs from a simple multi-level pyramid because, in the former case, even the top shareholder does not fully control any firm. At the very first (highest) level, his/her control of each firm in the highest block presupposes that he/she also already has control of other firms in the same block, which may be the case only hypothetically. A conglomerate head's control power over CAFs is, in a sense, a self-fulfilling artifact (i.e. control through a circular logic). The economy of hierarchy in corporate control is partially founded upon a presumption of hierarchy to begin with. This is the Achilles' heel in the organizational structure of the *chaebol* because perfect trust is required among main participants in the ownership and management of CAFs. Thus, the human core in a *chaebol* conglomerate includes only family/kin members and CEOs behaving like familial servants (*gasin*).[8]

What is called 'voting right multiplier' (VRM) is an indicator denoting the degree of exaggeration in ownership control over CAFs, and calculated as vote-entitled stock share divided by actually owned stock share. An investigation in 2005 by the Fair Trade Commission revealed that conglomerate heads' VRMs reached an average of 6.78 among those *chaebol* that had minimum assets of two trillion won and were regulated against mutual investment among affiliated firms (*Yonhapnews*, 12 July 2005). (The commission pointed out that VRMs of listed firms in major European countries only slightly surpassed one – e.g. 1.07 in France, 1.18 in Germany, 1.34 in Italy, 1.12 in England, 1.26 in Sweden, etc.) This means that conglomerate heads, by mobilizing stock shares owned by his/her family, trusted managers, and other CAFs, were exercising a decision-making power 6.78 times larger on average than their actual stock ownership would legitimately allow. The average share owned by the concerned conglomerate heads and their families was only 4.94 percent (2.01 percent for heads; 2.92 percent for families). Heads of the bigger *chaebol* tended to show larger VRMs. Incredibly, about 60 percent of these CAFs were managerially dictated by their respective head, who did not own even a single share.

This economy of hierarchy is highly effective in expanding conglomerate heads' control of CAFs and thereby aggrandizing their financial interests, realized through the various processes explained in the preceding subsection. If a conglomerate head's managerial capability and the interrelationships among CAFs are highly positive, then an economy of hierarchy can also exist in terms of CAFs' improved corporate performances. However, as these two conditions are not necessarily met in every *chaebol*, a diseconomy of hierarchy may occasionally destroy many CAFs and sometimes destabilize the national economy due to the sheer magnitude of the corporate breakdown. Such has been the case particularly when an unprepared son or daughter takes the head's position in the control hierarchy of the concerned *chaebol*.

Nevertheless, a conglomerate head's decisive yet rational leadership may enable CAFs to concentrate on firm-specific tasks such as product improvement and marketing, while relying on the head to mobilize financial resources, secure governmental cooperation, stabilize (or defend) management, and even discipline labor. These latter functions constitute a sort of *de facto* government over CAFs as its constituencies (and cannot be properly conceptualized as part of what Amsden demarcates as "economy of scope"). However, the conglomerate head has no *de jure* status. Most of his/her decisions and actions from the office of "group president" are legally fictitious, but take practical effect through managers of CAFs. Quite naturally, conglomerate heads' leadership is not always benign, candid, and wise. And their ambiguous formal status has often been abused as a way of evading legal responsibility for ruinous, deceitful, and/or illegal actions with respect to CAFs. This leaves prosecutors and judges in the awkward position of having to bring the fictitious bosses before justice, not with too much formal evidence but with abundant circumstantial evidence and strong conviction – very much like the cases against underground criminal organizations.[9] A critical component of the diseconomy of hierarchy consists in the fictitious nature of each *chaebol*'s governance itself. The conglomerate head, as ruler behind the shade, exercises practical power without formal responsibility, so that his/her leadership is easily degenerated into instances of what economists call "moral hazard."

3.4 *Chaebol* Reform as Democratic Politics

The sudden arrival of democracy in the late 1980s has spawned the ironic long-term consequence of empowering the *chaebol* in their relations with the government and civil society. The authoritarian developmentalist governments under Park Chung-Hee and his military heirs used to harness their rule with subjugated media and judiciary organs (Park and Chang 2001). These supposed whistle-blowers were not left free by the authoritarian regimes for an obvious reason: their political power had been illegitimately captured through coup d'état and their supposedly developmental alliance with the *chaebol* involved corruption on phenomenal scales. While the government itself was subjected to serious democratization since 1987, its former tools for authoritarian developmental rule – i.e. the *chaebol*, judiciary organs, and major newspapers – staunchly resisted progressive political and economic reforms. In fact, in this process of defying progressive democratization, the *chaebol* were able to form a new line of coalitions with dominant conservative elements in major newspapers, courts, economic ministries as well as military-originated conservative political parties.[10] While former democracy fighters managed to cling to state leadership through three consecutive presidencies since the early 1990s, the conservative coalition sometimes overpowered the progressive leadership by manipulating public opinion, dominating parliamentary and local governmental elections, inducing administrative concessions in economic policy, and overturning progressive causes through conservative court verdicts. Materially, this coalition pivots around the financial might of the *chaebol* and is basically "distributional" rather than developmental.[11]

In this context, regulating and/or reforming the *chaebol* has become as much a political project as an economic policy. Any effort by the state leadership for *chaebol* reform cannot avoid confronting internal sabotages by economic bureaucrats and judiciary officers and external criticisms by major newspapers and conservative politicians.

Of course, regardless of the *chaebol* issue, these groups would keep challenging the political viability of any progressive political regime. The *chaebol* have happily capitalized on such an antagonistic position of conservative state offices and newspapers, not to mention that of deposed conservative politicians, against the newly incumbent presidents, whose progressive political backgrounds were expected to facilitate progressive economic reforms. The inability of President Kim Young-Sam to bring this reactionary coalition under control spawned an economic runaway situation in the mid 1990s, which instantly resulted in national financial insolvency amid the sudden withdrawal of Japanese and Western lendings. It was not the firm political will of the next president Kim Dae-Jung but the national economic crisis, triggered by the *chaebol*'s careless overexpansion, that necessitated at least a modicum of reform in the *chaebol*'s ownership structure and managerial practice.

Regressions have not been limited to *chaebol* reform. In fact, the viability of democracy itself has been at stake. With the political ambition of military effectively removed, the *chaebol*'s unconcealed intention to buy over state power began to pose the next historical impediment to South Korea's fledgling democracy.[12] As pointed out in the preceding section, the basic organizational nature of the *chaebol* necessitates collusion with the administrative, political, and judiciary elites. Due to the unique politico-historical context of today's South Korea, many administrative, political, judiciary, and journalist elites colluding with the *chaebol* do so with an ideological conviction of self-righteousness. It is this ironic, anti-democratic attitude of professional operators of the supposedly democratic institutions that the *chaebol* capitalize on for their unjust interests, and, in turn, help to intensify. The deepening of South Korean democracy, which managed to rehabilitate democratic procedures for political competition only recently, is now critically conditioned upon democratic reforms in court, prosecutorial authority, media, etc. However, the latter's self-justified plutocratic collusion with the *chaebol* crucially impedes such political necessities and, instead, brews a possible degeneration of democracy into conservative oligarchy.

As the supposedly progressive political regimes disappointingly performed in their battle against the conservative coalition, and as the short-lived union-backed political party (Democratic Labor Party) continued to struggle with limited popularity, NGOs led by civil activists and critical intellectuals arose as the most effective countering force. In particular, as pointed out earlier, People's Solidarity for Participatory Democracy staged internationally famous campaigns against the *chaebol*'s controversial and corrupt practices. The NGO successfully brought to court numerous suspicious decisions and transactions by major *chaebol*'s CAFs and their ruling families. Besides, it also kept pressuring the government to fulfill its legal duties in supervising the *chaebol*.[13]

NGOs' impressive achievement in bringing the *chaebol* and their patrons to economic and political justice, however, has not fundamentally altered the national political landscape, over which the *chaebol*-backed conservative coalition appears to have strengthened its already dominant influence. Nonetheless, it is yet to be seen whether this coalition would be openly able to take over state leadership and, in such a case, whether the *chaebol* would actually dominate the government.[14] The political origin of most conservative politicians is not bourgeois plutocracy but developmental statist authoritarianism, in which industrial entrepreneurship used to be subordinated to political authority. It is also to be seen, in case the *chaebol* should take over political command as well, whether they would prefer a truly liberal democracy to a mercantilist one in which public service and support for private business is at any rate prioritized over grassroots social citizenship. Can South Korea ever have a genuine liberal bourgeoisie which, according to Barrington Moore, Jr. was the prime social requisite for democracy in Western political history?[15]

3.5 The *Chaebol* and Neoliberal Reformisms: South Korea's *Compressed Neoliberalization*

The main conservative party, succeeding the military developmental rule, managed to win two consecutive presidential elections in the democratic era, but the two administrations thereby elected had to withdraw from outright developmental authoritarianism and allow social voices and rights to be expressed against the entrenched economic and political interests. In particular, the removal of the military's protective political umbrella put the *chaebol* in an extremely vulnerable position, due to hostile public opinion and vengeful labor sentiment. Among the state apparatuses, economic ministries, prosecutorial offices, and courts were full of elite public officers, who had willingly or unwillingly cooperated in distorting public work for such authoritarian developmental politics. In civil society, the conservative private newspapers that had been offered lucrative business-linked compensations for collusive or dishonest journalism, albeit with the

THE *CHAEBOL* REPUBLIC

authoritarian state's occasional blatant harassment and censorship, found themselves in quite an uneasy position in the democratic era (Park and Chang 2001). These former functionaries and accomplices of developmental dictatorship either had to be fully reborn into clean and normal actors or strategically repositioned into a renewed developmental coalition, by which their prerogatives would be maintained permanently. The overall response consisted in the latter, so that a powerful new coalition arose, this time independent of the executive authority in Blue House. Its organizational and ideological center consisted in the *chaebol*, making the coalition a *distributional* (as opposed to *productive*) one, and inducing a plutocratic tendency in administrative and judiciary procedures (Olson 1971, 1982). Most importantly, this coalition would successfully obstruct or sabotage progressive demands and policies that began to bloom in the national economic and social affairs after democratization. Paradoxically, it was this neo-developmental coalition that embraced neoliberalism most enthusiastically, however not for liberal reform per se but for deceptive extension of the supposedly developmental yet pro-*chaebol* economic rule.

On the other hand, as the so-called "democracy fighters" had fought a long battle against *gaebaldokjae* (developmental dictatorship), an automatically given political mission of their own governments was to redress various social and economic injustices embedded in or intermingled with the authoritarian developmental political economy. Such injustices comprise a fairly long list: the *chaebol* issue, industrial monopoly, labor suppression, gender discrimination, welfare deficiency, financial discrimination, educational and cultural control, interregional disparities, and so forth. In a great paradox, the post-authoritarian (liberal) reforms on these problems also came to be espoused, in many aspects and significant degrees, by neoliberal prescriptions and measures. A sort of *situational progressivism* was claimed or found in apparently neoliberal reforms – whether or not perceived as such consciously and nominally – in corporate governance, industrial competition, labor and gender relations, welfare ("social safety net"), finance, education and culture, local developmental autonomy, and so forth. The democratic administrations supported and were supported by civil, local, and intellectual actors in pursuing these reforms as officially declared remedial justice.[16] Given a virtual impossibility of socialism and serious social democracy in the South Korean political context, such situational progressivism took on the status of each administration's main policy-line. However, to the extent that their reforms were guided and circumscribed by neoliberal principles, their pledges for remedial social and economic justice had to be compromised and even helped worsen the concerned injustices. It was in this context that the political heirs of the military-led autocratic developmentalist regimes – namely, Lee Myung-Bak and Park Geun-Hye – easily charged into state leadership after a decade of democratic neoliberal governance.

As far as economic governance was concerned, neoliberalism did have a potential historical role to play in South Korea's industrial and corporate reform. To the extent that the mercantilist developmentalism of the South Korean state required strategic distortions of the market economy, various economic, social, and legal problems were accumulating behind its rapid national economic development. While the West-derived neoliberal theories and policies were not exactly targeted at such structural problems of a developmental political economy, some of the basic tenets of (neo)liberalism may have had a potent rectification impact in the South Korean context as well. Besides, many activist economists have influentially pursued such (neo)liberal initiatives for corporate and industrial reform and thereby made the *chaebol* feel pressurized for transparent management and fair trade.[17]

In this context, it was rather paradoxical that the *chaebol* and their neo-developmental allies in the economic ministries and conservative media also embraced neoliberalism quite enthusiastically. The *chaebol*'s motivation needs to be interpreted in the specific post-developmental and democratic context since the late 1980s. That is, the democratized state began to be responsive to grassroots social demands and pressures for economic justice, whereas the *chaebol*, as already internationally competitive economic entities, often felt their national developmental relationship with the state to be cumbersome, and instead wanted to subordinate state policies and regulations to their own business interests (Chang, K. 2012b, 2018). The *chaebol* and their collaborators found neoliberalism so useful in manipulating the state's economic governance and social policy to their tastes and interests.

South Korea's *compressed neoliberalization* before, during, and after the "IMF crisis" of the late 1990s can be understood only by paying sufficient attention to such multi-party interests and motivations in pursuing mutually diverse and contradictory neoliberal reform(ism)s. This paradox was most distinctly illustrated in South Korea president, Kim Dae-Jung's positioning as "the IMF's man in Seoul" (Cumings 1998), mainly thanks to his satisfactory implementation of (neo)liberal reforms in the financial system, industrial structure, labor market as well as corporate governance largely in accordance with the "IMF conditionalities" for an urgent financial bailout. Kim was not alone as dear *allies-by-consequence* for the IMF and its global financial clients. Many critical civil activists and scholar intellectuals came to attract largely favorable attention from global finance by forcefully calling for *chaebol* reform toward a transparent and accountable industrial market economy.[18] The *chaebol* were not comfortable with such (neo)liberal reform(ism)s, but their financial stalemate could be overcome only through radical liberalization of both the industrial capital market and the labor market. They thus opted to frame and manipulate neoliberal reforms, whenever possible, toward their specific private interests. Ultimately, global financial capital's nearly instantaneous takeover of staggering proportions of major chaebol-*affiliated* firms' corporate stocks seemingly completed the long-demanded (neo)liberal *reform* of the *chaebol*, however, without seriously rectifying their controversial ownership and management structures, which began to be seen as potentially useful instruments to the now co-reigning global finance.[19]

3.6 Conclusion and Prospect

In order to understand how rampant politico-economic distortions pivoting around the *chaebol* have continued, in spite of South Korea's revived democracy, one should systematically analyze *the particular characteristics of democratization in the post-developmental authoritarian context and their relationship with neoliberalism*. In the democratization process of South Korea, the removal of "political soldiers" was not accompanied by fundamental reforms or purges of other collusive elements of authoritarian developmental politics, including the *chaebol* (as politico-bureaucratically nurtured capital) and their implicit functional accessories (such as technocrats, judiciary officers, journalists, and academics). Although their material interests and sociopolitical influences briefly shriveled during the explosive uprisings of democracy activists, organized workers, and even many middle-class citizens, they would soon realign themselves, in order to establish a sort of neodevelopmental ruling alliance, which has been, on the one hand, independent of the democratically elected, one-term-only state leadership, and, on the other hand, maneuvered by the *chaebol*'s ideological initiatives and financial payouts. It was this new developmental alliance that welcomed West-born neoliberalism most aggressively yet often deceptively. The *chaebol* and their functional accessories and political allies found neoliberalism not only economically desirable but also, once ideologically reprocessed into a sort of developmental neoliberalism, politically convenient. The antisocial and anti-proletarian tenets of neoliberal values and policies (symbolized by Margaret Thatcher's iron fist against British workers and citizens) were wholeheartedly embraced by these reactionary forces, in order to fend off the sociopolitical challenges and economic demands from ordinary workers and citizens, as well as from progressive intellectuals and politicians.

Even for the *chaebol*, however, such political utility of neoliberalism was far outweighed by its economic risks. When hasty financial liberalization, coupled with the *chaebol*'s propensity to overexpand on debts, was rapidly driving the national economy toward a total financial fiasco, none of the *chaebol*'s developmental neoliberal allies and functionaries was able to predict or prevent the unfortunate process. The resulting national economic crisis authorized global finance and its international regulatory patrons to impose more blunt versions of neoliberal reform on South Korea as the condition of financial bail-out. Among others, capital account liberalization would soon globalize the ownership structure of major South Korean firms as global investors rushed to buy their shares at crisis-set prices (i.e. under currency collapse and panic selling). Even the supposedly progressive governments, under Kim Dae-Jung and Roh Moo-Hyun respectively, helped to accelerate the *chaebol*'s corporate globalization, by intensifying trade liberalization and endorsing rapid transnationalization of production sites, and thereby betraying the economic interests of low-end domestic producers and local workers.

By contrast, the *chaebol* did not betray the *chaebol*-dependent state leaderships, as they expeditiously reestablished themselves as the world's most competitive exporters in numerous high-end industrial sectors – however, without shedding their controversial ownership structures and repeatedly illicit managerial practices. The proactive role of the democratically elected governments, whether rigidly conservative or partially progressive – behind the *chaebol*'s ascendance as neoliberal global subjects and their consequent indifference to the fate of their former and candidate employees, consumer citizens, and grassroots financiers in the domestic economy – seems to have manifested a sort of *empty democracy* in the making. Furthermore, the *chaebol*'s practical necessity to continually corrupt the state's regulatory and judiciary authorities for their dual rent-seeking tends to undermine even the minimum legal, let alone moral, integrity of the arduously revived democratic procedures. All such economic, social, and legal injustices are now rarely objected to or criticized by the openly opportunistic global finance, now as nearly half-owners of most profitable *chaebol*-affiliated industries in South Korea.

— 4 —

THE PROLETARIAN PREDICAMENT OF DEVELOPMENTAL COMPRESSION

Social Conditions of Flexibly Complex Capitalism

4.1 Introduction:
Labor under Compressed Industrial Capitalism

The linear life course of a proletarian working man (i.e. education/training, employment, and retirement) was conceived under twentieth-century Western capitalism. Major social institutions – education, employment, and pensions – supposedly made stable employment the typical life pattern. However, under the recent volatilities in the industrial structure and labor market and the concomitant job instabilities in individual life, the actual conditions of men's working lives require fundamental reexamination (Blossfeld, Melinda, and Bernardi 2006; Diprete 2002). The correspondence between one individual and one workplace/career is no longer the general case. The trend toward labor flexibility and the subsequent weakening of the working man's ability to support his family has led to the drastic erosion of the so-called family wage system (Crompton 1999), and to the generalized instability, fluidity, and individualization in social relations (Bauman 2000; Beck 1992; Castel 2000).

Likewise, since the unprecedented economic crisis and accompanying labor reshuffling and precariatization in South Korea since the late 1990s, public concern has seriously grown about the socioeconomic stability and sustainability of proletarian livelihood on the basis of the capitalist labor market. However, as analyzed in this chapter, South Korea's industrial workers and their familial dependants had endemically undergone fundamental structural difficulties in livelihood even without, or before, such an unexpected macroeconomic crisis – or, more correctly, because of the nation's thundering economic developmental compression, based upon incomparably swift, wide, and continual industrial restructuring. In South Korea's dramatic industrial take-off, its workforce was swiftly mobilized from rural population, whereas, in the mature stages of industrialization, the ceaseless upward restructuring of industrial capitalism has kept necessitating mass dismissal or peripheralization of workers in the sequentially abandoned or shrinking industries. *Labor reshuffling was embedded in industrial reshuffling*, so most of the production workers engaged in each sequentially declining industry, technology, and/or product, faded away long before their supposed retirement age.[1]

In this regard, South Korea's neoliberally driven wholesale financial crisis and unprecedentedly jeopardous socioeconomic aftermaths – in particular, radical labor shedding and reshuffling for hitherto employed adult workers and almost instantaneously generalized precariatic (under)employment for domestic young workers in combination with industrial capital's aggressive production offshoring – do not necessarily point to an essential historical transition or reversal in the socioeconomic status of its working population, but could instead imply a refashioning and/or intensification of labor's unremitting subjection to industrial capital's unilateral economic necessities and priorities, which, in turn, are normally equated with national developmental exigencies. This is not to deny that the economy-wide labor shedding instantaneously accompanying South Korea's acceptance of the so-called "IMF conditionalities" for an immediate financial bail-out was the only effective mechanism for rescuing most of the impendingly bankrupt industrial enterprises and their creditor banks and, accordingly, the entire national economy, which was similarly near-bankrupt.[2]

As a matter of fact, such developmental capitalist governance, without labor's stable industrial citizenship, was apparent as early as in the very beginning phase of industrialization, when *yeogong* (factory girls) in sweatshop light industries were massively recruited from villages, however, only to be shortly discharged on or before marriage, alongside the nation's nearly instantaneous industrial restructuring into capital-intensive, male-dominant heavy industries (Koo, H. 2001) While the size of stably breadwinning male workers in such industries increased accordingly, they did not necessarily constitute a meaningful majority of the industrial workforce (of men). Instead, even most of them ended up changing employers, occupations, or industries, while frequently, or chronically, confronting acute financial difficulties, which, in turn, necessitated their spouses' return to the labor market (mostly for casual employment) for some complementary income earning. A few decades later, basically all young women are now entering the labor market because the post-crisis neoliberal precariatization of labor normally necessitates their independent or complementary breadwinning under a severe shortage of stably capable male providers for familial livelihood (Chang, K. 2018, ch. 8).

Collectively, as a sort of postindustrial-cum-neoliberal reality, their structural difficulties in effectively consolidating the cohesive working-class identity and integrated class struggle platform continued to obstruct sociopolitically organized systematic solutions to such material problems (Chang, K. 2022b). South Korea's breathtaking economic transitions – from a predominantly agrarian society to a vibrant early industrializer in labor-intensive sectors by the late 1970s, a dynamic capital-intensive heavy industrial economy by the early 1990s, and a pervasively globalized and financialized economy with the state-of-the art high-tech sectors in the early twenty-first century – have indispensably subjected its laboring population to a seemingly impossible life project of occupationally surviving such repeatedly abrupt industrial transformations, as well as a fundamental sociopolitical difficulty in forming the stable and effective class solidarity needed for collective promotion of economic justice and social welfare.[3]

4.2 Developmental Compression and Proletarian Working Life Courses

Proletarian Working Life Courses under South Korea's Developmental Compression

Curiously, but not exceptionally, studies on the working life course in South Korea have focused mainly on women. South Korean women have generally had complex and discontinuous working lives, attracting keen scholarly attention (Choi and Chang 2004), whereas men's working life courses have usually been considered to be simple and uninterrupted, under an implicit assumption of their stable participation in the economy. The employment histories of South Korean men have been (mis)represented as "lifetime employment," as a result of the popular gender-based notions and stereotypes of East Asian labor regimes. The stability of a working life course may be understood as the extent to which income-earning activities continue uninterruptedly during the worker's lifetime. In the historical process of industrial capitalism, such participation depends not just on the socioeconomic

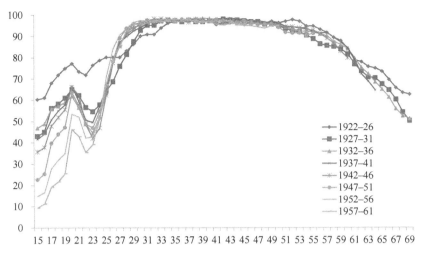

Figure 4.1 South Korean men's work participation rate by birth cohort (those born in 1922–1961) (Age, %)

Note: The work participation rate is the economic activity participation rate, analysed through the gainful worker approach, and calculated as the proportion of gainful workers over the targeted population.

Source: Generated from raw data in "Job History Survey" of *The Korean Longitudinal Study of Ageing* (2007).

conditions of employment but also on family norms, which vary according to gender and generation (Tilly and Scott 1987).

Figures 4.1 and 4.2 show the different trajectories of work participation by gender, and the progress of work participation by generation (birth cohort). From this, we see how patterns of work changed during the most dynamic stage of South Korean industrialization.[4] The work participation rates for men were shown to be very stable, with small variations by age and no significant differences between generations. For men in their mid-twenties to late fifties (that is, the prime period of the working life course), a participation rate upwards of 90 percent was maintained. The same was true for all generational (cohort) groups. But, ages outside the prime period (i.e. from fifteen to the mid-twenties and after the mid-fifties) showed a generation gap. There is a trend among males to delay the beginning of their working life to their mid-twenties, and advance the time of their retirement to the mid-fifties. Nonetheless, despite some radical changes in the economic structure and sociocultural conditions, the working life courses of South Korean men were revealed as stable patterns both at the individual and the historical level.

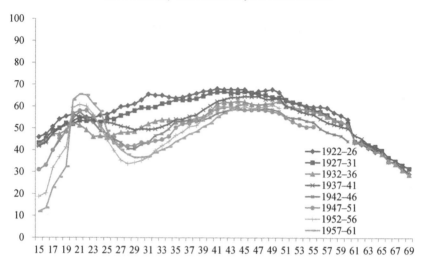

Figure 4.2 South Korean women's work participation rate by birth cohort (those born in 1922–1961) (Age, %)

Note: The work participation rate is the economic activity participation rate analysed through the gainful worker approach, and calculated as the proportion of gainful workers over the targeted population.

Source: Generated from raw data in "Job History Survey" of *The Korean Longitudinal Study of Ageing* (2007).

In contrast, women's work participation rate did not show stable patterns across generations. The work participation rates of the then youngest cohort of women showed a decrease when compared to those of their older counterparts. Also, the gap was widening between the work participation rates of women and men, particularly in the age bracket where the men's work participation rate reached ninety percent. A more long-term perspective, however, reveals this contrast to be more complex. During the late teen years and early twenties, women's work participation rate was higher than men's. This was because of male-only military service and gender-asymmetrical college education. For the generation born in 1957–1961, women's work participation rate was 65 percent at age twenty-two, while that of their male counterparts was only forty percent. The trajectories of the work participation rate by age would gradually change to manifest generation-specific groupings. Women born in the 1940s and 1950s showed a marked decrease in the work participation rate in their late twenties (namely, the period when most had married and become parents), but ten to fifteen years later these women re-entered the labor market and recovered their former economic activity level. Looking at the work participation rate by age, we can infer the specific rhythm of women's working life course by generation: it usually showed a break in their working life around the time of marriage and their reentry into the workforce at around the age forty.

The modern work–life separation used to be based on a gendered division of labor, which was often described as the male breadwinner and female homemaker model. The gap shown here between the work participation rates of men and women in their mid-twenties to mid-thirties may certainly be explained by such gendered division. During that life period, most men served as the main family provider and most women devoted themselves to housework and childcare. The different gender roles thus became normalized in the early phase of (universal) married life. But the resurgence of women's work participation rate showed that this gender arrangement did not last for long. In clarifying the relationship between men and women with regard to employment and family responsibilities, it is necessary to detect the correlations between the respectively significant changes in men's working life course and women's, and to uncover the concrete details of their occupational characteristics by industry, employment status, and so forth. A sort of hidden reality behind the seemingly 'continuous employment' of male workers needs to be systematically explained during the historic period of South Korea's developmental compression.

The Historical Nature of Men's Working Life Course and Its Familial Effects: Proletarian Patriarchy under a False Assumption

In this subsection, we explore the hidden reality behind men's greater than ninety percent participation rate in income-earning activities across all generations during South Korea's "miracle-paced" industrialization. It was routinely hypothesized that once a man entered the labor market, he would be able to maintain his job continuously, thereby accumulating work experiences and skills and moving up the occupational ladder. Sometimes, however, the expression "continuous employment" hid periods of instability, such as stints of unskilled, part-time jobs in the process of looking for better employment. To determine how many men fell outside the ideal suggested by "continuous employment," we must identify those men whose work status and progress were mutually identical, and assess their respective proportions in the total male working population. Those who deviated from this category and the trajectories of their deviations should then be specified to integratively assess the nature of employment fluidity.

A comprehensive analysis of historical data on South Koreans born between 1932 and 1961 – namely, those generations whose economic participation had mostly taken place during South Korea's most drastic period of capitalist industrialization and economic growth – shows that men's working life course differed from women's because it was marked by continuous labor participation, but underlying that continuity was an extensive instability (Choi and Chang 2004). Despite the constantly increasing proportion of formal corporate sector jobs in the national economy, men's individual working life courses had been characterized by their gradual exclusion from this sector before their middle age. The generation born between 1932 and 1941 began their working lives slightly before industrialization and thus had less opportunities to enter the modern labor market that emerged from industrial capitalism. But the generations born between 1942 and 1951 and between 1952 and 1961 had many opportunities to get formal wage employment, and many of them could enter the so-called internal labor market that developed after the mid-1980s, which offered higher wages, more stable jobs, and reduction in turnover rates (Jung, E. 1992; Song, H. 1991). But, even for the 1942 to 1951 cohort, only forty percent had gained formal wage employment at the time of marriage. While that generation enjoyed a relatively high employment stability, the proportion of formal employment was small. By contrast, the 1952 to 1961 cohort experienced a sustained expansion of formal wage labor and began their working lives with relatively high prospects of a decent corporate sector job.

An age-wise comparison of "occupation distributions" showed a qualitative difference in job distributions at the time of marriage and middle age (age 45 here). Those engaged in "marginal work," such as unskilled manual laborers, day laborers, and those self-employed without overheads, constituted a large segment of total employment distribution. In all generations, marginal work represented a high percentage of jobs, both at the time of marriage and at middle age. At middle age, fewer men had formal wage jobs (with the exception of managerial/ professional occupations) and, relatedly, more men were self-employed or involved in "marginal work." This trend did not reflect the historical development of the employment structure. In a typical historical process of (successful) national industrialization, there has been a sharp decline in agricultural employment and a rapid expansion of formal wage jobs in modern industry. Yet, when we compare men's employment at the time of marriage and at middle age within a single generation, these trends were in fact reversed: as they got older, fewer men had formal wage jobs and more were self-employed or performing peripheral jobs.

Across all generations, more than half of agricultural laborers, self-employed business operators, and those in managerial positions and semi-professional occupations retained their jobs until middle age. By contrast, those employed in the most common jobs then (office workers, sales and service workers, etc.) showed lower levels of occupational retention. Notably, the smaller the size of the employing organization, the lower the occupation retention rates of its office workers and laborers (see the subsequent section). Overall, the generations analyzed here confirm that jobs at the time of marriage were increasingly likely to be in the formal wage sector, that unemployment declined, and that the male working population was rapidly incorporated into the process of capitalist economic development. But, in terms of the individual life courses, the transition from young adulthood to middle age was accompanied by a decreased percentage of formal wage jobs and an increase in non-wage labor and marginal work.

In retrospect, to describe the destabilization of employment after the 1997 economic crisis as "the collapse of lifetime employment" or "the end of long-term employment" cannot but be an exaggeration, given the limited number of those engaged in office work at large companies. In South Korea, a stable working life course supported by long-term employment has always been a rare experience, even during the heyday of South Korea's industrial capitalism. The vast majority of the working population, who did not belong to this exceptional minority, experienced not a few occupational changes in their lifetimes. Their experience of occupational change can be gauged by the status of the job to which they moved. South Koreans in all employment categories showed a strong tendency, between the marriage age and the middle age, to move to self-employed business operation and marginal work, rather than remaining within the same occupational boundaries. Men who left the formal wage labor sector were no longer in a position to accumulate work experience within an organization, and frequently faced unemployment or demotion.

Our study showed, however, that such deviations in a man's working life course did not appear to lead to unemployment lasting more than one year. Rather, all generations showed a tendency to continue income-earning activities outside the formal wage labor sector. These activities were usually identified as "self-employed business operation" and, less frequently, as "marginal work." The formal wage labor sector and the informal sector became structurally segmented. In observing the intersectoral movements in men's working life courses, we see that the outflow from formal labor to informal labor was overwhelmingly greater than the reverse flow across all cohorts. Relatedly, the formal wage labor sector relied on relatively young labor, and the informal sector relied on relatively aged labor.

It is important to note that labor risks in South Korea's rapid industrialization period were not as much associated with unemployment as with continuous peripheral employment (Yoon, J. 1994). Its wide-ranging informal and peripheral labor market was closely related to the complex working life courses of men, consisting of their entry, termination, and re-entry. A review of the employment distribution by generation and in-company occupation change shows that the working life course of men since the 1960s was far removed from a supposed "standard working life," consisting of a preparatory period, an active period, and retirement. More than half of the surveyed men experienced occupational change, change of company, and status demotion before the middle age of 45 (usually considered the peak of a working life). In particular, their work in the non-formal sector was camouflaged under the guise of "continuous employment." This trend did not diminish even after the 1990s.

As is widely known, South Korea's rapid economic development was accompanied by big capital's concentration in some strategic industries in each respective stage. This helped to create an extensive informal sector outside the area of corporate capital concentration. The informal sector was sometimes seen as offering men better financial opportunities than the corporate sector wage labor they had engaged in as young men, so many of the surveyed workers willingly transferred to informal sector ventures. These provided, at least, an alternative to unemployment. Until the introduction of the general social insurances in 1998 (as part of the "social safety net" amid the radical economic restructuring during the national financial crisis), the only meaningful component of social welfare available to numerous ordinary workers was the government's retirement allowance, which took the form of a lump sum payment rather than a pension. As such, it functioned less as a stable source of income for the individual than as a potential investment fund in the creation of a small business. Self-employed small business operators mobilized their spouses and other family members, thereby making up for constraints on capital and increasing opportunities to enhance their income. Among those surveyed, if compared to those who turned to self-employment, men who transferred to marginal work were much more likely to suffer from a financial downturn. Blue-collar workers were more likely than white-collar workers to move to peripheral jobs.

The above analysis of the (in)stability of the supposedly most productive period in the working lives of South Korean men indicated a crucial weakening of the role of the male breadwinner, a role long taken for granted in terms of work ethic and gender norm. In this respect, we should analyze whether there was a correlation between the occupational mobility of the husband and the employment status of his spouse. According to the result of our analysis, when the husband's employment status unwillingly changed, this instability was introduced into the household economy, so that the household gender division in the early days of the marriage could not be sustained, and the wife had to re-join the workforce in order to support the household complementarily. The nature of the husband's job played a role in determining whether or not the wife returned to work. It was more likely for a wife to do so if her husband was involved in a job that could make use of the wife's labor, such as self-employed business or agriculture. But, even when husbands belonged to the wage labor sector or had peripheral jobs, changes in their employment often signaled a return to employment on the part of their wives. This trend was closely tied to differences in generation. Among those born between 1932 and 1951, the impact of changes in the man's occupational status on whether or not the wife turned employed was significant only when the jobs could use family labor (such as self-owned businesses, certain peripheral jobs, and agriculture). Among those born between 1952 and 1961, however, significant correlation was confirmed between all occupational changes by men (with the exception of those moving to better jobs) and the wives' employment.

The conclusions drawn from this analysis do not confirm that married women joined the workforce in pursuit of autonomy and personal fulfilment. Some American and European scholars in economic sociology have argued that the increase in the number of working wives in the second half of the twentieth century signaled a revolutionary change (Davis 1984; Goldin 2006). Their motives for seeking employment have supposedly switched from a (passive) desire to compensate for their husbands' insufficient income to an (active) desire to have their own income. Accordingly, women are seen to seek long-term employment in order to strengthen their autonomy (Goldin 2006). This view, however, did not correspond with the real working lives of South Korean women born from 1932 to 1961.The analytical result here at least confirms that their decision to seek employment was influenced by their husbands' job (in)stability. Married women's participation in the workforce could improve their social positions, but not necessarily as a self-conscious endeavor. It took a few more decades, or another generation, for women's genuinely liberal modernization began to take place in the economy and society.

4.3 Developmental (vs. Neoliberal) Precariatization: Social Conditions of Flexibly Complex Capitalism

In Arthur Lewis's (1954) seminal classic theory of industrialization, a populous undeveloped nation's capitalist industrialization is triggered and sustained by the lengthy (or "unlimited") supplies of socially transitional labor from subsistence family farms to capitalist urban enterprises. It is the very transitional nature of such migrant workers that enables capitalist industries to utilize very profitably – or, in Marxist class theory, exploit – their labor because only subsistence-level or slightly higher wages suffice in inducing them to enter into capitalist industrial employment as a way of escaping the increasingly worsening conditions of livelihood in their parental families under rapid population growth. Some non-Western countries did succeed in such Lewisian industrialization, which then would effect urbanized proletarian families' propensity to reduce fertility (i.e. procreation of children, who need to be raised and educated at increasingly high costs, without a clear prospect of being rewarded in old age out of filial piety) and, ultimately, increasing shortages of laborers (in particular, flexibly exploitable ones as in their earlier years). Economically speaking, if labor supplies are *limited* as such under industrial growth, the changing labor demand–supply ratios should inevitably keep raising the average wage of industrial workers. It is crucially important to emphasize that such processes would initially begin with respect to socially transitional labor (i.e. villager-turned workers) and expand to involve all urban workers (including former villagers and their urban-born children).

As such economic possibilities were actually realized, structural challenges imposed on the currently industrialized nations led them to rephrase currently poor and populous nations' population burdens as "demographic dividends," apparently as a sort of euphemistic retrospect on their own past. However, for such possibilities to become a meaningful proletarian history, workers could not simply rely on (natural?) economic possibilities, but had to fiercely or desperately stage sociopolitical struggles against various attempts by industrial capitalists (and their political and administrative allies in the capitalist state) to slow down, or even nullify, the (market) economic processes. Such attempts, above all, have been designed to permanently elongate, or even flexibly reinvent, the transitional social nature of workers, which has coalesced with endemic industrial fluctuations (including disguised industrial depressions, with massive diversion or concealment of accumulated profits), organizational and/or technological subordination of human labor to unilaterally mechanized production systems, women's generalized but segregated labor participation, permanent and/or circulatory import of foreign migrant workers, neoliberal flexibilization (or precariatization) of employment conditions and relations (to which youths are particularly vulnerable), and so forth (Chang, K. 1995, 2019). If national economic development has, fortunately, been accompanied by, or helped to strengthen, effective democracy in political and industrial conditions – namely, political parties, governments, and trade unions (in industries, firms, and regions) representing and serving workers' interests systematically and stably – it could have helped to prevent, or reduce, the adverse consequences of such adverse forces and environments to the proletarian population, and even to advance to the welfare state system for "decommodifying labor," with comprehensive socioeconomic protections and entitlements. Needless to mention, such has been far from the case in a staggering majority of capitalist countries, both in the developed and undeveloped regions.

In the modern capitalist world's general socioeconomic context, the transitional social nature of industrial workers has been generated, reproduced, intensified, and/or regenerated as a nearly universal feature or condition. Likewise, the recently popularized notion of "precariat" (Standing 2011) for denoting mostly young, casually or unstably (under)employed workers in the neoliberalized economy, may be more broadly applicable to *wide varieties of precariat*, detectable across diverse historical and social contexts. In fact, the turbulent and vulnerable socioeconomic conditions of South Korean workers during the nation's compressively developmental era (analyzed in the previous section of this chapter), as opposed to those of their children and younger siblings during its neoliberal crisis era, may necessitate the category of *developmental precariat* in that such status was highly symptomatic of a complex capitalist industrial system, enmeshed with the developmental state's comprehensive and aggressive intervention for industrial takeoff and upgrading. Relatedly, the following three issues need to be systematically addressed in explaining South Koreans' developmental precariatization as a serious structural phenomenon.

First, South Korean industrial workers' concentration in SMEs (small and medium-sized enterprises) and instabilities and fluidities of their jobs therein (analyzed in detail in the preceding section) can be understood in a great part in terms of structural differences in the basic laboring practices and relations in them, vis-à-vis those in large, mostly *chaebol*-affiliated enterprises. Most of the so-called permanent employees in the pre-IMF crisis period belonged to large firms of the *chaebol* as managerial officers or high technology personnel (besides public sector organizations). The specific systemic nature of SMEs has not simply consisted in their organizational and financial smallness but, no less importantly, in the particular patterns and conditions of industrial work that are marked by widely informal, flexible, and even improvisational practices (see Cho, S. 2004; Jung, E. 2007; Lee, J. 2013; Gim, E. 2012). Such practices may enable many SMEs to survive or prosper, but they also tend to make industrial employees find it difficult to establish and sustain a lifetime proletarian career. This is not necessarily because the SME employees feel unfairly exploited and alienated. Given their certain human endowments of diplomas, skills, and/or experiences, with which they may not be hired by the so-called *daegieop* (meaning big companies), many of them usually presume that employment in SMEs incurs a sort of qualitatively hierarchical disadvantage.

While such disadvantages may be tentatively escaped by many SME employees in terms of finding new employers, entering different sectors, or shifting to self-employment (as described in the previous section), they are far from sufficiently replaced by the new generation of their children and younger siblings, due to the latter's educational overqualification, expectation of decent (but expensive) life, avoidance of the so-called 3D (dirty, dangerous, difficult) jobs, demographic tapering, and so forth (Lee, J. 2013; Gim, E. 2012). Relatedly, the human dimension of South Korea's sudden economic transition to aggressive globalization, particularly after the IMF crisis (1997–1998), has consisted most crucially in sufficiently and flexibly securing variously precariatic foreign workers to urgently relieve the SMEs from their worsening labor shortages. This has led South Korea to spearhead the whole of Asia, both in the (managed) opening of the domestic labor market to foreign guest workers and the production offshoring to numerous demographic giants in the region (Chang, K. 2019, 2024).[5] Most of the foreign guest workers (euphemistically called "industrial trainees") have been hired by manufacturer SMEs (and some farmers facing seasonal labor shortages) and frequently found to suffer from sweatshop conditions of work; whereas a large majority of locally hired industrial workers in South Korean FDI firms across Asia (now numbering more than domestically hired Korean workers) are employees of a sort of *multinationalized SMEs* (Chang, K. 2019, ch. 8).

Second, the chronically flexible, or precariatic, labor regime in South Korean SMEs may not be sensibly explicable by focusing singularly on the employers' ordinary business interest or propensity. In an interesting political economic twist, South Korean SMEs have continually complained and protested about their own subjection to unfairly, and often illegally, exploitative relationships with the *chaebol daegieop* (big enterprises of *chaebol*), and this has been politically and administratively acknowledged as a fundamentally legitimate concern, making *gyeongjejeongui* (economic justice) in the industrial order a key policy agenda under many recent governments of both progressive and conservative positions.[6] Quite curiously, economic justice is never mentioned in media or by politicians as an issue of labor–capital relationships, which are instead addressed in terms of labor–capital conflict or harmony, quite falsely implying the two parties' potentially countervailing positions in a capitalist economy, where a large majority of industrial workers struggle helplessly under the precariatic conditions of SMEs. The nation's industrial system, pivoting around the *chaebol*, necessitates most SMEs' intermediating roles in aggressive labor utilization and control.

Given a handful of mega-conglomerates' overwhelmingly dominant positions in the national economy, combined with their massive global shares in export, not many SMEs can prosper, or even survive, without entering systematic hierarchical relationships, with them as subcontractors of parts, services, logistics, and so forth. As compared to the recently popularized notion of "global value chains" in the world economy, a sort of *domestic or national value chains* involving the *chaebol* and their subcontractor SMEs in hierarchically organized transactions has long characterized the South Korean industrial system in its simultaneous pursuit of import substitution and export promotion.[7] Just as the latest global value chains are heavily oriented toward preferential terms of labor use (or exploitation) particularly in Asian economies, South Korea's domestic value chains have long required SMEs as subcontractors to very flexibly use and control industrial workers in desperately winning and maintaining the monopolistic *chaebol*'s consent in business with them.[8] Such SMEs' functions in complex labor management culminate when labor shedding and reshuffling, necessitated under South Korea's ceaseless industrial restructuring, usually become their lopsided burden. On the other hand, South Korea's recent production offshoring in terms of innumerable South Korean SMEs' (as well as many *chaebol* firms') relocation to or new establishment of factories in China, Vietnam, etc., in fact, has effected such domestic value chains' transformation into global (or Asianized) value chains, now additionally involving precariatic industrial workers from across Asia, whether hired in South Korean, locally owned, or jointly owned SMEs abroad (Lee, J. 2024).[9]

Finally, the incomparably heavy entrance and concentration of (formerly or circulatorily) industrial workers in highly diverse areas and forms of self-employment (*jayeongeop*) should be carefully explained with respect to the economic systemic nature of laboring as such. Self-employment in South Korea's self-employed sectors is quite purely characterized by self-employment – that is, most of self-employed business units are unlikely to hire many or long-term employees. *Self-employment is much more a labor regime than a business regime* in that intense self-exploitative laboring is the most crucial aspect or condition of self-employed population's economic maintenance and survival. The business nature of self-employed units is undoubtedly serious because they usually operate in virtually unconstrained market-competition against each other, but their limited entrepreneurial inputs and/or technological resources are compensated mostly in terms of intensities in own labor exploitation.[10] In this sense, self-employed population in ever growing numbers and proportions is positioned as the bottom layer of precariatic labor, for which competition and self-exploitation are escalated in mutual reinforcement.

In recent years, the rapid expansion of standardized service franchises (for convenience stores, bakeries, fried chicken shops, and so forth) pervasively threatens individually operated local counterparts, further *deentrepreneurializing* the concerned self-employed services (Cha, Y. 2023). Also, the so-called platform labor, whose occupational status as self-employed business vs. employee (without a clearly specifiable employer) is fundamentally controversial, adds to similar influences through the centrally organized intermediation between service self-employees and physically remote clients, usually by requiring standardized forms and/or conditions of service provision.[11] Interestingly, these recent trends have been very readily accommodated by South Korean self-employees, in a large part due to their propensity to manage self-employment as a self-exploitation labor regime, rather than an entrepreneurial business regime. In a sense, most of them have preferred a sort of *flexible self-exploitation,* without being burdened too much about the initial technological, organizational, and/or financial requirements for an independent business.

4.4 Conclusion: The Proletarian Predicament of Developmental Compression

The unstable working life course of South Korean men, as systematically documented in this chapter, should be viewed first in the context of unprecedentedly rapid capitalist industrialization (and deindustrialization). In the process of rapid economic development, South Korean society continuously saw radical structural changes to its industries. A series of breathtaking shifts has taken place – from agriculture to labor-intensive industries, to capital-intensive industries, to ICT and service industries. The fact that these changes all occurred within a few decades, the length of an individual's occupational life, suggests that most workers have inevitably encountered chronic job instability. Moreover, the rapid economic concentration into a handful of gigantic export conglomerates (i.e. the *chaebol*) have not necessarily represented enhancement in employment and occupation. Instead, as Tat Yan Kong incisively observes (in comparison with Germany and Japan), it has often accelerated technological and labor force outsourcing, limiting the demand for long-term skilled labor. According to him:

> Korea had not yet made the transition to "quality" mass production (QMP) of the Japanese and German types ... German and Japanese QMP were based on the symbiosis of advanced production technologies, high skills, and reciprocal labor relations (i.e. cooperation between stakeholders based on recognition of shared long-term interests). Advanced production technologies involved highly skilled processes that could not easily be relocated. The high labour skills required for these processes could only be acquired by training. Skill acquisition entailed the existence of frameworks for cooperative labour relations based on reciprocity. In Japan, this cooperative framework was enterprise-based. In Germany, it was industry-based and mediated by the state.
> (Kong, T. 2012: 241–242)

The popular characterization of the East Asian labor regime(s) has been only controversially, if not impossibly, applicable to South Korea's developmental compression, predicated upon continually radical industrial restructuring and accompanying labor reshuffling.

That is, lifetime employment was an exceptional privilege for a tiny minority of the South Korean working population.

In retrospect, as indicated earlier, to describe the destabilization of employment after the 1997 economic crisis as "the collapse of lifetime employment" is now an apparent exaggeration. South Korea's "developmental miracle" achieved through its dramatic industrial takeoff and continual radical industrial restructuring indispensably necessitated most of the production workers (outside the corporate internal labor market for seemingly aristocratic managerial workers) in the sequentially rising and then declining industries to collectively confront structural vulnerabilities and instabilities in skill utility, job status, and livelihood. Their occupational dismissal and socioeconomic peripheralization, frequently before reaching the middle age – not to mention the supposed retirement age – were an almost built-in feature of the South Korean mode of industrial advancement, or developmental compression.

South Korea's democratization (more precisely, democratic institutional restoration) in the late 1980s seems to have made this hitherto built-in labor shedding very problematic for socioeconomic and politico-legal reasons. On the eve of the "IMF economic crisis," labor market flexibility – while it had been far from non-existent before the neoliberal era, on the one hand, and would become the key rubric of socioeconomic governance under the neoliberally driven state policy of economic crisis management, on the other hand – was all of a sudden orchestrated into explicit legal stipulations, under the concerted efforts between the developmental(ist) state (then under the democratic, or self-proudly *munmin* (civilian), president, Kim Young-Sam) and mainstream industries of the *chaebol*. However, this move was practically nullified due to the nearly society-wide support for organized labor's resistance, threatening the political fate of the Kim government. Nevertheless, the national economic crisis accompanying his economic policy blunder in heedless financial liberalization would force the next government (under the supposedly progressive Kim Dae-Jung) and national labor unions to agree to immediate radical labor reshuffling, as well as long-term labor market flexibility, as an IMF conditionality in bailing out the South Korean economy. In a sense, the earlier era of *developmental precariatization* was thereby succeeded by the latest era of *neoliberal precariatization*.

As another social constraint of South Korean industrialization, working-class patriarchy was materially defective, even for those generations who lived through South Korea's most drastic period of capitalist industrialization, paradoxically because of the very success of rapid industrial takeoff and continual restructuring. By analyzing the working life courses of such men, this chapter showed a fundamentally limited relevance of the male breadwinner model in South Korean society, even before the 1997 economic crisis. It also showed that insecurity in the male working life course encouraged or even forced wives to rejoin the workforce. The limitations of the male breadwinner family under South Korea's compressed industrial capitalism may be explained as a process in which the risks of the unstable working life courses of men were *familialized* in the form of their wives' reemployment in mostly peripheral and/or menial jobs.

The so-called "M-curve" in the working life course of Korean women reflected not only labor market discrimination against married women with family responsibilities but also pointed to the rapid economic restructuring that made men's breadwinning chronically unstable. As labor market policies and family policies were formulated under the false assumption of men's stable breadwinning, women used to be doubly burdened by discriminatory employment conditions and onerous familial duties. The post-IMF crisis period has paradoxically reduced the gap between assumed (or hoped for) and actual conditions of male workers' job status, not in terms of improving the latter to match the former, but rocking the former myth to match the hard reality. Consequently, the currently young generation shows widespread deferral and abandonment of marriage (which is, in turn, the main cause of the country's "lowest low" fertility) and virtually all young women enter and stay in the labor market, regardless of their marital expectation and/or status. This trend has an interesting ramification for most women's higher education and its labor market consequences: better educated women are more likely to remain unmarried into their thirties and after and thus should provide for themselves, so that South Korea's earlier idiosyncratic nature as the world's only country of better educated women's higher chance of becoming full-time housewives has disappeared (*The JoongAng*, 1 June 2024). This gender-equalization, however, takes place at a time of worst precariatic condition, pitting young men and women hostilely against each other.

Part II

Culture, Family, Life Risk

— 5 —

REFLEXIVE POSTCOLONIALITY

Intellectual and Cultural Contradictions of
Compressed Modernity

5.1 Introduction:
Knowledge, Culture, and Compressed Modernity

The rise of Asia, mostly in economic terms, briefly enlivened political
as well as scholarly discourses among Asians themselves, on capitalism, democracy, and welfare systems, with some supposedly Asian
cultural characteristics – in particular, Confucian capitalism, democracy, and welfare system (e.g. Kim, K. 2017; Han, S. 2019).[1] However
much similar to the earlier, West-initiated, academic debate on Asian
capitalism and industrialism, argued particularly with respect to
Japan's phenomenal economic success (Dore 1973; Vogel 1979),
the later Asianist discourses by and large have failed to establish a
long-lasting and/or broadly accepted treatise, either academically or
politically, on any particularly Asian line of modernity. What remains
evident is that the (formal) institutional as well as the (urban) physical façade of the economically rising Asian nations tends to negate a
comprehensive and/or sustained societal effect of any uniquely Asian
cultural factors. Despite East Asian countries' phenomenal economic
success and concomitant societal modernization, the region's early
modern ideal (ideology) of philosophical self-preservation combined
with an instrumental(ist) emulation of the West – for instance, *dongdoseogi* in Chosun (Korea) – does not seem to have materialized
meaningfully.[2] Their recent interest in and promotion of the so-called
"soft power" does not seem to enable them effectively to revitalize
such early modern aspiration.[3]

The vague manifestation and largely unclear effect of Asian culture
and philosophy in modern societal transformations do not necessarily imply that Asian societies and citizens have instead incorporated

Western culture and philosophy earnestly for such transformations. The ideology of *dongdoseogi* seems to have at least justified a broad tendency of instrumentalism, under which the utilization of Western knowledge, technology, goods, and social institutions intentionally omits or conveniently bypasses the deep understanding and accommodation of their cultural and philosophical foundations in the Western civilizational and societal contexts. Thereby arose a historical process of *aphilosophical* liberal modernization and development in which the nationalist goal of *catching up* with the West became a surrogate philosophy in itself, and the technocratic rules and means kept replacing or overriding the moral concerns and civilizational considerations of civil society (Chang, K. 2022a, ch. 4).

In an ironic consequence of the broad disembedding (or even nullification) of culture and philosophy from the institutional and material order, South Korean society and people have been exposed to nearly unconstrained varieties of culture, however, in routinely reifying settings and formats. Under what may be termed as *complex culturalism* (Chang 2022a, ch. 6), South Korean institutions and citizens have liberally incorporated into themselves various historical and civilizational sources of culture, which are indigenously Korean, Asian, Western, or global, on the one hand, and traditional, modern, or late/post-modern, on the other hand.[4] For instance, the Koreanness in South Korean cinemas, television dramas, "K-pop" songs, and other genres of popular culture has been found or enjoyed in terms of the dynamic complexity of life experiences and emotions as to extremely diverse civilizational elements, both in world-regional and historical terms. *The remarkable diversity and plurality of cultural experiences have been ironically conditioned upon the practical irrelevance or insignificance of culture and philosophy in the institutional and material world.* At the societal level, culture and philosophy have been routinely reified as purely superstructural objects, so that their diversity and plurality would not disturb the dominant sociopolitical and political economic order. Both classic and popular arts of all possible genres have been actively learned and played by South Koreans, both within and outside their country; so have philosophies and literatures of all historical and world-regional origins. Such cultural and philosophical richness, unfortunately, does not seem to have meaningfully helped to establish and strengthen the systematic ideational basis of dominant political and social institutions.

At the private (personal and familial) level, however, the disembedding or nullification of culture from the everyday practical world is not necessarily the case. In the country's hyper-popular television dramas, personal and familial lives are always portrayed as morally framed and contested arenas of intense social interactions and material conflicts. Such representation of South Koreans' private world is not at all mistaken. Parents' moral authoritarianism, usually framed in Confucian norms, governs both the daily and lifelong processes of familial interactions, whereas children's plural values of life are incorporated into the daily and lifelong familial interactions, both through filial dependency and care.[5] It should be noted that South Koreans' strong familialism – in particular, parents' heavy and long influence over children – is not to suppress individuals culturally or materially. Familial pressure – usually perceived or interpreted as family members' reciprocal sacrifice – is meant to maximize individual family members' socioeconomic success; whereas individuals feel obliged to make the most and best efforts for socioeconomic success as a sort of familial duty.[6] In this way, South Koreans – elites and ordinary people alike – consciously or unconsciously compensate for the generalized lack of societal philosophy and culture in economic and sociopolitical activities by familial values and norms.

5.2 (Statist Liberal) Reflexive Social Sciences and Social-Institutional Dephilosophicalization (Ideologicalization)

Japan's swift rise as a formidable imperial force, to whose militarized capitalist expansionism Korea (then Chosun) first fell prey, induced Korean elites to take on an instrumentalist position in civilizational conversion – namely, *dongdoseogi* (Eastern spirit, Western instrument). On the one hand, Japan was unmistakably seen by Chosun elites to have successfully incorporated Western technologies and institutions into its post-feudal revolutionary transformation; and, on the other hand, Japan's ostentatious political self-identification, through the ideology of *wakonyosai* (Japanese soul and Western skill), reminded Chosun elites of the viability of a sociopolitical future in which traditional philosophy would maintain its hegemonic status in governing the nation and society. In fact, such an instrumentalist approach to Western modernity was even more welcome in China because of both its zealous civilizational pride and its repeated humiliation under Western colonial encroachments. *Zhongtixiyong* (Chinese body and Western utility – namely, learning Western science and technology with Chinese (mainly Confucian) philosophy sustained at the center) was intellectually upheld as the core paradigm for transforming China developmentally (Yoon, S. 2017).

None of these East Asian nations would be able to remain politico-philosophically autonomous or indigenous under the radical historical transformations of the twentieth century and after. Japan's ambition for militaristically conquering (and then economically controlling) the Asia-Pacific region only led to its catastrophic defeat to the United States, which, in turn, carried out forceful measures for a fundamental politico-societal transformation of Japan according to American liberal principles; China's conservative (Republican) revolutionaries would ultimately be defeated by Communists, who then began a violent attack on China's Confucian heritages; Korea would be coercively colonized by Japan, which ruthlessly denied any politico-philosophical and sociocultural autonomy of Koreans, and its liberation following Japan's defeat to the United States only led to a division between two ideologically opposing and militaristically conflicting states (i.e. state socialist North Korea and liberal capitalist South Korea). While China and North Korea became ideologically driven Leninist nation-states, Japan and South Korea by and large accommodated American liberalism only as a political gesture for cajoling American political patronage and economic support.

Under the broad sentiments for politico-philosophically and culturally reviving the damaged nations, the West-oriented national development and modernization of Japan and South Korea were executed with a gross (and often intentional) neglect of the philosophical and sociocultural foundations of Western knowledge, technology, and institutions. Particularly in South Korea, where ideologically coherent political parties and doctrines have been virtually nonexistent (perhaps except for Park Chung-Hee's improvised national(ist) developmental authoritarianism), *dongdoseogi* only led to the generalized justification of a sort of *mudoseogi* (no spirit, Western instrument) reality. South Korea's West-dependent compressed development and modernization have been self-evaluated, not in terms of the philosophical and historico-social appropriateness of such societal transformations, but in terms of their physical rapidity and volumes. In a great paradox, the aphilosophical approach to dependent modernization and development would critically facilitate a very broad and prompt, however superficial, accommodation of Western knowledge, technology, and institutions.

Besides such historical contexts and experiences for South Korea's culturally and philosophically circumscribed West-oriented modernization and development, there are additional logistic, practical, and political conditions that have helped to intensify, and complicate, its civilizationally unbalanced or deformed transformations. First, as explained in detail in my other work (*The Logic of Compressed Modernity*, ch. 4), *compartmentalized institutional simulation* as the core mechanism for compressed institutional modernization has systematically discouraged academic and public attention to the ideological–philosophical foundations and historico-social milieu of Western modernity as a whole.[7] An holistic approach to learning and replicating Western modernity as a civilizational system is not intentionally avoided, but the rigidly compartmentalized structures and processes of scientific, technological, and institutional replication have induced mutually segmented academic disciplines, professions, industries, and administrative departments/ministries to concentrate narrowly on the development, expansion, and protection of monopolistic resources, authorities, and powers within each respectively controlled institutional space. Thereby arose universities/colleges, scholarly communities, administrations, and civil society, each of which would remain merely a mechanic aggregation of mutually isolated compartments, devoid of an organically integrative meta philosophy, theory, or ideology, whether borrowed from the West or developed indigenously.[8] This macro-ideational void is often complemented by the strong introverted allegiance or loyalty of individuals to each discipline, profession, industry, or department/ministry of occupational belonging, which in turn is socially reinforced through disciplinarily segmented university education networks. A sort of *institutionalized rentier consciousness* governs nearly all entrenched compartments of the state and society, many serious confrontations among whom may not be resolvable by any deductive principles or dialogic deliberations, but are usually reproduced and reinforced through mutual hostilities and bigotries, reflecting their memory of earlier confrontations.[9]

Second, as touched on in Chapter 2 of the current book, perhaps as the most crucial contradiction in South Korean modernization, its national economic development has been triggered and sustained by institutional arrangements that chronically deviate from and even frontally contradict the condensively accommodated Western (liberal) institutions in legal, political, social, and economic management. Its liberal institutional modernization has been pursued and achieved for its own sake, but this institutional accomplishment has not served as a sufficient condition for national economic development. Despite international scholarly debates and public controversies, South Korea's phenomenal economic development, particularly under Park Chung-Hee, has offered a fertile ground for influential (political) economic arguments that emphasize the essential interventionist role of the state and its relationship with economic and social actors in initiating and upholding capitalist economic development (Amsden 1989; Evans 1995; Rueschemeyer, Stephens, and Stephens 1992; Wade 1990; Chang, H. 2014). Such illiberal or heterodoxical experiences have been neither comfortably accommodated in the country's formally replicated (liberal) institutions nor theoretically taught or justified by Western academic or ideological orthodoxies about such transnationally replicated institutions. The situationally driven utilitarian dualism between formal institutional modernity and practical developmental improvision has further reinforced the generalized inattention to the ideological–philosophical foundations and historico-social milieu of Western modernity.

Third, the Cold War, both at the global level and the (Korean) national level, by coercively (or illiberally) necessitating a politico-ideological monopoly of *jayuminjujuui* (free democracy, implying, in practice, anticommunist liberalism), has ironically prohibited genuine ideological and philosophical discussions on liberalism, democracy, and capitalism – not to mention socialism and communism.[10] In particular, the military-dominated state during the Park Chung-Hee era forced South Korean citizens to abide by the militarized rule of "free democracy" without being allowed to openly question the historico-social relevance and philosophical–theoretical superiority of such (absolutized) liberal order.[11] In another irony, the politico-ideological coercion by the rightwing state induced civil society to be reactively influenced by dogmatic (?) leftwing ideological forces (some of which allegedly allied with North Korea and underwent harsh persecution by the authoritarian police state).

Given South Korea's achievement of compressed economic and sociopolitical transformations under or through such particular conditions and processes, it has had to reckon with the long-term civilizational desirability, or institutional viability at the least, of its aphilosophical modernization. Apparently, also as implied in the earlier chapters in Part I of this book, the state, economy, and society are saturated with such material forces and political interests as would refuse any fundamental reforms to the improvised or deformed liberal order for coherently reconstructing the nation into a civilizationally or historico-socially truthful entity.[12] On the other hand, its very turbulent neoliberal transition – in particular, its totally unexpected slippage into an unprecedentedly devastating financial crisis in the late 1990s – briefly subjected all elite and grassroots subjects in nearly all sectors to an internal awakening (and external scolding) about the fundamental structural pitfalls and risks of their national developmental and institutional orders. Some local scholar-intellectuals and social activists, as well as the incumbent state leader, Kim Dae-Jung (who, as I have said, was described by Bruce Cumings as "the IMF's man in Seoul"), would take on even global prominence with contextually persuasive arguments for rectifying the nation's economic order by apparently liberal – or arguably neoliberal – measures and rules.[13] The neoliberally driven closing of South Korea's lengthily systematized gap between the formal institutional and the (frequently illicit) practical orders, however partial or short-sustained, has unfortunately (or fortunately?) fallen short of reconstructing the nation into an ideationally coherent entity. Nonetheless, in nearly two decades after the "IMF crisis," the self-assertively reformist government of Moon Jae-In recycled these intellectual advocates of (neo)liberal economic restructuring as key government figures, but would end its term without any apparent achievement, either in institutional and/or ideational reform.

5.3 Generalized Reification of Humanities and Arts

In major South Korean universities, academic departments of humanities are institutionally segmented from those of social sciences, often through the mutually separate colleges of social sciences and humanities. Within a college of humanities, the departments of history, philosophy, and literature/linguistics are internally segmented between Korean, Oriental, and Western majors – with some universities even having separate departments of Korean, Oriental, and Western studies in each humanities discipline. Relatedly, academic departments of social sciences are predominantly staffed by West-trained South Korean PhDs, whereas most of the faculty in charge of Korean and Oriental humanities subjects are either domestically trained PhDs or some South Koreans with PhDs from other Asian or Western universities. Ironically, if not surprisingly, it is the West-trained social scientists, not the locally trained humanities scholars, who are routinely engaged in real world matters, through institutionalized relationship with state organs, political parties, business, professional, and civil organizations, and so forth. By contrast, humanities are researched and taught in a socially isolated, museum-like setting, without systematic references to immediate social realities. Interestingly, such social disarticulation has situated both Korean/Oriental and Western humanities in the same condition of *automatic reification*. Without being organically interactive either with social realities or with intellectual and public reflections upon them, the utility of both Korean/Oriental and Western humanities has been reduced to the individualized appropriation of intellectual and cultural heritages under elitist and/or consumerist orientations.

The individual consumerist mode of humanities nonetheless has been offering a large market for higher education and public culture under the combined effects of the country's Confucian literary atmosphere and intellectually dependent modernity. In modern Korea, much like in Chosun, educationally certified cultural statuses have constituted an independent social hierarchy.[14] This used to be particularly significant for college-educated women who, after using their college degrees for educationally assortative mating, used to remain at home in greater proportions than those with less education (see Chapter 6).[15] In most universities and colleges, women used to be disproportionally concentrated in humanities and other "soft" majors.[16] In a sense, South Korean women's social isolation used to be educationally institutionalized in conjunction with the systematically reified condition of humanities and other gender-skewed majors in various institutions of higher learning. From the 2010s, the distribution of South Korean women's tertiary education majors has broadly converged with those in other industrialized countries, which, however, does not imply its achieving of gender-neutral conditions of higher education and labor participation, but its assimilation with more general patterns of gender differences across the industrialized world (Shin, S. et al. 2020).[17]

Despite the practical ineffectiveness of the *dongdoseogi* approach to West-simulative modernization and development, there has been a historically framed moral impetus for formally extolling traditional philosophy, literature, and history through ritualistic cultural displays in the educational, civil, and national spheres. This is rather a general practice in most of the aged historical societies, but postcolonial nations with particularly bitter memories of colonial subjugation and strong aspirations for developmental catch-up – South Korea being an exemplary case – have been understandably distinct in this regard.[18] Furthermore, many local scholars and intellectuals have tried to reanalyze and reinterpret Korean history and philosophy by focusing on their supposedly foregone effects for indigenously propelled or hybridized modernization. Broadly, there have been three lines of related scholarship: (1) the study of Chosun *silhak* (meaning practical scholarship) in the late seventeenth to the mid nineteenth centuries, as an indigenous middle-age paradigm for pragmatist socioeconomic reformation (e.g. Jeong, I. 2012; Shin, Y. 1998), corresponding to what Clifford Geerts (1973) dubbed "internal conversion" in the Southeast Asian context; (2) the thesis of (foregone) indigenous development, indicating the historical potential of late Chosun society for autonomously initiating its own capitalist development (e.g. Kim, J. 2010; Kwon, N. 2015) and the historical preemption of such potential by Japan's colonial invasion; (3) the theses of Confucian capitalism and democracy (e.g. Kim, K. 2017; Lew, S. 2013), suggesting a sort of hybridized modernity in economy and politics. Despite vibrant investigations and discussions in each scholarship and intense debates and criticisms between them and other perspectives, these arguments have not been clearly successful in convincing other academics and general masses about the indigenous potentials, origins, and conditions for modernization and development.

Despite their situational limits as founding, framing, and/or sustaining forces for the social institutional and political economic orders in South Korea, Western philosophy, literature, and history have been rather extensively accommodated in the educational, intellectual, and cultural spheres. Studying Western intellectual and cultural heritages has been held as a goal in itself – namely, a sort of intellectual modernization vis-à-vis institutional modernization and economic modernization (capitalist development). This understanding has entitled those with related college or higher degrees to demand a sort of cosmopolitan cultural citizenship from the state and society, in terms of their trained knowledge fields being positioned, acknowledged, and accepted legitimately.[19] Paradoxically, *their practical inconsequence has led to an uncircumscribed culturalist consumption* of them by academics, students, journalists, social commentators, and so forth.[20] In particular, Western philosophies ranging from Greek philosophy to postmodernism have almost exhaustively been taught, discussed, and recited in South Korea. The intellectual and cultural accommodation of latest Western thoughts has always been prompt, but many of them have been subjected to slippage into oblivion no less promptly.[21] Not infrequently, Western philosophies and ideologies have been aggressively appropriated in political competitions and intellectual and social movements – for instance, social democracy, neoliberalism, feminisms, environmentalisms, as well as classic liberalism and Marxism. But, such sociopolitical appropriations usually fall short of establishing a systematic organic relationship with local realities through self-reflectively propelled reconstruction of Western philosophies and ideologies. Through a Baudrillardian simulative consumption of them (Baudrillard 1994), many South Korean politicians, activists, and intellectuals have used Western philosophies and ideologies as mechanically indicative signals for (frequently disguised) social and national transformations.

Whereas the intellectual reification of humanities is critically assessed here, what is much more serious consists in the acontextual and asocial nature of – or way of practicing – social sciences. In fact, such situational predicaments of humanities and social sciences tend to escalate each other, in proportion to their mutual intellectual-cum-institutional isolation. As discussed elsewhere (Chang, K. 2020a, chs. 1 and 4), social sciences in South Korea have been dominated by a West (U.S.)-dependent institutional(ist) modernization regime, which heavily prioritizes the mechanical learning (memorizing) of the theoretical, conceptual, and methodological substances of Western social sciences (Kim, J. 2015). In recent years, this tendency has been far intensified in East Asian universities, in conjunction with the (neo-liberally propelled) global competition among the so-called research universities of major industrialized nations (now including China) because of the West-biased evaluation criteria set by those nations, to which a majority of Asian and other students have been headed for advanced degrees of learning and research.[22] Western knowledge has thereby been simulatively and repeatedly recited as a sort of cultural consumption, whereas South Korean realities are often avoided from (the supposedly mainstream scholars') scientific research, as shown most seriously in the discipline of (neoclassical) economics.[23] Besides, as (data on) South Korean realities are simplistically subjected to mechanical analyses using contextually irrelevant Western theories and/or concepts, such analyses often end up generating scientifically meaningless details (without theoretical conclusions or implications) and prevent the cosmopolitan evolution of social sciences in conjunction with such local realities.

The common nature of social (dis)articulation shared by Korean/ Oriental and Western humanities, as indicated above, has produced a sort of congeniality among their practitioners in the broad academic order of intellectual authorities and institutional resources. However, such situational congeniality rarely engenders serious long-term endeavors for collaboratively innovating or inventing new perspectives, approaches, theories, and philosophies for civilizationally (re)evaluating and advancing South Korean society (and the world).[24] In a sense, *social disarticulation is the very structural condition for their independent institutional existence*, often through separate collegiate academic units. The rigid institutional segmentation between Korean/Oriental and Western humanities has induced their practitioners to assume the social identity and behavioral pattern of *institutionalized cultural islanders* toward each other. As the main temporal-and-spatial references of the two groups of humanities are mutually conflictual, audiences (such as students, masses, media, etc.) are often asked or even forced to *epistemologically compartmentalize* their understanding of the world, history, and life.

Broadly speaking, social disarticulation is also a shared property between humanities and arts (such as music, painting, etc.) in the formal educational, scholarly, and professional spheres. Under the rubric of "pure arts," both Korean/Oriental and Western arts in the institutionalized spheres have routinely been studied, taught, and practiced, without active engagement with or critical reflection on historical realities and social purposes. In no surprise, individualized consumerist appropriation has been the main mode of institutionalized access or approach to arts among students, masses, (non-artist) intellectuals, etc., whereas women students' disproportionately high representation in arts education has been the combined (interactive) outcome of the gender-segregative social order and the social disarticulation of arts. Also, the historically contextualized moral primacy of practicing and remembering indigenous arts and the learning and appreciating of Western arts as an independent goal of cultural modernization are social phenomena parallel to the above-explained situation of humanities. The institutional segmentation between Korean/Oriental and Western arts is even more rigid and their mutual temporal–spatial incongruities are even more structural. Needless to emphasize, this is structurally enmeshed with the respective art spheres and markets in society.[25] These similarities between arts and humanities clearly indicate their common social limits and intellectual contradictions under South Korea's compressed modernity, but the related institutional liabilities are much larger for humanities than those for arts, mainly due to differences in their formally declared social purposes.

5.4 Alternative Intellectual and Cultural Fields

Undoubtedly, it is an immense challenge to manage one's life under the condition of compressed modernity. South Korea's West-simulative institutional modernization in radically fast and expansive manners has required not only technocratic and professional experts directly in charge of institutional transplantation but also ordinary citizens to keep struggling in understanding and accommodating incessant rapid flows of new institutions, which are seldom contextually justified by locally adjusted theory, ideology, and/or philosophy. Nonetheless, South Koreans still have had to extensively learn Western philosophy (as well as history and literature) as a requirement of intellectual modernization that is mainly enforced through formal educational curricular (and school exams). In a painful dilemma, due to numerous reasons explained earlier in this chapter, South Koreans are chronically unable or routinely unallowed to actively use their knowledge of Western thoughts in debating, determining, and utilizing West-derived institutions. South Korean citizens have been doubly alienated, precisely because of their everyday hard work in reality and rigidly educationalized learning in the mutually segmented institutional settings.

The wide popularity and zealous readership enjoyed by *jaeya* humanities and social sciences (outside the formal institutional academia) mainly feed on such double alienation of ordinary South Koreans.[26] This used to be an impressive extra-institutional phenomenon among educationally dissatisfied students, socioeconomically frustrated young adults, societally conscientized workers and citizens, and so forth – each such group, in turn, being sociopolitically active and contentious.[27] In retrospect, it was quite remarkable that extra-academia social analysts and historico-political critiques used to influence the public heavily with massive readership of their books. This trend even involved university students' intense thirst for organic knowledge on their lived social realities, aside from each academic discipline's formal curricula. Frequently released from many university libraries are the book-lending statistics by which books by many influential *jaeya* scholar-intellectuals, as well as literary writers, are ranked far above those of regular university academics. Such extra-institutional knowledge fields seriously shrank after South Korea's (re)democratization and continual developmental upsurge, but the totally unexpected national financial crisis and its shocking social aftermaths – such as radical labor reshuffling and precariatization, rampant socioeconomic inequalities and destitution, and widespread suicides and other social pathological conditions – began to rekindle public needs and desires for persuasively sensible explanations and answers on hard-to-believe unprecedented difficulties and instabilities in sheer material survival.[28]

Such rekindling of *jaeya* social science from the beginning of the twenty-first century has been espoused, quite interestingly, by a new cultural-cum-intellectual trend in which South Korean cultural elites have forcefully and skillfully reprocessed social and historical realities into globally celebrated masterpiece cinemas, dramas, and other cultural genre products. The most distinguished figure so far is, without dispute, Bong Joon-Ho, whose movie, "Parasite" – a social satire on South Korea's inequality, class, and family – won the best film award at the Oscar in 2020. When Bong was earlier awarded the Palme d'Or, the top award at the similarly prestigious Cannes Film Festival in 2019, the jury president Alejandra Inarritu praised that this film spoke in a "funny, humorous and tender way of no judgment of something so relevant and urgent and so global" (*Korea Herald*, 26 May 2019). Even the South Korean president then, Moon Jae-In, joined the applause by remarking, "Director Bong's movies start from our everyday environment to show the dynamism and values of everyday life" (*Korea Herald*, 26 May 2019).

In a sense, Bong's social influence, based upon his cultural mastery, had been conversely evidenced by his inclusion in the previous Park Geun-Hye government's blacklist of key cultural leaders to be banned from governmental support. One may wonder why the conservative Park government's blacklist was confined only to cultural creators and producers, not including academic and *jaeya* social scientists and critiques. However, given the earlier military-era history of pervasive surveillance and censorship, fabricated or manipulated incrimination, and occupational expulsion of innumerable critical academics, intellectuals, literary writers, and social activists – mostly by (ab)using the National Security Law (*Gukgaboanbeop*) – the supposedly democratic era's not-so-secretive blacklist of major cultural figures and organizations signaled both continuity and change in the conservative state's control of knowledge and culture. On the one hand, it continues to feel compulsively tempted to (unconstitutionally) contain and counteract undesirable or unfavorable sociopolitical impacts of the culture and knowledge fields under whatever groups are now decisively popular and influential. On the other hand, it now judges that cultural figures and organizations are much more impactful on the public's sociopolitical opinions and attitudes than social analysts, critiques, and academics, whose public influences have nonetheless been rekindled in the recent period (as mentioned above). The conservative political power's insatiable temptation to subdue even the now globally distinguished and celebrated figures in various cultural genres is in direct contradiction to its ostensibly chauvinist (?) desire to tout and co-opt them for propagandic and developmental utilities.

Bong is not necessarily an exception to be globally as well as nationally recognized for excellence in persuasively empathetic cultural productions and performances reflecting South Korean realities and experiences. Even a special term of "the Korean wave" (*hallyu*) had to be devised, in order to signify the globally popularized Koreanness in great numbers of South Korean films, television dramas, novels, various performing arts, and so forth (cf. Yecies and Shim 2011).[29] Within South Korea, some cinemas and television dramas have turned into social phenomena themselves. They not only draw record numbers and rates of viewers but also stir society so drastically that intense media coverages, public opinions, and even policy debates on the concerned social issues follow for substantial durations. Distinguished recent examples are countless: *Squid Game* (2022), *Sky Castle* (dealing with class, family, and education; 2018–2019), and so forth. All of them have similarly left huge social, political, and/ or cultural impacts on the public mind through their critically creative reflection and representation as to liberal, or illiberal, realities and contradictions.

Popular culture's such social weight may even surpass that of academic social sciences during their earlier heydays, when various *reflexive possibilities* of national and/or social progress were earnestly introduced and hotly debated, amid a blurring of academic scholarship and public intellectualism.[30] Furthermore, the global prominence of the Korean wave (*hallyu*) in cinema, drama, music, etc., implies that its social weight is now highly cosmopolitan, which is ordinarily unthinkable for both West-oriented academic social scientists and locally focused critical intellectuals. It should be clarified that these phenomena are far from an outcome of anything like "socialist realism." On the other hand, it is somewhat suggestive that many persuasive scholarly analyses of the Korean wave productions have utilized *compressed modernity* as their theoretical and/or analytical framework (Chang, K. 2022a, ch. 1). That is, according to such studies, compressed modernity is embedded or detected in various forms of cultural representation of South Korean society and people. If such is the case, the Korean Wave, as the worldwide viewing, watching, reading, feeling, liking, sharing, and discussing of Korean popular culture productions, potentially implies that compressed modernity may be a globally shared reality, expectation, and/or imagination, albeit in diverse forms and substances. Is cultural production a much more effective form of intellectual reflection on social life than increasingly mechanical academic social sciences, especially in the context of compressed modernity, which tends to chronically defy conventional social sciences' temporal, spatial, and causal suppositions on human life and society?

5.5 Moral and Cultural Hyping of Family

The most decisive cultural, if not intellectual, parameter for ordinary South Koreans' daily and lifelong management of life consists in their intense and pervasive familialism.[31] While social life under aphilosophically replicated and managed institutions – and sometimes under illegitimately established and reproduced powers and interests from above – rarely enables South Koreans to gratify themselves spiritually, their private life is lived under highly moralistic terms and conditions centered on familial (and quasi-familial) relationships (Chang, K. 2018). Much like nation (i.e. the Korean nation) at the macro-level, family has been the central unit of material survival and spiritual integration at the micro-level throughout the modern as well as the premodern Korean history. Traditional mechanisms for enforcing familialism – such as Confucian philosophy (or ideology), with its prime moral emphasis on familial order and solidarity, family-based farming as the main mode of production, family-based control and mobilization of population, and so forth – are not only still operative but also have been more expansively and systematically reinforced in various aspects.[32] In particular, postcolonial Koreans as a whole ended up culturally *yangbanizing* (aristocratizing), or neotraditionalizing, themselves by commonly asserting in family life the Confucian social identity and cultural practices, regardless of their precolonial castes (Chang, K. 2022a, ch. 4; 2018, ch. 3). Relatedly, practically all major religions – Buddhism, Protestantism, Catholicism, as well as neo-Confucianism (as religion of familial relationships extended to deceased ancestors-as-deities) – endorse, glorify, and/or mobilize family-oriented values and attitudes among South Koreans.[33]

Furthermore, the perplexing and distressing experiences of grassroots under repeated political turbulences (i.e. Japan's colonial invasion, the Korean War, abusive state leaderships, etc.) have intensified the family-centeredness of South Koreans as the main survival strategy-cum-norm.[34] As conceptualized and analyzed as familial liberalism in my earlier work (Chang, K. 2018), even the latest developmental processes (such as the unprecedentedly rapid capitalist industrialization in the 1960s to 1980s, the sudden national economic crisis and attendant neoliberal economic restructuring in the late 1990s, and so forth) have required all social classes, ranging from self-employed urbanites to the *chaebol*, to proactively organize family relationships and resources for economic success and survival. The thereby accumulated wealth, as the prize for their developmental endeavors, has naturally been spent and invested in highly family-centered manners – with family housing and children's education held as the prime purposes of every South Korean's hard work.[35] While Confucianism does not refute any of these practices, various West-derived family ideologies (such as affectionate familism and individualist familism) have also been accommodated, in order to ambitiously constitute and flexibly justify familial desires and purposes.[36] With such flexibly complex ideational (or ideological?) platforms, family seems to have been accepted by most South Koreans as the only social sphere or institution in which practical behaviors (reality) and moral values (philosophy) organically coalesce, enabling them, if under auspicious conditions, to feel fundamentally and consistently gratified at familial interactions and relationships.[37]

In the country's hyper-popular television dramas (and movies), personal and familial lives have almost always been portrayed as morally framed and contested arenas of familial social interactions and material sacrifices and conflicts. Such representation of the private world is far from erroneous – as is amply evidenced by South Koreans' sustained high viewership of such dramas.[38] In fact, many South Koreans tend to *proactively consume* such family dramas by frequently demanding drama producers to accommodate their (usually moralistic) wishes as to the remaining episodes, and sometimes do succeed in receiving acceptably revised storylines.[39] Whether in drama or real life, parents' moral authoritarianism, usually framed in Confucian norms, governs both daily and lifelong processes of familial interactions, whereas children's plural values of life are incorporated into daily and lifelong familial interactions, both through filial dependency and pious care with parents. The next chapter in this book will analyze such – and other – aspects of South Koreans' family-centered personal life and social order in terms of liberal modernity's extensive familialization and its sociopolitical ramifications in the life world.

— 6 —

COMPRESSED MODERNITY, GENDER, AND OBFUSCATED FAMILY CRISIS

Individualization without Individualism

6.1 Introduction:
South Korean Women in Revolt or Retrenchment

South Korean capitalism – or South Korean modernity in general – has undeniably been characterized by hostilities to both labor and women. Whereas the anti-labor tenet in the national economy (and politics) has been politically fostered by Cold War liberalism, the subordination of women in society and families used to be culturally nurtured, if not determined, by the country's Confucian heritage. Labor retaliated first in the late 1980s, riding the high tide of democratization, but the national economic crisis and the subsequent neoliberal rescue measures seem to have effectively debilitated the once globally prominent activism of South Korea's organized labor forces. From the late 1990s onwards, women took their turn by staging offensives against their country's chauvinist capitalist modernity (Moon, S. 2024). Their offensives, however, have been much less confrontational. They have utilized their personal freedom in seemingly *sabotaging social reproduction*, a domain which has been conceived and deployed almost exclusively as a private concern by the South Korean state as well as its citizens. Since social reproduction has remained in the private realm without significant public support or intervention – at least since the termination of the aggressive family planning program – women's personal inclinations and decisions exert a quiet but critical impact (Chang, K. 2018).

By radically deferring, forgoing or ending marriages, by sternly refusing to produce more than one or two offspring (or to procreate at all), or by courageously rejecting family relationships beyond the nuclear unit, South Korean women have taken their society – and, to some extent, the world – by surprise. All of a sudden, these tacit yet pervasive trends have begun widely to be worried about (and implicitly criticized) by policy officials and academics alike as a potential threat to the social sustainability of the national economy, and that of the nation itself. Thanks to the strong, organized feminist voice in the government, as well as in civil society, however, these trends have seldom been openly branded as a manifestation of women's individualism. In this incomparably family-centered society, individualism used to be readily associated with moral defects, and was almost equated with egoism. In addition, few convincing studies exist showing the societal rise of women's coherent individualism *per se* (even though the conceptualization of individualism attracts serious controversies). Nonetheless, in international scholarship, the trends described above are usually considered to be components of individualization.[1] Innumerable survey reports, media articles, and social commentaries have converged on the observation that South Korean women have been individualizing at an unprecedented velocity. How, then, can we make sense of this seemingly contradictory trend of South Korean women's *individualization without individualism*? This puzzle can be addressed by examining the gender implications of South Korea's family-centered modernity (and late modernity).

As extensively discussed above and elsewhere, South Korean modernity has been a highly compressed one, for which South Korean families have functioned as a highly effective receptacle (Chang, K. 2010a, 2022a). In this context, it is as much due to the success of South Korean families as an engine of compressed modernity as due to their failure that they have become functionally overloaded and socially risk-ridden. Such familial burdens and risks are particularly onerous to South Korean women because of the fundamentally gender-based structure of family relations and duties that has in part been recycled from the Confucian past, and in part manufactured under industrial capitalism (Chang, K. 2018). Under these complicated conditions, South Korean women have had no choice but to dramatically restructure their family relations and duties, as well as their individual life choices. A visible trend of *defamiliation* – reducing the effective scope of family life and relations – has thereby taken place as a matter of practicality rather than ideational change. More recently, on the other hand, South Korean families appear to confront additional institutional threats from the radical new world dubbed by Ulrich Beck "second modernity" (Beck and Grande 2010). As the social institutions of (first) modernity, such as the state, industrial economy, firms, unions, schools, and welfare systems, exhibit seemingly irreparable weaknesses in delivering social functions and individual utilities once taken for granted, families are left with even more expanded functions and duties for their loved ones. As families experience the adverse forces of second modernity on top of the burdens of compressed modernity, many South Koreans – women in particular – observe family relations converting from a social resource to a source of individual risks, and thus are encouraged to minimize such family-associated risks by extending or returning to individualized stages of life. A notable trend that may be called *risk-aversive individualization* has thereby been triggered. Like defamiliation, this is also a matter of practicality rather than ideational change.

These complicated patterns of relationships between different stages of modernities, familial relations and functions, and women's life choices are not limited to South Korean society alone. In East Asia particularly, Japan and Taiwan share many of the historical processes and social characteristics of South Korean modernity and second modernity. The compressed nature of modernity, condensed transition to second modernity, family-centered personal and social life, women's innumerable duties, and tendencies toward individualization are symptomatic, albeit in different degrees and periods, of Japanese and Taiwanese societies as well. That is, a brief observation of the neighbor (capitalist) societies reinforces the conclusion that individualization without individualism, particularly among women, is a broader East Asian phenomenon. It is, however, essential to acknowledge the diversity in familial norms and values in these three societies, which, thanks to individualization *without* individualism, continues to characterize their distinct cultural characteristics.

6.2 Compressed Modernity, Second Modernity, and Women's Individualization

Variations of Individualization: Ideational, Practical, and Demographic

In this chapter, I intend to show that South Korean women's practically driven *defamiliation* and (risk-aversive) *individualization* fall short of representing a deeply ideational transition in their familial and individual lives. Thus, it is essential to distinguish conceptually between ideational and practical individualization. In addition, demographic changes in family forms, individual life courses, and fertility–mortality trends, while physically reflecting other tendencies of individualization, can independently produce individualization effects, as people find themselves living considerably longer, confronting extended periods of the "empty nest" stage, and so on. Given these distinctions and possibilities, I suggest the following categories of individualization and defamiliation as the guiding conceptual tools for our analysis of individualization without individualism. While not all of these categories are referred to in the current chapter, it is important to contextualize this individualization without individualism (in terms of risk-aversive individualization) in relation to other categories of individualization with which it might be compared.

Firstly, risk-aversive individualization is a social tendency, whereby individuals try to minimize family-associated risks of modern life (or modernity) by extending or returning to individualized stages of life. It can be distinguished from reconstructive, nomadist, institutionalized, and demographic individualization.[2] Reconstructive individualization is defined as a social tendency in which individuals actively redesign their life courses and structures in order to assertively confront (second) modernity through their autonomous individual life.[3] I define nomadist individualization as a social tendency in which individuals try to defy the adverse social forces of (second) modernity by disengaging their life from modern social institutions and structures such as family, state, industrial economy, education, and so forth.[4] Institutionalized individualization, in accordance with Beck and Beck-Gernsheim (2002), is a social tendency that modern social structures, services, and policies induce individuals to pursue individualized living arrangements and lifestyles. Finally, demographic individualization is a social tendency in which demographic changes, such as increases in life expectancy and the empty-nest period, result in individuals spending increasingly lengthy periods of their lives alone. Risk-aversive individualization and demographic individualization do not have to be preceded by 'positive individualism' (i.e. a social norm whereby individualized patterns or styles of life are regarded as inherently valuable) as a generic culture.[5] By contrast, reconstructive, nomadist as well as institutionalized individualization are all predicated upon the cultural establishment of positive individualism of one sort or another.

Secondly, I define defamiliation as a social tendency in which individuals try to reduce the familial burden of social reproduction by intentionally controlling the *effective* scope and duration of family life.[6] Defamiliation here denotes a *decrease* in family life and relations rather than a complete abandonment or abolition of them. Defamiliation can be conceived as a type of *refamiliation*, denoting various patterns of demographic, social, and psychological restructuring of families.[7] (Parts of the subsequent discussion on South Korean women's defamiliation and individualization will allude to other trends of refamiliation as well, albeit, without always conceptually demarcating them.) Just as with individualization, defamiliation may be subdivided into various types. Although our focus on South Korea is risk-aversive defamiliation, I can also speak of institutionalized and reconstructive defamiliation. In the South Korean context, institutionalized defamiliation seems to be best illustrated by the state-promoted project of family planning from the 1960s to the 1980s.[8] It seems reconstructive defamiliation has been accommodated most zealously by young married women who want to lead an independent nuclear family household unfettered by patriarchal interferences from extended kin members.

Family-Centered Compressed Modernity, Gender, Defamiliation

Beck and Beck-Gernsheim, after carefully examining the historical relationship between macro-social conditions and familial and individual concerns in order to systematically explain individualization under Western (late) modernity, conclude that individualization is much more an institutionalized social change than a cultural or moral modification. Briefly, they observe that "individualization is a compulsion, albeit a paradoxical one, to create, to stage-manage, not only one's own biography but the bonds and networks surrounding it, and to do this amid changing preferences and at successive stages of life, while constantly adapting to the conditions of the labour market, the educational system, and the welfare state and so on" (Beck and Beck-Gernsheim, 2002: 4–12). They extend Talcott Parson's concept of *institutionalized individualism* in order to describe this trend. The view of Beck and Beck-Gernsheim on institutionalized individualism is mainly focused on the (late-modern) social, ecological, and political economic conditions of individually tailored personal lives, whereas Parsons emphasizes the voluntaristic nature of social actions and relations associated with (modern) social institutional arrangements.[9] To elaborate, industrial capitalism, the welfare state, democratization of politics and social relations, and even globalization, all induce or force modern individuals to plan and live "a life of one's own," entailing individualized efforts and risks (Beck and Beck-Gernsheim, 2002: 22–29). Institutionalized individualism inevitably induces the restructuring of individual-family relations and alters the modal attribute of families. As Beck and Beck-Gernsheim emphasize, "The family is becoming more of an elective relationship, an association of individual persons, who each bring to it their own interests, experiences and plans and who are each subjected to different controls, risks and constraints" (Beck and Beck-Gernsheim, 2002: 97).

The above is far from analogous to what has been experienced by South Koreans. Institutional individualism – not to mention cultural individualism – is not what governs the life of contemporary South Koreans. While some of the historical conditions for individualization in the West (e.g. industrial capitalism, democratization of politics and social relations, and globalization) have also existed in the South Korean context (and may have induced some trends of individualization), many additional structural factors (e.g. minimal public welfare, familial responsibility for social reproduction, and family-based social and economic competition) have simultaneously functioned to support what may be called *institutionalized familialism*. It is through this institutionalized familialism that South Koreans' family-centered life has been structurally integrated into the compressed modernity of their society. In the particular sociohistorical context of South Korea, family relations and functions have turned out to be both essential components and consequences of compressed modernity. South Koreans' extremely family-centered life has been structurally interwoven with rapid rates of capitalist industrialization, urbanization, and proletarianization, and with aggressive educational pursuit and privatized welfare protection (Chang, K. 2010a). In sum, South Koreans have lived through family-centered compressed modernity, and thereby remain unrivalled *familialists*.

Compressed modernity has led South Koreans to come into contact with many different family ideologies prescribing complex, and often mutually contradictory, roles and responsibilities that beset their everyday life. More specifically, as explained and illustrated in detail in my earlier work (Chang, K. 2010a, ch. 2), (neo-)Confucian, instrumental, affectionate, and individualist *familisms* have governed South Korean life in extremely complicated ways.[10] The kernel of Confucian familism – family values and norms along Confucian principles, such as individual submission to family, age/generation-based hierarchy, and gender division – arises from the inheritance of traditional family values and norms of the Chosun era (that became generalized across society as a sort of equal sociocultural status in the modern era); instrumental familism – the ideology that family relations and resources should be used as the instrument for individual family members' social success, which in turn is identified as the collective goal of all family members – is a sort of life philosophy that has evolved out of various family-reliant survival strategies of South Koreans in the turbulent twentieth century; affectionate familism – the ideology that the family should be an institution and/or arena for subjective interactions of an emotionally nurturing quality – was originally established in the process of capitalist industrialization and social modernization in Western countries and later incorporated into late industrializing countries in Asia and elsewhere; individualistic familism – the ideology that individual self-realization and/or gratification is the *raison d'être* of family relations and formations – is, in South Korea, hinged upon two social trends, namely, social democratization nurturing the development of individuality with regard to women and youth, and also the commercialization of domestic life amid the rapid expansion of consumer capitalism. While each of these family ideologies separately imposes burdens and pains on family life and relations, chronic mutual discrepancies and contradictions lead to additional social and psychological strains. Even the state has strongly advocated familialism, albeit in an inconsistent manner, thereby exacerbating the psychological and functional difficulties of families.[11] Most governments have tried to use family as a core instrument for diverse social policies, but none has seriously shared its heavy material, not to mention psychological, burdens. In this way, South Koreans' institutionalized familialism has directly reflected the sociocultural and political components of compressed modernity.

Interestingly, the Confucian, instrumental, affectionate, and individualist families – or, more precisely, the Confucian, instrumental, affectionate, and individualist *characteristics* of (virtually all) South Korean families – have a common attribute of emphasizing women's functionally dominant but socially subordinate role in family life. Confucian familism dictates a rigid gender division of labor, under which women's morally prescribed duties in filial care for elders, spousal care for husband, and motherly care for children constitute the functional axis of family life; instrumental familism tends to be sustained frequently on the basis of women's *chimabaram* (skirt wind, meaning women's aggressive activities for promoting familial interests outside home); affectionate familism requires women to become the spiritual axis of family life, by which other family members can be emotionally nurtured and mentally regenerated; individualist familism may have bolstered women's premarital status but, after marriage, it burdens them with contradictory mutual expectations and demands from their children, spouses, as well as themselves. A functioning South Korean family, under compressed modernity, is both proudly and wearily bustling with all these ingredients of family life. A stably married South Korean woman, under compressed modernity, is almost made hysterical by such complex ingredients of family life.

Not surprisingly, as stress and fatigue are inevitably endemic in the family life of almost all South Koreans, various efforts are made to avoid or, at least, ease family burdens, creating a visible tendency toward *defamiliation*. It is also no surprise that the most critical symptoms of defamiliation are directly enmeshed with women's life choices. For instance, the widely worried and increasingly prevalent phenomena of marriage deferral and avoidance, combined with extremely low fertility and increasing childlessness, are much more critically propelled by women than by their male counterparts. These trends of defamiliation, however, do not suggest a fundamental transition to an individualist society but rather manifest the continuing primacy of institutionalized familialism and women's attitudinal attachment to it. In most cases, South Korean women try to reduce, postpone, or remold *the effective scope of family life* because they intend to cling to it rather than desert it.

Compressed Second Modernity, Gender, Individualization

According to Beck, second modernity is a civilizational condition in which various (mostly negative) "side-effects" of (first) modernity add up to a qualitatively different situation, in which the fundamental values of first modernity are still respected, but have to be pursued with radically different social means and institutions under a cosmopolitan paradigm.[12] This new stage of human civilization is characterized by global free trade and financialization, deindustrialization and corporate deterritorialization, informatization and cyberspace, bioscientific manipulation of life forms, borderless ecological and epidemiological hazards, transnational demographic flows, and even globally financed and managed regional wars (Chang, K. 2010b). (To the extent that second modernity is an outcome of intensification of first modernity, which, in turn, has pivoted around liberal capitalism in an overwhelming majority of nations, neoliberalization may be considered a critical manifestation of second modernity.) Under second modernity, many social institutions of (first) modernity – the state, political parties, market economy, welfare system, schools, industrial enterprises as well as families – abruptly become ineffective or dysfunctional. As these institutions increasingly show seemingly irreparable weaknesses in delivering social functions and individual utilities once taken for granted under first modernity, it becomes necessary for individuals to (re)design their biographies in terms of permanently individualized endeavors, pursuits, and existences. In this way, individualization becomes essential in social change under second modernity.

Just as with early modernity, South Koreans have entered second modernity in a highly condensed manner. Compressed second modernity has been as much South Koreans' own developmental pursuit as an irresistible outcome of their subordination to external (or cosmopolitan) forces. In a sense, a developmental internalization of cosmopolitanized reflexivity has taken place (Chang, K. 2010b). Under a strong nationalist sense of developmental urgency, new bandwagon projects – such as *segyehwa* (globalization), *gaebanghwa* (opening), *jeongbohwa* (informatization), and *jisikgyeongje* (knowledge economy) – have governed South Korean life since the early 1990s, but not without serious economic, social, and even political side-effects.[13] While these proactive initiatives have been instrumental in rapidly ushering South Korea into a new civilizational stage and providing new sources of economic growth, there have also been disastrous consequences for society and individuals alike. In particular, the highly impulsive and thus haphazard way second modernity has been brought about for immediate developmental effects has crucially aggravated such risks – the national financial meltdown of 1997 being an indelible marker. Even after South Koreans astounded the world with their enviably swift macroeconomic recovery, they have, however, been critically affected by a range of diverse institutional problems involving the state, industrial economy, labor market, business enterprises, trade unions, schools, and, equally importantly, families.

Above all, in post-crisis South Korea, the highly developed industrial economy suddenly ceased providing more and better jobs for one of the world's most motivated and best educated populations. Instead, as earlier indicated in Chapter 4, many labor-intensive industries have been relocated to low-wage countries such as China and Vietnam, whereas industrial technological progresses have usually been realized through labor-saving measures. In the private sector, aggressive neoliberal labor reform measures have been undertaken, and long-term regular employees have suddenly become a rarity. Even the public sector, where jobs continue to be zealously coveted by an ever-increasing number of applicants, is under mounting pressure to follow suit. Along with labor market restructuring (or 'flexibilization'), the so-called conservative welfare state-type social security system, which is predicated upon stable regular employment, is of little use to those already experiencing un(der)employment

(Chang, K. 2019, ch. 4).[14] With their ever-worsening economic and social status, fewer and fewer South Koreans rely on labor unions and other class-based social organizations to promote class interests through organized social struggle. Civil society, which once mightily erupted to restore democracy, remains largely quiescent in the face of mass economic disenfranchisement and social injustice.[15] As school diplomas, even from colleges, rarely help match graduates to jobs for which they are qualified, public education has been subjected to increasing scrutiny regarding its social utility.

Families are not immune from this general social deterioration. The majority of parents and adult children are now less capable of providing financially for their dependants. In addition, familial cultural resources have become increasingly ineffective in protecting family members against social challenges and in helping them to achieve communal as well as individual goals. Furthermore, families are also beset with increasing societal demands resulting from the decline of other institutions of modernity. The worsening failure of the state, industrial economy, corporations, unions, schools, and welfare programs to ensure the basic conditions of material livelihood and social status inevitably leads individuals anxiously to turn to their loved ones again for assistance.[16] Although the familial capacity for offering such help may vary by class, most families do try to provide assistance of some sort according to their means. In doing so, however, families end up overburdening themselves further, and, as a result, family relations ultimately convert from a social resource to a source of individual risks. In such a scenario, family members may find it necessary to consider physical, material and/or emotional separation from one another, either temporarily or permanently.

This *risk-aversive individualization* is all the more compelling for women, due to their continuing bondage to family as its *masterminding servant*. The adverse forces of second modernity have been particularly disturbing to South Korean women because they have had to confront disproportionately its familial hazards on top of their existing burdens under compressed (first) modernity. In fact, in order to supplement the functional decays of other institutions of modernity, second modernity often tends to intensify the simultaneously Confucian, instrumental, affectionate, and individualist characteristics of South Korean families and women's complex burdens embedded in such familial characteristics. It is true that various patriarchal norms and practices in society, markets, and firms, as well as families have been seriously weakened amid the radical tendencies constituting second modernity. However, women's almost exclusive liabilities in managing familial care work, home management, and socially oriented instrumental support (in education, etc.) have not yet seen any serious transitions (Chang, K. 2010a). As the trend of women's (risk-aversive) individualization has occurred in a highly condensed way since the mid 1990s, its demographic manifestations are not easily differentiated from those of defamiliation, a process still ongoing for numerous South Korean women. In fact, the simultaneous occurrence of women's defamiliation and (risk-aversive) individualization is another essential component of South Korea's compressed modernity.

6.3 South Korean Women in Compressed (First and Second) Modernity

South Korean women's defamiliation and risk-aversive individualization are far from difficult to detect. Thanks to the strong feminist political influence in the post-democratic transition period, such visible changes in women's life patterns and family relations are no longer publicly subjected to traditionalist and/or conservative criticisms. But the tenacious conservative discourse around a supposed decline of the family (which is often deemed responsible for the deteriorating living conditions of the elderly, children, etc.) used to remain indirectly targeted at women. Unsurprisingly, in the private domain, blaming women for family misfortunes and personal mishaps remained much more prevalent, and this private 'gender-bashing' itself has further accelerated women's defamiliation and individualization (Bae, E. 2009, 2010). The implicit suspicion that South Korean women may be "cultural runaways," however, is not borne out by any clear evidence showing their moral and emotional detachment from family. As the following examination of recent data on individual life and family relations shows, contemporary generations of South Korean women have attempted to live and think pragmatically, in order to *remain familialist*, not individualist.[17]

More specifically, in line with those problematics about family and gender addressed earlier in this chapter, I intend to probe the broad situation of the mid 2000s and the mid 2010s (as revealed in some internationally standardized national surveys), in order to reflect the historical forces of both compressed modernity and (compressed) second modernity. For this purpose, we have used the data generated by the Korea General Social Survey (KGSS) in 2006 and 2016. Japan, Taiwan, and China also carried out the corresponding surveys in the same years, using basically the same questionnaires. The statistical data presented here have been produced by the direct analyses of the original survey results of the Family Module.[18] The South Korean survey in 2006 covered 891 women and 714 men; the Japanese survey in 2006 covered 1,166 women and 964 men; the Taiwanese survey in 2006 covered 1,047 women and 1,055 men. The corresponding figures for women and men in the 2016 surveys were respectively 576 and 475 for South Korea, 1,405 and 1,255 for Japan, and 1,012 and 1,012 for Taiwan. The use of these data needs to be justified with regard to a possible criticism that such cross-sectional data may not be appropriate in probing a supposedly longitudinal process like women's individualization without individualism. While we do not deny that individualization involves a chronological process of change, our focus here is on *the recently emergent patterns* of South Korean women's life choices, family relations, and personal and social values that attest to the seemingly contradictory but internally coherent relationship between their individualized life courses and enduring family-centeredness.

Family Over Individual?

One of the most direct ways of checking an individual's attitude to family is to ask them whether the welfare of their family is more important than their own. When South Korean women were asked this direct question, an overwhelming majority of them in 2006 responded positively. South Korean women's such positive emphasis on family welfare priority turned out to be only slightly weakened after ten years (i.e. in 2016). While this was more strongly the case with older age groups, even younger age groups were predominantly familialist, not individualist. (In a separate analysis of our data, even among those who had experienced marriage irregularities such as divorce, separation, and widowhood, only a tiny minority thought otherwise.) South Korean men turned out to be even more strongly familialist. This is not at all difficult to understand because South Korean families, as explained earlier, have operated under diverse gendered ideologies for prescribing women's understanding and care for men. Women's strong allegiance to family thus needs incisive and comprehensive explanations.

One of the most compelling indicators of a married person's adherence to family is their endurance of a difficult marriage in consideration of their children's welfare. When asked in 2006 whether divorce should be avoided until children grow up, a majority of women in middle or old age agreed, but a small majority of those under twenty or in their twenties disagreed. In the subsequent ten years, only the disagreement of those women in their twenties grew stronger to a clear majority, but all other age groups' agreement rather became stronger. (Men in all age groups also showed strengthened positive positions.) Among those women who were unmarried or who had divorced, their opinions in 2006 were almost evenly divided (with very slightly stronger agreement overall). Divorced women's objection grew fast in 2016, whereas divorced men's objection in the same year also turned bigger than agreement. As divorce is increasingly seen as a (rational or democratic) readjustment of family relations and individual life (as opposed to the view where breaking up marriage and family is deemed irresponsible), younger generations of women were more likely to consider it undesirable to endure a problematic marriage simply because of the presence of young children. South Korean men were again more conservative with regard to divorce where young children were involved. In a society where women's share of family care and household labor remains incomparably high, men may have felt it as much less of a burden in insisting on the endurance of a difficult marriage for the welfare of children.

Delaying or Questioning Marriage

While individuals rarely ask themselves whether they are familialist (or individualist), the question of whether and when to enter marriage – that is, whether and when to form a family of their own – has remained an issue consciously reflected upon. In fact, the increasing deferral of marriage and sustained expansion of marriage refusal among South Korean women have often been considered a key indicator of their (subjective as well as demographic) individualization. While the proportion of unmarried women aged thirty or more was still much lower in South Korea than in neighboring East Asian capitalist societies, the speed at which the age-at-first-marriage has been rising in this country is rather alarming.[19] This, however, is not due to women's prevalent pessimism about marriage as a life choice. Both in 2006 and 2016, only about one in five South Korean women across all age groups (excluding those in their twenties) thought negatively about the happiness of their (previous, current, or future) marriage. In 2016, teens of both genders were slightly more negative. The relative (but still very minor) ambivalence of twenty-somethings in 2006 could be understandable because most of them were approaching marriage as a decisive choice in life, but even this group turned slightly more positive about marriage in 2016. A clear majority of South Korean women still thought that marriage can make them happier, but they also seemed concerned about the practical conditions for a happy marriage.

Conversely, their premarital life did not seem to be characterized by personal independence or freedom from family. Both in 2006 and 2016, nearly 80 per cent of the never married women were financially dependent upon their parents, with about 60 percent receiving such financial support often or very frequently. Most of them, however, would hope or expect to become financially independent upon marriage. Most of the never married women were even receiving personal care from their parents, with nearly one in seven in 2006 doing so often or very frequently. This became 75 percent in 2016, perhaps reflecting their fulltime work in the world's most intensive capitalism that required parental rescue service. In Japan, the protracted dependence of young (and not-so-young) adults on their parents led a Japanese sociologist to introduce an extremely derogatory but heavily popularized concept of "parasite singles."[20] While there has certainly arisen a similar social trend in South Korea, this Japanese concept – unlike numerous other Japanese concepts describing new social trends commonly shared in South Korea and popularized by South Korean media and scholarship – has never been openly accommodated by South Koreans. This seems to indicate a psychological and/or cultural readiness on the part of South Koreans to agree to an extended parenthood role (particularly in relation to daughters), regardless of its social acceptability. Also, as daughters' generalized labor participation, while necessitated by the neoliberal liquidation of young men's patriarchal capabilities, signals an important parental achievement, most of their parents gladly offer assistance in managing their life chores, including grandchild care in particular. Besides, the unprecedentedly serious squeeze on the job market for young people in the crisis-hit and neoliberally restructured economy may have further justified the extended parental support for young adults.

Patriarchal Marriage Challenged

Many young women's dependence on parents may not have ended even as they prepare for marriage. Parents seem to have exercised an almost absolute authority over the choice of marriage partners for women aged 60 and over as of 2006 (most of whom may have married while in rural areas). Even most of the younger women of marriageable age (as of 2006), many of whom rapidly entered urban areas, could not refuse such parental authority altogether. Although South Korean parents used to be less interventionist with respect to their sons, a majority of sons were also subjected to parental influence in deciding marriage partners. It was noticeable, for both women and men, that those in their twenties were subjected to even stronger parental influence in deciding marriage partners than those in their thirties. To most South Korean parents, children in their twenties may have appeared too young to decide a marriage partner independently. (This question was not asked in the 2016 survey.)

Upon marriage, South Korean women's dependence on parental support and influence used to turn into their subjection to the patriarchal division of labor vis-à-vis their husbands. A majority of South Korean women in middle or old age, as of 2006, considered it important to help their husbands for their career advancement. However, a majority of those aged under thirty clearly disagreed with their older counterparts in this regard. This changed dramatically in 2016. Only those in their sixties agreed more; those in their fifties were divided evenly; those in their forties clearly opposed; and those in their thirties and below overwhelmingly opposed. Responses also varied with marital status. A high majority of never married women, as of 2006, objected to such patriarchal stipulation of a woman's role, whereas a majority of women currently or previously married were inclined to compromise with patriarchy. In 2016, even currently married women only slightly more agreed, while never married, divorced, or separated women very strongly disagreed. While most South Korean women used to end up marrying, they have gradually rethought the rigid patriarchal prescription of women's role in *naejo* (assisting husband from inside). Younger generations seemed to be more *democratically familialist* than their elder counterparts. Most crucially, younger women were not at all different from younger men as regular and permanent participants (with very high educational qualifications) in South Korea's extremely competitive and volatile capitalist labor market (Chang, K. 2018, ch. 8). South Korea used to be the only country where more education led to less work for women. This pattern changed in the twenty-first century, not because of increased supplies of decent work for women matching their high education, but because higher educated women are less likely be married in each age group and thus need to provide for themselves by working in the economy (*The JoongAng*, 1 June 2024).

CULTURE, FAMILY, LIFE RISK

Forgoing or Retrenching Parenthood

Intergenerational differences were much less noticeable with respect to another tenacious patriarchal norm – that of son preference. When asked in 2006, the necessity of having at least one son in a family was objected to by only about one in three women aged less than thirty, whereas the remaining women were divided fairly evenly between acceptance and ambivalence with respect to this norm. (Given that South Koreans' fertility rate fell near and then below the level of one child per family, having at least one son inevitably implied having no daughter.) In fact, women in their thirties were slightly more likely to oppose this patriarchal reproductive norm than younger women, whereas women aged fifty or higher predominantly accepted this norm. When asked the same question in 2016, disagreement grew much bigger, however, except for women in their sixties.

South Korean young men were even more startling in displaying their preference for sons even in the twenty-first century. Only around fifteen percent of young men aged less than thirty as of 2006 were opposed to the necessity of at least one son in family, whereas this was opposed by around twenty percent of men in their thirties to fifties. But, in 2016, men in their forties, fifties, and sixties agreed more, whereas men in younger ages disagreed more (but less so than women in the same ages). Across all age groups, at least a half of the surveyed men in 2006 accepted this patriarchal reproductive norm. Even in 2016, yes was clearly more than no among men. (Even for women across all age groups in 2016, yes and no were almost similar.) Younger men's son preference (in 2006) may not have been unrelated to their own patriarchal attitude, built up through their socialization into the male-dominant social structure and political culture, but it could also have been a critical reflection of their mothers' active collusion with the patriarchal social order and family support norm, which may have induced them to seek the key meanings of life through their sons' social success and filial allegiance. This situation, however, would not last long, particularly because increasing numbers of lovingly raised and highly educated daughters have already begun successfully to challenge male competitors, above all, in the public and professional sectors, whereas young men's gendered advantages have been liquidated under the downward levelling (i.e. *precariatization*) of young working population.

As a demographic and, for that matter, ethical dilemma among South Korean women (and men), their total number of desired children and total number of desired sons were not too different. For

South Korean women aged under forty in 2006, the ideal number of children in marriage was less than 1.5, and even those in their forties and fifties did not consider it desirable to have more than two children. (While not shown in this table, men held roughly the same view.) Roughly half of the surveyed women in their twenties to fifties favored only one child, whereas the remaining women were divided between preferences for two children, three or four children, and none, in a declining order. (In 2016, the concerned question was not asked, but innumerable other surveys have revealed women's further declining desire of multiple children.) While 'far-below-replacement fertility' was by then a phenomenon widely shared across East Asia, South Koreans' strikingly low fertility expectation has been unparalleled in the region. The actual fertility level of South Korean women has been much lower than these preferences – stagnating at barely above the 1.0 level in the mid 2000s and then slipping to the world's lowest level in the early 2020s – namely, the total fertility rate (TFR) of 0.72 in 2023 as officially tabulated (https://www.index.go.kr/unify /idx-info.do?pop=1&idxCd=5061).

Since both the desired and actual levels of fertility were extremely low, in spite of the persistent norm of wishing to secure at least one son, numerous unborn daughters used to be sacrificed by (illegal) abortion. This simultaneously pragmatic and patriarchal behavior was directly manifested by extremely skewed sex ratios, in particular, among higher-order births.[21] Their son preference seemingly manifested a *will to parenthood*, which, under the patriarchal order in family and society, may have been tantamount to a Nietzschean "will to power."[22] In an *unfortunately fortunate* development of the post-financial crisis era, however, the swift deindustrialization, radical labor market restructuring, and widespread un(der)employment of young people began ostensibly to negate men's socioeconomic advantages, thus helping to dilute South Koreans' son preference (Chang, K. 2018).

It is critical to acknowledge that South Korean women's extremely low levels of desired and actual fertility were not yet accompanied, or facilitated, by any noticeable increase in childless marriages. Almost all South Korean women still intended to marry, and their marriages were rarely without children (even though it was usually limited to rearing only one). Childless marriage may have been readily regarded as a symptom of (subjective) individualization in the South Korean context, but it did not constitute a significant social trend yet.

Rampant but Covert Divorces

The widening divergence between family norms and the realities of family life in South Korean society was perhaps most strikingly illustrated by the explosive increase in the number of divorces, despite the surprisingly enduring anti-divorce attitude of women (and men). Since the economic crisis of the late 1990s, South Korea rapidly caught up with Western societies in the crude divorce rate, and then stood second only to those Western liberal societies in which divorce assumes a fundamentally different meaning as an active individual choice.[23] Despite such a huge increase in divorces across generations and classes, South Koreans' intense moral uneasiness about divorce remained largely intact. When asked in 2006 whether divorce is the best solution for an unworkable marriage, South Korean women (and men) in their twenties to forties and in their sixties and over were more likely to disagree than agree. Women in their fifties and under twenty were more likely to agree than disagree.[24] This changed dramatically in the next ten years. When asked the same question in 2016, only women in their sixties and over were more opposed, but those in the other ages all agreed by clear majorities. Men in their sixties or over, and teens, were more opposed (the latter being in the child ages). In our separate analysis, most of the divorced women did not disqualify their decisions or experiences in retrospect (whereas their male counterparts were less content with such decisions or experiences). Nevertheless, the social stigma attached to divorcee still remained formidable, inducing many newlyweds to enter marriage without filing the nuptial documentation with the state during the practical test period of their marriage's sustainability. On top of such cultural discrimination, most female divorcees had to confront chronic material hardship in the pervasively gender-discriminatory economy, which usually necessitated their financial dependence on aged parents. Divorcees, popularly called "returnee singles" (*dolsing*), often returned to their parental families, instead of becoming a sort of liberated individualist.

6.4 Individualization without Individualism in East Asia: Similarities and Varieties

East Asia is often conceived as being a homogeneous cultural region, due to the very long historical exposure of societies here to common civilizational elements such as (neo-)Confucianism, Chinese statecraft, and so forth. However, numerous scholarly observations have instead revealed mutually different patterns of traditional family forms and relations in Korea, Japan, and Taiwan. Interestingly, it is during the modern and late (second) modern era that these societies have shown similar patterns of family forms and relations and, as discussed here, common trends of defamiliation and (risk-aversive) individualization. At the core of such similarities is the gendered nature of their family structures and ideologies, which reflect modern and second modern social forces as much as their cultural traditions (Hong, C. 2013, 2017). In particular, the compressed nature of (capitalist) modernity and second modernity in the three countries is intricately enmeshed with the simultaneously subservient and masterminding status of women in the highly family-centered systems of (political) economy, social care, educational competition, and so forth. In the same vein, women's defamiliation and risk-aversive individualization as a practical – not ideational – reaction to the social burdens and risks emanating from compressed modernity and second modernity are also commonly observed in the three countries. As a result, women in South Korea, Japan, and Taiwan have commonly been held responsible for spreading marriage deferral, declining fertility, and increasing divorce, all at staggering levels, regardless of the clear fact that they still show a strong subjective attachment to conventional, if not always traditional, familial norms and values. Interestingly, these familial norms and values are what most critically distinguish the three countries from each other. I will briefly indicate in the current section that individualization without individualism in (capitalist) East Asian societies is a social process that simultaneously homogenizes and dissimilates the region.

While both Japanese and Taiwanese women in 2006, like South Korean women, were more likely to prioritize family welfare over individual happiness, the intensity of Taiwanese women's family-centeredness was much stronger than that of Japanese women (and slightly stronger than that of South Korean women). In fact, nearly half of Japanese women in their twenties, thirties, and fifties were simply ambivalent about this question. This did not change too much in 2016. (The concerned question was not asked in 2016 in Taiwan). When asked whether divorce should be avoided until all children grow up, a clear majority of Taiwanese women in all age groups except those aged sixty or over, as of 2006, were opposed to this norm (or idea). In 2016, even those aged sixty or over objected more, and no age group had a high proportion of ambivalence. By contrast, a large majority of Japanese women were divided between ambivalence and agreement to the same norm, both in 2006 and 2016. In 2016, "yes" and "no" were similar across most age groups, with those aged in their forties and fifties clearly displaying more objection. It has already been observed that South Korean women showed clear intergenerational contrasts in this regard, with older women agreeing to this norm more, and with younger ones refuting it more. Looking at the possible happiness arising from marriage, a not-so-ambiguous majority of Japanese women across all age groups in 2006 were simply ambivalent about it. This majority became 66 percent in 2016, while only 13.7 percent expected a happier life by marriage. Taiwanese women in 2006 were most and overwhelmingly pessimistic in this capitalist region about the possibility of a happy marriage (whereas South Korean women used to be largely optimistic about this possibility). Their pessimism grew even stronger in 2016, with 62.6 percent of pessimism as opposed to only 27.2 percent of optimism.

To conclude, the evidences above unfailingly indicate that Japanese, Taiwanese, and South Korean women remained *differently family-centered*, despite – or, more correctly, because of – their common experience of individualization without individualism.[25] Taiwanese women were most consciously family-centered, but turned quite liberal about individual rights. Japanese women were most ambivalently (or most cautiously) family-centered, but seemed to place family concerns before individual interests. South Korean women were most optimistically family-centered, but marked intergenerational differences made it difficult to generalize or predict the overall nature of their familial devotion. In spite of these contrasts in the individual–family relations as perceived by Japanese, Taiwanese, and South Korean women, the overall patriarchal structure of family life seems to have remained common to all these societies. It appears that patriarchy, albeit *in much mitigated and pragmatically modified forms*, survived into East Asia's twenty-first century, in spite of forceful transformative influences of (compressed) modernity and second modernity.

— 7 —

COMPLEX RISK SOCIETY

Risk Components of Compressed Modernity

7.1 Introduction:
Compressed Modernity and Its Risk Components

In the mid 1990s, paradoxically upon South Korea's acceptance into the OECD (i.e. the world's group of industrialized nations), the global fame of South Korea for its miraculously rapid industrialization and economic growth was crucially tainted by numerous gigantic physical accidents, each of which demanded the lives of tens or hundreds of people, ruined invaluable public facilities and private properties, and destroyed natural environments irrecoverably. Referring to the 1990s alone, for instance, a large luxury department store in Seoul (Sampoong Department Store) collapsed, killing several hundred people; underground gas exploded in Daegu and Seoul, demolishing busy urban streets of a few square kilometers respectively; a big bridge over Han River (Seongsu Grand Bridge) plunged into water, claiming the lives of tens of people; a super large oil tanker sank into the sea, polluting hundreds of kilometers of the southern shoreline; an express train derailed over an underground construction site, bringing tens of people to death; suspected leakage in nuclear power plants was reported all too often (Lim, Lee, and Chang 1998; Hong 1998). Even in more recent decades, South Korea has kept shocking the world as well as its own population by such scandalous disasters as the Sewol Ferry's sinking in 2016 (Suh and Kim 2017), claiming youthful lives of 304 high-school students (on a school travel) and also the Itaewon stampede disaster in 2022 (Kim et al. 2023), instantly sacrificing 159 innocent lives of mostly young citizens (wishing to refresh themselves after a long period of the stressful Coronavirus quarantine).

Apart from these gigantic accidents, traffic accidents and industrial accidents have continued to cause everyday anxiety to most South Koreans (Lee and Yoo 2007; Lim, Lee, and Chang 1998).[1] Construction sites have kept claiming so many lives of passers-by as well as construction workers. Propane gas explosions in neighborhood streets and apartments have been endless. Drinking-water pollution has worried innumerable cities and towns almost every year. Dangerous medical and industrial wastes have been illegally dumped in so many agricultural lands, and even neighborhood streets. Severe chemical and heavy metal poisoning has been reported across the country. The further list of chronically disturbing accidents and hazards is nearly inexhaustible.

The flip side of South Korea's development strategy for rapid economic expansion has been to neglect or ignore various noneconomic aspects of civil life such as culture, welfare, environment, safety, and so forth (Chang, K. 1999, 2022a). Consequently, it has continually been criticized in news media and academic literature that the actual quality of life lags far behind the level of economic development as measured in monetary terms. In particular, as indicated above, South Koreans have been put in recurrent collective panic by numerous man-caused disasters (*injae*) that frequently make news headlines all over the world.[2] It is no wonder that very few South Koreans feel safe about traffic and transportation, construction, foodstuffs, water, air, and, not least seriously, digital and other late-modern technologies.[3] Workers', consumers', and other ordinary citizens' endemic subjection to unidentifiably diverse risks, accidents, and disasters simultaneously constitute their class-based sacrifice and exploitation. That is, injuries, damages, and sacrifices in this "accident republic" have comprised a crucial part of its worsening social inequalities.[4]

A careful look at rampant safety incidents reveals that South Koreans have been experiencing a highly diverse set of accidents and hazards, encompassing those common to developed and undeveloped societies respectively and those very particular to South Korea. As a result of its compressed capitalist development and social change, various types of accidents and hazards that tend to exist separately across different historical periods and social places have been found simultaneously in contemporary South Korea. It somehow appears unavoidable that South Koreans experience such accidents and hazards in a similarly compressed manner like the nation's developmental and other compression.[5] More crucially, the very attempt to compressively achieve such collective goals in various arbitrarily strategic manners has caused many uniquely South Korean types

COMPLEX RISK SOCIETY

of accidents and hazards.[6] In particular, as explained in my earlier work on *Transformative Citizenship in South Korea* (2022b), a sort of *developmental contributory risks* have prevailed in South Korea's compressed national development, in which frequently unlawful acts of developmental contribution or participation are accompanied by socially perilous results, however, without due regulatory or legal sanctions.

In this chapter, South Korea is characterized as a *complex risk society*, in which physical risks of both undeveloped and developed societies, as well as physical risks somewhat unique to South Korean society are being found simultaneously.[7] Complex risk society, in turn, is a crucial component of South Korea's compressed modernity. In particular, its developmental experience is a much compressed one in that it has impressively saved the required time and space for expanding the capitalist economy, whereas some of its archaic/indigenous social and economic characteristics have been rather reinforced, to coexist with modern, postmodern, Western, and global characteristics. Such compressed nature of South Korean modernity is intricately linked to various risk dimensions of economic development and social change. Relatedly, this chapter characterizes South Korea in accordance with four major types of risks found in the country (and, in fact, increasingly across the world) – namely, as *developed* risk society, *un(der)developed* risk society, *condensive* risk society, and *slapdash* risk society.

The social realities against which I initially developed the concept/theory of complex risk society were drawn from the mid 1990s, when South Korean society became exposed to an unprecedented array of appalling accidents and disasters. This period will be maintained as the main temporal reference for the current chapter – with selective updates on the latest developments and situations – because it appears particularly pertinent in displaying the complex array of risks to which South Koreans have been subjected under compressed modernity. In spite of South Korea's entry in the twenty-first century into the apparently post-developmental phase, its multifarious risk structure has not been meaningfully alleviated, but, in fact, has frequently been complicated or aggravated by neoliberal socioeconomic policies and practices for coping with economic downturns and instabilities. Long after South Korea's democratic restoration in the late 1980s, the chronically unabating order of *risk injustice* seems to challenge the socioeconomic integrity of South Korean democracy.

While I think that Ulrich Beck's (1992) concept of "risk society" quite relevantly points out one of the most crucial dilemmas of the

147

modern industrial civilization, and that my modification and extension of this concept in terms of complex risk society could be a useful attempt to delineate the disastrous condition of South Korean society, its people's everyday experience is far more forceful than these conceptual constructs in arousing chronic public concern about the disturbing risk order.[8] The safety crisis in South Korea is so obvious that perhaps a more straightforward term, such as the widely mentioned "accident republic" (*sagogonghwaguk*) may also suffice in pointing out the concerned phenomenon. Nevertheless, Beck's problematics presented in his risk society argument, if some modification and extension are applied to incorporate the particularly compressed and dependent nature of South Korea's capitalist development, offer an invaluable scholarly insight for South Korea, a society he was so earnestly asked to visit a few times, and to deliver intensive lectures for.

7.2 South Korea as Complex Risk Society

South Korea as Developed Risk Society

Cheomdangisul (state-of-the-art technology) has been one of the most cherished words among South Korean elites, ordinary citizens, and media alike in the industrial era. Ranging from nuclear energy to bio-engineering, South Korean society as a whole has shown a sort of *high-tech fetishism*. News media hurriedly carry, as loud headlines, stories of South Korean companies and researchers making supposedly significant new technologies and scientific discoveries, often before or without their validity being scientifically confirmed. Besides, South Korean industrialists and economic technocrats have been quite aggressive in spending money to learn and borrow new foreign technologies. Their economy and society seem to have been operating under the extensive use of high-efficiency – and, for that matter, high-risk – technologies.

South Korea's success in compressively achieving many aspects of a hyper-advanced industrial system warrants that various modern and late-modern risk factors indicated by Ulrich Beck, Charles Perrow, and other influential scholars are also closely applicable to its own social realities. Ceaseless accidents, involving virtually all types of "advanced" technologies, indicate that South Koreans cannot avoid the crucial social and physical costs of the high-efficiency, high-risk industrial system, while only enjoying its material benefits. This is particularly so because many of the utilized theories and technologies have hurriedly been borrowed from Western countries, without sufficient knowledge and information concerning their internal scientific reliability and contextual relevance.[9] Besides, as elsewhere, the bureaucratic, corporate, and/or professional interests of techno-scientific experts routinely manipulate and/or distort scientific and technological judgments, and consequently endanger public safety.

Needless to mention, the nation's high-tech fetishism is structurally entangled with its politicized capitalist developmentalism, whether under authoritarian conservative or democratic liberal leaderships. In fact, it was during the national presidency of the self-proudly democratic Moon Jae-In, who was elected after the political failure of two conservative developmentalist presidents (i.e. Lee Myung-Bak and Park Geun-Hye), that South Korea became, in 2017, the world's first national adopter of "the Fourth Industrial Revolution" as an official national developmental paradigm (Chang, K. 2022a: 72).[10] Moon's such high-tech developmentalist rhetoric took an interesting turn during the Coronavirus pandemic, when the nation's (globally envied?) early success in effective quarantine, based upon intrusive digital surveillance of citizens and prompt development of Coronavirus test kits, impulsively led him to declare that his nation was supposedly set to take off as a global leader in coping with the formidable health risk era of humanity with aggressive technological innovations. That is, the government's quarantine accomplishment was instantly reinvented into a bio-industrial policy of the Fourth Industrial Revolution era, whereas its significance in the protection of collective health and safety as social citizenship was soon to slip into both governmental and public oblivion (Chang, K. 2022b, ch. 1).[11]

South Korea as Un(der)developed Risk Society

Unbalanced growth is not only an economic theory but also a core mandate in South Korean development.[12] Significant imbalances have been pronounced between industrial and agricultural sectors, between material and cultural development, between economic growth and welfare provision, between urban development and environmental protection, and, not least importantly, between production/consumption expansion and safety promotion. Such imbalances imply that South Korean society has remained much un(der)developed in various noneconomic aspects. Much like the conservative developmental drive of "growth first, distribution later" (*seonseongjang hubunbae*), a *de facto* policy regime of *growth first, safety later* has characterized

South Korean realities in physical and industrial safety, public health, environmental protection, and so forth.

A brief survey of frequent physical accidents in this society immediately reveals that it suffers from many symptoms of an un(der) developed risk society. Let me take some examples: chaotic cross-sections without proper norms, regulations, and facilities for guiding traffic; dangerous construction and public work sites exposed to passers-by without due cautions or barricades; home and industrial energies (in particular, various types of gas) supplied and used with rampantly lax observance of safety regulations; and rivers and shores endemically polluted with organic wastes, plastics, and chemicals. Due to these (and other) factors, as indicated below, South Koreans still find themselves suffering some of the worst levels of traffic and industrial accidents, ecological disasters, health problems, and so forth.

Another symptom of an un(der)developed risk society, though it has recently been redressed to some extent, is the lack, or under-development of the public service system for emergency rescue and ambulance care at accident sites. In a traumatic example, when Sampoong Department Store collapsed in 1995 with more than fourteen hundred people stuck and jammed under concrete debris, neither the municipal government of Seoul nor the national government was ready to deploy an emergency rescue and relief system, leaving the perilous lives of the casualties (resulting in 502 deaths) only in the hands of many brave volunteer rescuers (Lim, Lee, and Chang 1998). When Sewol Ferry sank in 2004 with 476 passengers, a majority of whom were high-school youth on a group excursion, neither the vessel's crew nor the coast guard was meaningfully prepared to execute rescue work, ultimately leaving 304 human lives sacrificed or permanently missing (Suh and Kim 2017). When the extreme overcrowding in an Itaewon alley on the Halloween day in 2022 was destined to cause a fatal mass crush – ultimately claiming 159 innocent young lives – neither the municipal police nor the district government took due precautionary measures (Kim et al. 2023). All in all, these appalling disasters make it clear that South Korean citizens have been dealing with public safety governance institutions of an archaic (in)capacity.[13]

South Korea as Condensive Risk Society

There are two subgroups in the uniquely South Korean – or, more broadly, compressed modern – types of risk.[14] First, there are risks

COMPLEX RISK SOCIETY

accruing to the simple fact that South Koreans have condensively experienced Westerners' historical development of two or three centuries over merely several decades. This condensing of history has, of course, been centered upon economic growth and industrialization. In other words, as South Koreans have undertaken production, construction, transaction, and consumption activities on unprecedentedly massive scales within the shortest time imaginable, they have concomitantly confronted various risks associated with such economic and social activities in similarly massive and fast manners – thereby constituting a condensive risk society. While South Korea still remains a condensive risk society, its most dramatic manifestation was experienced up until the eve of the "IMF economic crisis" in the late 1990s. Let us examine below various risk conditions of this key period of condensive development.

The most familiar examples of the risk symptoms of explosive economic expansion were found in the accidents accruing to the amazing increases of factories, automobiles, and other modern facilities in the mid to late twentieth century (as shown in *Changes in Social and Economic Indicators since Liberation*, compiled by the National Statistical Office, 1996).[15] The number of factories grew from 5,249 units in November 1946 to 91,372 units at the end of 1994; whereas that of automobiles grew even more rapidly from 14,700 units in 1948 to 8,469,000 units in 1995. Such increases in numbers of factories and automobiles were accompanied by no less explosive increases in industrial and traffic accidents. The number of people injured (including deaths) by industrial accidents was only 1,489 in 1964, increased to 156,972 in 1983, and subsequently declined to 90,288 in 1993. The number of deaths caused by industrial accidents changed even more dramatically, i.e. from merely 33 in 1964, through 2,429 in 1992, to 2,210 in 1993. The number of people injured (including deaths) by traffic accidents was 10,184 in 1954, only fluctuated for a decade to become 11,244 in 1964, and then precipitously increased to reach 348,081 in 1993. The number of deaths caused by traffic accidents changed at similar schedules, albeit less abruptly, i.e. from 2,240 in 1954 through 2,385 in 1968, then 13,429 in 1991 (at its peak), to 10,402 in 1993. However, the number of deaths caused by traffic accidents among every million people began its precipitous hike since the mid 1980s and reached one of the highest levels of the industrialized world around 1990, i.e. 313 in 1991. As of 1998, Greece was the only country among all OECD countries that surpassed South Korea in the per-million-persons killed in road accidents – namely, 210 in Greece and 195 in South Korea (National Statistical Office, 2000: 93).

151

Most South Koreans believe that substantial proportions of these accidents and disasters could have been reduced if more concerns and efforts had been shown to increase safety facilities and improve the public institutional capacity and sociocultural environment for managing safety matters. However, a society's public institutional capacity and sociocultural environment for managing safety matters would not greatly improve overnight, unlike commodity production and other economic capacities. Broadly speaking, this social constraint may reflect a sort of "cultural lag" (Ogburn 1922).[16] Also, the rapid national economic, corporate, and social restructuring and diversification experienced by South Koreans has resulted in the distressing dilemma of *repeated inexperience*. Workers, managers, administrators, and even professionals have ceaselessly confronted new tasks in which their inexperience is directly linked to mistakes and accidents.[17] In particular, as discussed in Chapter 4, the rapid transitions in international product cycle have required exceptional entrepreneurial and technological adaptabilities from South Koreans.[18] Their apparent success in this regard means that they constantly shift to new industries, technologies, and occupations, often before they master the current ones in skillful and safe manners.

South Korea as Slapdash Risk Society

Far more problematic than these sheer change-caused risks is a pervasive attitude among South Koreans to consider various safety measures cumbersome and unnecessary, in making quick profits and in fulfilling corporate or administrative targets without any delay. The rapid increases of accidents and calamities in South Korea may not altogether have been inevitable, in spite of its explosive growth in economic and social activities. But there seem to have been somewhat intentional acts of ignoring and even sacrificing safety matters, in order to achieve the maximum fast growth of the national and local economies, industries, and business enterprises.

The so-called extensive growth strategy in South Korea/East Asia used to emphasize the quick mobilizational use of labor and natural resources, as opposed to the systematic improvement in efficient and safe production.[19] Also, the mercantilist state ideology of "catching up" (with advanced industrial economies) used to remain responsible for a risk-generous attitude of public officials in carrying out administrative activities and supervising private economic activities (Chang, K. 2022b, ch. 9). In this context, capable entrepreneurs and bureaucrats have been the ones who can complete the given economic targets within the shortest time possible, no matter what costs or risks may be caused in industrial and public safety. *Their notion of efficiency has remained fundamentally time-based.* In this way, South Koreans have amazed foreign observers (and even themselves) by producing industrial commodities and constructing mega-size skyscrapers, high speed motorways, power plants, and other mega infrastructures for both South Korea and the world, at previously unimaginable speeds. Even when obvious legal wrongdoings by these heroic entrepreneurs and bureaucrats are revealed by prosecutors or in court, their punishment would rarely go beyond a nominal level (see Chapter 2 in this book).[20] Thus it should not take South Koreans or foreign observers by surprise that some of these physical constructs have collapsed, claiming lives and fortunes at massive scales.

Besides, developmentally or organizationally driven violations of safety principles and rules have been practically normalized in the everyday undertakings of public transportation workers, heavy equipment operators, and even hospital nurses. In this respect, South Korea may be seen as a *utilitarian risk society*, broadly corresponding to its utilitarian institutional dualities, addressed earlier in Chapter 2. Subways, railways, and buses have been operating under a routine compromise of safety in scheduling and boarding (*Kyunghyang Daily*, 24 November 2022). Most operators of heavy equipment such as tower cranes and trailer trucks have been practically forced to work beyond legally allowed durations (*Newsis*, 23 March 2023). So many hospital nurses have been implicitly ordered or expected to undertake numerous functions that professionally and/or legally belong to physicians, besides working many more hours than legally allowed (*Hankyoreh*, 23 May 2023). In a great paradox of South Korea as a slapdash risk society, such industrially or organizationally routinized violations of safety principles and rules would not be upheld by the respectively concerned workers at times of frontal class conflict. As a form of class struggle for promoting their working-class interests, they collectively stage what is called *junbeoptujaeng* (law-abiding struggle) of strictly keeping safety principles and rules to effectively counteract serious deterioration in their working conditions and compensations (Oh, M. 1997; Kim, S. 2016). (This does not imply that they are not interested in socially promoting professional expert activism for public safety.) In a further twist, their employers or contractors – often being the government itself – would threaten to materially and even legally punish them for supposedly harming corporate or public interests by such lawful class acts of safety-respecting work.[21]

153

From the late 1990s, due to the unprecedented national economic crisis and its radical neoliberal ramifications in social and economic conditions, South Korea's quality as a (condensive and slapdash) risk society has been structurally transformed. A sort of *neoliberal risk society* has been on the rise, with such symptoms of *risk neoliberalization* as "subcontracting of risks" (Heo, I. 2013) and "migration of risks" (Lee, Y. 2023). The latter may be more specifically dubbed *migrantization of risks*. Those workers engaged in neoliberalized labor regimes, such as employment with subcontractors, dispatched labor, work as "industrial trainee," and even illegal migrants' casual work, all have been disproportionately exposed to fatal accidents, injuries, or deaths. In particular, the proportion of (formally known) foreign workers among all deaths due to industrial accidents grew rapidly from 7.0 in 2010 to 9.2 percent in 2022 and 10.4 percent in 2023 (*Seoul Economic Daily*, 28 June 2024).[22] These problems have astounded South Korean society, such that they have been addressed not just as a labor policy issue but also as a basic human rights concern (https://www.humanrights.go.kr/base/main/view).

7.3 Compressed Modernity, Transformative Contributory Risks, and Social Inequalities

Now the nuclear power industry here faces a war time ... During a time, we need to discard the bureaucratic mindset of prioritizing safety. (South Korea President Yoon Suk-Yeol strongly exhorted the related ministers and high-level officers accompanying him to a nuclear power industrial firm.)

(*Hangyoreh*, 23 June 2022)

South Korean citizens' exposure to multifarious risks, dangers, and threats are practically expectable from South Korea's multi-front, expeditious transformations and their personal, communal, and organizational lives situated in such transformations. Unless the nation had pursued an exceptionally risk-averse line of developmental, institutional, and civilizational advances, its citizens would not have been exempted from ordinarily contingent risks from all such modern activities. A systematic investigation into the structural nature of South Korea as complex risk society, however, leads to a crucial realization that nearly all categories of risks have seriously reflected the pragmatic, strategic, and/or urgent efforts to expedite and aggrandize developmental, institutional, and/or civilizational purposes and utilities in the nation's quite distinct historical and international contexts.

For instance, those risks normally associated with Beckian advanced risk society have been drastically amplified amid South Korea's aggressive endeavor for technoscientifically and industrially catching up with the West, often by arbitrarily compromising or even ignoring risk-assessment/management principles. Many of those un(der)developed society risks have not been inescapably attributable to South Korea's (now improbable) technoscientific, organizational, and/or other backwardness, but pragmatically or conveniently neglected, or even extended, in order to developmentally (and some-times politically) concentrate in certain strategic sectors and areas under the premise, if not a pretext, of "unbalanced growth," or by the implicit policy line of *growth first, safety later* (corresponding to the Park Chung-Hee government's explicit developmentalist policy of "growth first, distribution later"). Most of those condensive society risks are simply taken for granted and widely accustomed to, as South Korea's phenomenal success in temporal condensation and growth maximization in socioeconomic development has resulted from a sort of national *survivalist* paradigm in the extremely tumultuous post-colonial and post-Korean War era (Kim, H. 2018). Those slapdash society risks have practically been manufactured under the specific developmental, institutional, and civilizational purposes and utilities that are narrowly, exclusionarily, and/or hurriedly decided, defined, or improvised by the often opportunistic yet dominant political, cor-porate, and/or local interests.

Since such diverse risks are considered and accommodated with respect to various transformative utilities, those citizens, communi-ties, and organizations otherwise accountable for or deliberately sacrificed by them are often praised and rewarded in *risk-reflective citizenship*.[23] Above all, as mentioned earlier, a sort of national fetish-ism prevails in glorifying those experts with some supposed scientific, technological, and/or industrial contributions (particularly for catch-ing up with the West), at whatever risks and costs would be revealed later on. Many of those managers, workers, farmers, researchers, and local residents, who have proactively or even bravely overcome or sacrificially endured dangerous outmoded conditions in carrying out either explicitly prioritized or conveniently neglected, yet essential functions, have been lauded as indispensable national, industrial, and/or organizational heroes under their tacit acceptance (or forced excuse) of such otherwise problematic dangers. Those hard-working South Koreans – with the world's longest hours and incomparable intensity in work, study, human care, and so forth – have been portrayed domestically and internationally as model citizens of the nation's miraculously compressive economic and other progresses. Those South Koreans who have conjoined or contributed to executing (over)ambitiously targeted and often irregular or illicit activities and operations (without regulatorily or legally challenging them) have been preferentially offered stable employment, positional promotion, extra wages or revenue, and so forth, on top of inner-circle honors and influences. In such diverse recognitions of risk-based transformative contributions, both public arenas and personal spheres have been inundated by political, organizational, and private discourses on what may be considered a sort of *transformative risk citizenship* (Chang, K. 2022b, ch. 9).

Since South Korea as a complex risk society is still driven forward under the premise of multifarious risk citizenship, its citizens are deeply sensitive to risk-associated social inequalities, as below (Chang, K. 2022b). First, those individuals with weaknesses in educational credential, occupational knowledge, industrial skill, and/or even legal residential status, have had to accept risk exposure as a compensatory leverage in economic participation – as exemplified by the so-called 3D (dirty, difficulty, dangerous) jobs predominantly occupied by undereducated, less trained/skilled, less experienced, and/or non-Korean workers, who are already under disproportionate alienation and destitute. Second, the frequent (or even usual) inconsistencies between risk-generators/profiteers and risk-receivers/victims tend to constitute crucial and even increasing parts of South Korea's social inequalities, often under the strategic, yet unfair or irregular, intervention of the developmental and/or plutocratic state, as exemplified in labor disputes, environmental damages, product hazards, and so forth. (This line of inequality in risk citizenship then also breaches the very basic liberal principle in legal citizenship, namely, all citizens' equality before the law.) Third, the developmental state has been asymmetrically protective of corporate risks (vis-à-vis workers', farmers', consumers' and local residents' risks) practically as a sort of *industrial policy*. This practice is in direct contrast to the welfare state's protection of the latter groups' livelihood risks through various social security programs. Finally, as consumer citizens, they have, on the one hand, manifested conspicuously risk-averse patterns of consumption, indulging in high-rise apartment homes, large passenger cars, high-intensity drugs, habitual hospital visits, and so forth, and, on the other hand, expressed particularly strong social anger when unable to fulfil such patterns of consumption. Apparently, all these risk-based inequalities assume a much more problematic sociopolitical nature than sheer material inequalities of an ordinary capitalist system.

South Korea's structural nature as a complex risk society, and its people's multifarious risk citizenship and risk-associated social inequalities, do not exclusively characterize it in the international context – particularly in the East Asian context. In fact, East Asians have kept mutually oxymoronic gazes at each other with respect to various physical, ecological, and health risks and inequalities associated with national (under)development. For instance, Japan has long served South Korea (and other societies in the region) both as model for emulation and warning for caution with respect to rapid national development's costly risks in safety, health, and environment – with the Fukushima nuclear disaster chillingly reminding them that Japan is no exceptional entity in perilous risk management. On the other hand, South Koreans have shown a very derisive view in discovering that Chinese citizens are endemically exposed to serious risks in safety, health, and environment – despite, or due to – China's explosive industrialization and economic growth, whereas they would not hide a similarly derisive collective feeling about themselves when confronted with appalling domestic disasters. East Asia's compressed modernity as a regional civilizational and political economic trait inevitably implies the region's common, if sequential, reality of complex risk society.

Part III

Prospect

— 8 —

A BECKIAN METAMORPHOSIS?

8.1 Antinomies of Compressed Modernity

What implications are derived from these multifarious manifestations of compressed modernity and its crucial structural risks, as analyzed in the previous chapters of this book? Have they not been uninevitable or even avoidable, without necessarily giving up most of South Korea's key accomplishments in modernization and development? Are they (ir)reparable or rectifiable now, without giving up the same? If neither of the above questions is positively answerable, does South Korea have to conceive and execute an entirely new mode of transformation, be it conceptualizable as modernization and development or not – or even *remodernization*, if not revolution? Otherwise, had South Koreans better *satisfice* (Simon 1947) themselves – for instance, in consideration of the undisputably worse social and other conditions of life in so many other postcolonial nations and societies?

Wide and intense global attentions to South Korean realities and transformations, both in the public and scholarly spheres, have consisted in the following three spheres:

(1) Needless to say, historically and comparatively, unprecedented accomplishments in industrialization, economic growth, social modernization, and so forth.

(2) Quite puzzling tendencies and symptoms of alienation, desperation, and frustration in highly diverse spheres of social and private life, as evidenced by: the world's lowest fertility rate; the pervasive trends of (formal) marriage avoidance, delay, and dissolution, without any correspondently rapid rise in cohabitation

161

and partnership, whether heterosexual or not; the world's worst level of elderly suicide, matched with the developed world's worst level of (relative) elderly poverty and rampant morbidity (in contradiction to South Korea's highest rapidity in population aging); the youth population's scandalous levels of suicide and mental ill health; adult workers' prevalent sudden deaths, endemic fatigue, and frequent industrial accidents, in combination with their long working hours, rivalled by only a few other societies; the highly frequent killings of familial dependants (namely, children and elderly) by their socioeconomically frustrated parents (incapable of breadwinning) or adult children (incapable of caregiving) before their own self-killing; the world's best-educated women's subjection to the developed world's worst socioeconomic discrimination and political alienation; the world's best educated young labor market entrants' subjection to the developed world's worst precarity in employment (that is, a virtual generalization of *bijeonggyujik*, or non-regular jobs); one of the world's worst unaffordability of urban housing (especially to those in such ages as urgently need it for independence, marriage, childrearing, etc.); some of the developed world's worst levels of inequality in income and asset between social classes, between and within generations, between genders, between regions (urban vs. rural and center vs. local), and so forth. It needs to be emphasized that the above-mentioned realities present not only socioeconomic policy concerns and social pathological symptoms but also reflect micro-level sociopolitical reactions and protests.

(3) A wide array of repeatedly staged social, political, and cultural spectacles that attest to the robustly defiant forces of civil society organizations and movements, organized labor, critical intellectuals and professionals, progressive activist students, sociopolitically concerned religious preachers, sociohistorically reflective cultural producers, as well as enlightened ordinary citizens in consciously counteracting the otherwise unilateral or top-down elite forces in the nation's political, economic, and sociocultural spheres. Above all, a series of nationwide social uprisings against some corrupt political regimes' revealed and/or suspected attempts at sabotaging constitutional principles and democratic procedures and distorting the basic socioeconomic justice for their business-collusive interests, have actualized dramatic political transitions in which a few autocrats (including Rhee Syng-Man, Park Chung-Hee, and Park Geun-Hye) were

literally evicted from state office, while a few other presidents had to concede to popular democratic demands for political and/or socioeconomic reform (including Chun Doo-Hwan and Lee Myung-Bak).

How, or whether, can any observer or analyst logically connect the above-explained three conspicuous, seemingly antinomic dimensions of South Korea's compressed modernity? Let me reflect on Ulrich Beck's latest insight into humanity's genuinely liberating transformation, as dubbed the "metamorphosis" through "emancipatory catastrophism" (Beck 2016), in order to explain whether compressed modernity's diverse risks and havocs, as described above in this book, have any comparable potentials for driving South Korea into socially (and civilizationally) desirable directions – that is, if they are, or can be, emancipatorily catastrophic.

8.2 Ulrich Beck:
Risk Society, Emancipatory Catastrophism, Metamorphosis

While Ulrich Beck's thesis of risk society was presented to alert the world to modernity's built-in structural dangers and perils, he ultimately argued that humanity's exposure and reactions to such risks would render itself to fundamentally restructure or regeneratively transform, albeit in widely unpredicted or unforeseen directions, and thereby keep proceeding into the next civilizational stages. In his final book, published post-mortem in 2016, *The Metamorphosis of the World*, he theorized such process as "metamorphosis" (of the world or humanity) and explained its diverse conditions and incidents. The logical kernel of this optimistic sociohistorical argument is "emancipatory catastrophism," which is most emphatically illustrated in his very intuitive account of the global climate crisis. Such an holistic crisis, according to Beck, would inevitably lead humanity to a collective awakening as "risk community" and prompt cosmopolitan efforts for collective existential survival and even associated civilizational rebirth.

In Ulrich Beck's emphatic argument:

> [M]etamorphosis is not social change, not transformation, not evolution, not revolution and not crisis. It is a mode of changing the nature of human existence. It signifies the age of side effects. It challenges our way of being in the world, thinking about the world, and imagining and doing politics.

> (Beck 2016: 20)

PROSPECT

Metamorphosis then also means that the past is reproblematized through the imagination of a threatening future. Norms and imperatives that guided decisions in the past are re-evaluated through the imagination of a threatening future. From that follow alternative ideas for capitalism, law, consumerism, science (e.g. the IPCC), etc.

(Beck 2016: 125)

Due to its inherently unconstrained, unavoidable, and unpredictable nature, the historical impact of metamorphosis could be even more fundamental than revolution.

Such puzzling historical possibilities can be conceivable in terms of "emancipatory catastrophism," which is most crucially disclosed with respect to the global climate crisis as follows:

A double process is unfolding. First, there is the process of modernization, which is about progress. It is targeted at innovation and the production and distribution of goods. Second, there is the process of the production and the distribution of bads. Both processes unfold and push in opposite directions. Yet, they are interlocked. This interlinkage is produced not through the failure of the process of modernization or through crises but through its very success. The more successful it is, the more bads are produced. The more the production of bads is overlooked and dismissed as collateral damage of the process of modernization, the greater and more powerful the bads become.

(Beck 2016: 68)

Global risks – like climate change or the financial crisis – have given us new orientations, new compasses for the twenty-first-century world. We recognize that we have to attach central importance to the dangers that we have repressed as side effects until now ... Climate change is not climate change; it is at once much more and something very different. It is a reformation of modes of thought, of lifestyles and consumer habits, of law, economy, science and politics. Whether presenting climate change as a transformation of human authority over nature; as an issue of climate (in)justice; as concerning the rights of future generations; or as a matter of international politics and international trade; or even as an indication of suicidal capitalism – all this is about the dramatic power of the unintended, unseen, emancipatory side effects of global risk, which already have altered our being in the world, seeing the world and imagining and doing politics.

(Beck 2016: 116–117)

Such global normative opportunities or necessities do not have to be recognized and practiced only in collective ways, but may sometimes be attuned to some countries' national-cum-cosmopolitan developmental initiatives, as exemplified by "the agility with which the

164

Chinese today are promoting the boom in the trade in renewable energy sources" (Beck 2016: 117).[1] Under a sort of critical historical optimism, Beck argues emphatically that the global climate crisis, as an emancipatorily catastrophic side-effect of modernity, "could usher in a rebirth of modernity" (Beck 2016: 117). Likewise, can we infer a rebirth of compressed modernity from what have been critically analyzed in this book as its various structural risks?

8.3 Postcolonial Reflexive Rationality, Compressed Modernity's Risks, and a Prospective Metamorphosis: From "Intended Unintendedness" to Unintended Intendedness?

In this concluding section, let me reexamine if the diverse societal risks embedded in or enmeshed with South Korea's compressed modernity, as analyzed in the current book's previous chapters, have structural potentials for what is suggested by Ulrich Beck as *emancipatory catastrophism* and thus enable it to proceed to post-(compressed) modern stages of fundamentally meaningful social progress – namely, a Beckian civilizational and/or systemic metamorphosis. More specifically, given South Korea's globally conspicuous dynamism in sociopolitical, industrial, techno-scientific, and cultural affairs – with all quite recent national or societal crises in the concerned areas – should we carefully reexamine if all the contradictions and risks of compressed modernity analyzed above are or can be emancipatorily catastrophic?

In South Korea, as explained in Chapter 1, remarkably potent and contentious civil society's efficacy has been manifested whenever the ruling political and administrative blocs in the state, and sometimes their collusive business allies, crucially derail or disrupt essential constitutional principles and democratic procedures, often alongside their arbitrary distortions of key socioeconomic policies to the sacrifice of ordinary citizens' basic rights and interests. Such political activeness of civil society, however, simultaneously reflects formal political parties' chronic failure and dysfunction in rationally, justly, and effectively representing sovereign citizens' interests and purposes. When millions of citizens took to the city streets to demand the recovery of democracy, the punishment of corrupt autocrats, and/or the rectification of fatally harmful state policies, they rarely welcomed formal party politicians' participation and instead ended up nearly realizing *direct democratic politics*, while various social movements and advocacy organizations, progressive professional reform groups, activist intellectual and student groups, organized labor and other class struggle organizations often functioned as a sort of *provisional political party* in their respective main activity domains. Similarly, the very swift and wide formation of online political spaces involving nearly unlimited national, social, and personal issues reflect not only the urgency of late (compressed) modernity's new challenges and agendas but the formal polity's incapability and even indifference about them. South Koreans' ostentatious sociopolitical activism, whether online or in the streets and squares, is certainly an emancipatorily catastrophic outcome of its stultified formal democracy, but the unintended emancipation effect is not likely to uphold itself lengthily unless systematically institutionalized or organized into socially sustainable or reproducible forms.

In the societal order of normal corruption, as analyzed in Chapter 2, socioeconomic inequalities reflect not only market capitalism's inherent dynamic of disequalization but also politico-legal discrimination by often unclearly justified technocratic considerations conflated with political influences. The anger and protest about *mujeonyujoe yujeonmujoe* (guilty if with no money, innocent if with money) are understandably intense in the particular South Korean context. Ordinary citizens' criticism on *jeonggyeongyuchak* (politics-business collusion) constitutes not only democratic consciousness against systematized corruption but also class consciousness in logical connection to their own everyday socioeconomic status vulnerable to routinely normalized socioeconomic-cum-legal discriminations. The generalized conflation of class status with socioeconomic and legal discriminations often trigger existentially generated intense political emotion and reaction whenever corruption scandals are revealed at the ruling elite level – as dramatically evidenced by the imprisonment of Park Geun-Hye and Lee Myung-Bak, two recent presidents, on corruption charges (and a few *chaebol* heads on bribery and embezzlement charges) under the mounting pressure of critical public opinions.[2] Is this apparent political-cum-economic catastrophe emancipatory whether or not the capitalist market economy-generated inequalities are meaningfully redressed?

South Korea's illiberally liberal capitalist order, as signified by the *chaebol*'s economic predominance shown in Chapter 3, paradoxically preempts (even monopolistic and oligopolistic) capital's sociopolitical hegemony, at least at the formally declared or disclosed level. Formal political elites and parties, however ineffective or indifferent in their democratic social representation, remain hesitant to allow or concede any major share of political power to the *chaebol* although they would not mind permanently protecting the *chaebol*'s business interests often under the rubric or pretext of national economic prosperity, competitiveness, and/or recovery. On the other hand, the *chaebol*'s harmful political side-effects and disruption of the transparent and accountable economic order frequently induce civil society and ordinary citizenry to become and remain keenly alert on the actually operating capitalism's undesirable potentials for seriously derailing or compromising the nation's basic political and socioeconomic integrity. Then, are the *chaebol* – ironically unlikely to worry South Koreans about possible capital flight precisely thanks to their legal-organizational irregularities – emancipatorily catastrophic in sociopolitical terms with all their unjustly exclusive usurpation of national wealth? Is this South Korean situation preferable to, say, the American reality of preponderant and multifarious bourgeoisie domination? What are the implications of many West European national systems of monopolistic/oligopolistic capital's coexistence with heavily organized labor and subjects of comprehensive social welfare?

The working population's pre-neoliberal and post-crisis (neoliberal) social transformations accompanying South Korea's developmental compression, as analyzed in Chapter 4, may have engendered two major emancipatory tendencies. First, during the globally unprecedented period of compressed capitalist industrialization in the late 1960s to the mid 1990s, a majority of South Korean citizens underwent the so-called proletarianization process, in which the proletarian class experience, no matter how transitory it was for a majority of them, was nearly generalized as a sort of subaltern (*minjung*) history and the authoritarian state's anti-proletarian stance was widely experienced in direct infringement of each laboring citizen's sovereign rights to freedom and welfare.[3] As a combined outcome of such processes, the working class – at least, those robustly organized groups – has developed a highly organic citizenship identity as a subaltern, democratic, and anti-(neo)colonial (or nationalist) entity. Second, the national financial crisis and its abrupt neoliberal rescue measures – including, above all, radical labor reshuffling across the national economy and generalization of non-regular employment for next-generation workers – all of a sudden came to normalize social precariatization or even economic disenfranchisement of rapidly increasing proportions and numbers of able-bodied/minded workers across generations. Such trends, while often responsible for abruptly bloated self-employment sectors, have interestingly triggered various "post-materialist" and "post-(developmental) capitalist" socioeconomic pursuits such as returnee farming (*gwinong*), back-to-village migration (*gwichon*), work-leisure and work-home balanced life, formal and informal social economy, co-op production movement, and so forth. The abrupt transition from the strong industrial proletarian identity and solidarity during the early decades of industrialization to various alternative forms of livelihood and lifestyle among young and not-so-young adults, accompanying their increasingly vague and transitory working-class status, appears undisputably double-sided in seriously enhancing, if not emancipating, the economic, social, and cultural conditions of this turbulently capitalist nation's ordinary yet sovereign life-world citizens.

As discussed in Chapter 5, both situationally and proactively West-reflexive (compressed) modernity's scientific, intellectual, and cultural conditions and consequences have often been shadowed by its stunning industrial and technological facades. To many reflectively concerned scholars, intellectuals, artists, writers, musicians, actors/ actresses, producers, students, readers, and audiences, such lopsided appraisal and/or pursuit of their society's modernity has been much problematic. Ironically, the instrumentalist obsession of the developmental state and the West-reflexive institutionalist dogma in nearly all universities and the supposedly liberal professions have indifferently left various organic cultural sectors to themselves in unfettered and even prosperous conditions and ironically allowed *jaeya* (civil) thinkers and analysts to command huge influence among choicelessly disenchanted students and citizens.[4] Such free or autonomous cultural domains and extra-university spheres of social thought and analysis, though their exclusion from the reflexively institutionalized mainstream sectors and organizations often implies alienation from due social and governmental recognition and unstable livelihood (which are, at least, personally catastrophic!), have served as valuable spaces for social, intellectual, and human emancipation.

Familialized compressed modernity, as explained in Chapter 6, while enabling the effective social and economic structural incorporation and the stable cultural and sociodemographic reproduction of society and population, has manifested numerous social side-effects, many of which are often ironically simplified as family crisis, individualization, and so forth. In particular, young women (who are the only child or have only one or two siblings) and their mothers have concurred on an undesirability of intergenerationally repeating the mother generation's socioeconomic status both within (patriarchal) family and across (patriarchal) society in the daughter generation's life.[5] Women's such intergenerational agreement, in turn, has engendered quite dramatic reversals and accelerations in various demographic and socioeconomic trends such as widespread postponement, denial, and dissolution of marriage, normalization of childless or mostly one-child only families, the world's lowest fertility (accompanying the previous two trends), young women's universalized entrance and remaining in the labor market, young women's further heightened and (gender-)equalized tertiary educational attainment, young women's unsurprisingly proactive solidification of democratic social identity (whether diversely feminist or at least post/anti-patriarchal), and, in no surprise, young men's gradual adaptation to or acceptance of post-patriarchal gender norms in family, work, and society, albeit alongside with some young men's subscription to anti-feminist collective emotions (spreading mostly through online networks). These tendencies seemingly coalesce to lead to South Korean women's hitherto delayed yet forceful process of liberal modernization (or emancipation?) and a concomitant metamorphosis of South Korea into a gender-neutral or gender-fairly democratic society. Another welcome, though frequently turbulent, social trend is that women's increasing presence and participation in nearly all types of public institutions, social organizations, and industrial sectors not only redress gender inequality and discrimination in them but also help to trigger holistic structural transformations or (re)adjustments in them out of immediate social ecological necessities.

As suggested in Chapter 7, complex (physical) risk society's citizens cannot but develop correspondingly complex traits in perceiving, reacting, cooperating, revolting, colliding, and enduring under potential risks and actual disasters and accidents. First, the profit-driven arbitrary prolonging of un(der)developed society risks – in particular, endemic industrial accidents and rampant environmental pollution and destruction – continues to serve as a critical basis for working-class consciousness and life–world communal consciousness.[6] Second, South Korea's compressed arrival at the (high-tech and high-risk) advanced developmental stage has helped form late-modern, post-materialist civil activism in ecological conservation, anti-nuclear movement, renewable energy promotion, and, in an interesting twist, "green growth." Third, South Korean citizens' exposure to enormous physical risks, accidents, and disasters accompanying their nation's condensive and repeatedly new or unfamiliar transformations in the economy and society has required them to be constantly vigilant and, under actual emergencies, decisively counteractive about them.[7] This civic culture or atmosphere is reinforced paradoxically due to the state's and its industrial partners' opportunism in pursuing maximum economic development and corporate growth with routine neglects of industrial, social, and ecological safety. Fourth, the shared economic opportunism of the state and business is frequently revealed to have involved grave violations and nullifications of basic or crucial protocols, regulations, and laws about safety and security in industrial production, as well as in social service and protection (which are often entrusted to tacitly profit-seeking entrepreneurs or professionals). This comprises a crucial part of the order of normal corruption (explained above in Chapter 2). In this context, workers', consumers', and other ordinary citizens' endemic subjection to unidentifiably diverse risks, accidents, and disasters simultaneously constitutes their class-wise sacrifice and exploitation. In the latest tragedies of the Sewol Ferry's sinking and the Halloween day crush in Itaewon, the sacrificed victims and their families and friends would be further immiserated by the responsible public organs' denial and evasion of (ir)responsibility, which, in turn, would help form the democratic civil networks and forums for politically rectifying the corruption-based "accident republic."

With all the above-explained social risks and reactions combined, South Korea may also be a spontaneously constructed republic of risk-conscious citizenry. Their basic sense of national belonging and social citizenship may be shaped no less decisively by individual and collective risk consciousness than by developmental status and pride. Needless to say, such risk consciousness may vary widely in nature, generality, and intensity across different social communities, sectors, classes, genders, and, not least crucially, generations. In particular, it has come crucially to demarcate today's young generation in work, living, marriage, procreation, and so forth. In recent years, young people's disproportionate subjection to socioeconomic uncertainties and industrial hazards have made them a sort of *risk generation*, but their sociopolitical criticism and resistance tend to be expressed in more individualistic manners than those of older generations. On the other hand, the sociohistorical role of intellectual political entrepreneurs is indispensable in effectively weaving together compressed modernity's all such potentials and dynamics for human, social, and ecological emancipation into a decisive metamorphosis of this already two-millennium-old civilizational entity.

Perhaps such metamorphosis would also be desired for the neighboring East Asian societies (China and Japan in particular) not only by their respective citizenries but also by Koreans. This is because Koreans have been very sensitively affected by various political, economic, social, and ecological turbulences and crises in China and Japan, especially from the late nineteenth century and well into the

A BECKIAN METAMORPHOSIS?

twenty-first century. Beyond dispute, the entire East Asia constitutes a Beckian cosmopolitan risk community. The respective dominance of political and economic elites vis-à-vis variously frail civil society in each East Asian nation apparently effects a critical obstacle to their mutually synergic or integrative metamorphosis into a cosmopolitan post-rivalry human community. For the same reason, East Asia's nationally contained or arrested civil societies need to reach out earnestly for one another, as indispensably cosmopolitan neighbors, for their truly meaningful civilizational metamorphosis.

NOTES

Introduction: Compressed Modernity and Its Structural Risks

1 See Chang, K. (2012c), "East Asia's Condensed Transition to Second Modernity."

2 Broadly speaking, Ulrich Beck's thesis of "risk society" under "reflexive modernization" also shares this neo-Weberian problematic. Ahead of modernity's such unintendedly regressive tendencies, Weber referred to the social effect of *unintendedness* in his essential interpretation of Protestantism as the key impetus for capitalist modernity, according to MacKinnon (1993: 216):

> For Weber, it is a worldly calling alone that "disperses religious doubt and gives the certainty of grace" ... Weber used unintendedness to explain away an apparent contradiction in ministerial writing. On the one hand, this writing exhorts followers to pursue profit assiduously in worldly calling; on the other hand, this same writing is crammed with cries of antimammonism, that the accumulation of riches is evil in the eyes of the Lord. Weber's strategy is to concede the antimammonism of the pastoral literature but to circumvent it with unintendedness: "I have attempted to show in spite of its anti-mammonistic doctrines, the spirit of ascetic religion nevertheless ... gave birth to economic rationalism." "Of course, this was not the purpose of the Puritan ethic, especially not the encouragement of money-making; on the contrary, as in all Christian denomination, wealth was regarded as dangerous and full of temptation."

Extending Beck's epistemology, Weber may be interpreted as pointing to a sort of *unintended intendedness* in the sociocultural function of Protestantism in the rise of liberal capitalism as opposed to a sort of *intended unintendedness* in the sociopolitical degenerations of liberal modernity in its later stage as criticized by various neo-Weberians (Chang, K. 2017b).

3 Intellectually and politically, the most prominent among them were various lines of (neo-)Marxists, including dependency theorists in particular (e.g. Samir Amin, Paul Baran, Andre Gunder Frank, etc.).

NOTES TO PP. 6–23

4 In an interesting twist, some successful West-emulators (or West-simulators) – particularly in East Asia – have been hesitant in advancing beyond such civilizational and institutional dependency, even when they are apparently capable of doing so. See Rezrazi and Andaloussi (2020) on South Korea's such reservation in the area of ODA (overseas development assistance), in spite of its global reputation as a highly proactive innovative developmental actor, and Kim and Kim (2024) on some subtle sociopolitical advances in South Korea's ODA in Southeast Asia.

5 For a most influential observation in this line, see Hamza Alavi (1972), "The State in Postcolonial Societies: Pakistan and Bangladesh."

6 See Chang, K. (2023), "Compressed Modernity and Its Life World Predicaments."

7 Beck's enthusiastic attention to the phenomenon of reflexive cosmopolitization and ardent endeavor for "methodological cosmopolitanism" conversely reflect the social institutional centrality of nation-state in first modernity and its structural decline and replacement in second modernity. According to Beck, Bonss, and Lau (2003: 4), "[f]irst modern societies are nation-state societies defined by territorial boundaries," and "[m]odern social relations are conceived as 'contained' in a national territory and most institutions boast an integrated relation to the nation-state." On the other hand, "Globalization undermines ... the idea of society as nation-state" (Beck, Bonss, and Lau 2003: 6) and "in second modern society the discrepancy between the national past and the global future will only grow" (Beck, Bonss, and Lau 2003:11). It is because the nation-state used to basically demarcate social relations and institutions in modernity that globalization (or reflexive comopolitization) engenders such pervasive and potent changes to virtually every dimension of human life. Seen in this perspective, Beckian globalization involves a societal transformation in internal and external entirety and consequently necessitates an entirely new methodological paradigm in social science, which Beck has strived to help establish in his final years of scholarship under the rubric of "methodological cosmopolitanism" (Beck 2000, 2011b).

1 Borrowed Democracy, State-Projective Politics, and Institutional Functional Conflations

1 South Korea's National Intelligence Service (NIS; formerly The Korean Central Intelligence Agency) formally displays the slogan of "We work in the shady and aim the sunny." Quite ironically, numerous types of public intelligence agencies have been utilized in such contradictory politics. Relatedly, major conservative newspapers have habitually (ab)used their intelligence capability in extracting informal political power in line with such shady politics. Park Chung-Hee, the military dictator in 1961–1979, once told Bang Il-Young, the president of a key conservative newspaper, *Chosun Ilbo*, "Although I am the president during the day, you may be the president of the night," emphasizing his power in controlling information and manipulating news (*Ohmynews*, 8 August 2003, "The Honored and Disgraced President of the Night Folds His Wings").

2 See Erik Mobrand (2019), *Top-Down Democracy in South Korea*, for a lucid account in this line.

173

NOTES TO PP. 25–31

3 This does not mean that Koreans' autonomous efforts at political institutional rebirth had not existed until then. But the *Imsijeongbu* (Provisional Government) group that had represented united independence movement activists most broadly and legitimately was outmaneuvered by Rhee Syng-Man and his strategic allies with colonial collaboration backgrounds and/ or entrenched socioeconomic interests. Rhee tactfully nullified its legacy and initiated America-modelled political and economic modernization under the American military occupation authority's tutelage. See *Haebangjeonhusaui Insik* (in Korean; *Understanding of History Before and After Liberation*), vols 1–6.

4 About the case of South Korea, see Helgesen (2003), "Imported Democracy: The South Korean Experience."

5 When these protestors kept chanting, "The Republic of Korea is a democratic republic, and sovereignty rests with people," throughout the several-month candlelight revolt, it above all reflected their collective anger at such arrogantly corrupt state-projective politics. Moon Jae-In, the president elected thereafter and awarded The Global Citizen Award of The Atlantic Council a few months later, seemed to be seriously aware of this fact when he remarked "The Global Citizen Award is received not by the individual of Moon Jae-In, but on behalf of South Korean candlelight citizens, who protected democracy by the candlelight revolution." See Ha, T. (2017), "The Candlelight Citizen Revolution That Will Last Forever in History."

6 Such massacres occurred in Jeju Island (1947–1949), in Yeosu-Suncheon (1948), and, during the Korean War, heavily in the Providences of Gyeongsangnamdo and Gyeongsangbukdo. In 2005, the National Parliament passed the Basic Law for Past History Examination for Truth and Reconciliation, by which the Truth and Reconciliation Commission was established "as an independent body to investigate and uncover the truth about the anti-Japanese independence movement, overseas Koreans, mass atrocities during the Korean War, various human rights violations that occurred during Korea's authoritarian rule and killings by hostile forces" (https://www.jinsil.go.kr/en/bbm/bbs/selectBoardArticleView.do?nttId= 23429). Many conservative ideologues opposed to such historical rectification and reconciliation, after supporting Yoon Suk-Yeol's election into national presidency, tried to practically occupy the Commission as well as other public institutions for promoting democratic citizenship and sabotage various purposes for historical and social justice.

7 This is, as debated by Ulrich Beck (2016), "emancipatorily catastrophic" and constitutes a crucial dimension of South Korea's Beckian metamorphosis (see Chapter 8 in this book).

8 Out of this tragic history arose numerous respectable "human rights lawyers," whose devotion in assisting and protecting the most alienated, exploited, and harassed under the successive tyrannical governments would evolve into their own political careers as national president (Roh Moo-Hyun and Moon Jae-In), mayor of Seoul (Park Won-Soon), and so forth.

9 See Han, G. (2021), "Discussion on the Conservatization of Men in Their 20s, Their History and Implications."

10 In regions subjected to such state atrocities and even genocides in this and later periods, there has been formation of distinctly anti-statist liberal

NOTES TO PP. 31–34

communities – in particular, the Provinces of Jejudo and Jeonlanamdo, which are now regional strongholds of democratic sociopolitical self-representation. See Choi, J. (2005), *The Gwangju Uprising*, as a forceful analysis of Gwangju's sociopolitical tribulations and evolutions.

11 The National Security Law used to function as a super or meta law in this regard. As the state's abuse of this law in infringing on or virtually nullifying the constitutionally declared basic liberal (democratic) citizenship rights continued without any serious legal sanctions, it was practically a law above the constitution. Such degeneration of the rule of law was responsible for generalized strategic silence among entrenched elites, including ordinary civil servants and opportunistic social scientists (Park, Y. 2012).

12 This effort sometimes took on a (disguised) social movement format, as exemplified by *Saemaul Undong* (New Village Movement) during Park Chung Hee's reign. See Moore (1984), "Mobilization and Disillusion in Rural Korea: The Saemaul Movement in Retrospect."

13 During the 2022 presidential election race, Yoon Suk-Yeol argued openly that the state takes precedence over *gukmin* (national citizenry), igniting wide controversy. Yoon, as a hardline state prosecutor, seemed to share a similar statist ideology to that of military-turned politicians. His actual presidency has been replete with unrestrained attempts at overriding basic citizenship rights and institutions of the ordinary liberal polity, which, after all, has been constructed after the American model. See Jhee, B. (2023), "Korea 2022: Yoon's Administration and Democratic Backsliding." On the comparison of *gukmin* (national citizen/citizenry), *simin* (citizen), *inmin* (people), and *minjok* (ethno-nation) in South Korea's particular historical and sociopolitical context, see Park, M. (2014).

14 In no surprise, such branches of national(ist) social sciences have become very unpopular or belittled in the recent neoliberal and/or global era.

15 Particularly influential was W. W. Rostow's (1959) theory on "the stages of economic growth." Other influential theses included Currie's (1974) "leading sector theory," Lewis's (1954) "dual sector model of industrialization," Streeten's (1959) "unbalanced growth," Hirschman's "linkage approach to development," and so forth. It is important to note that most of these arguments or studies on the late developing economies, no matter how critically or conservatively they saw the world and Western economies, did try to take into account particular economic and social conditions of the concerned developing economies. Some South Korean economists managed effectively to accommodate such careful attention of leading Western scholars in development economics, thereby getting appointed to key policymaker positions in the government. Also, the government set up various para-governmental research institutions, such as Korea Development Institute and Korea Institute for Industry and Technology, designed to connect Western ideas and policies to South Korean realties.

16 See Chang, K. (2022b), *Transformative Citizenship in South Korea*, ch. 3, "Political Citizenship without Democratic Social Representation."

17 See Lee, S. (2006), "The History of Using Korean History Textbooks as Political Means: Focusing on the Rhee Syng-Man and Park Chung Hee Dictatorship."

18 For instance, there continued attempts to control books read by soldiers in the military as follows:

175

NOTES TO PP. 36–41

Ten years after the publishers and authors of the Ministry of Defense-specified "seditious books to be banned from the military" filed a law suit in 2008, the court's compensation verdict was finally confirmed. The 8th Civil Affairs Division of the Seoul High Court . . . made the confirming verdict in partial favor of the plaintiff on 19 December 2019. As the Government gave up appealing on 8 January 2020, the verdict was finalized for good.

(*Hankyoreh*, 8 January 2020)

Similar censorship has continued to be disclosed and protested also in the prison (*Hankyoreh*, 11 November 2019).

19 North Korea has also been explained as a theater state in Kwon and Chung (2012), *North Korea: Beyond Charismatic Politics*.

20 See Kim, Y. (2007), "The Party Politics and Presidential Leadership after Democratization in Korea."

21 See Thompson (1995), *The Media and Modernity*, for a systematic comprehensive account of technical mass media's effects in shaping social and political relations in (late) modernity.

22 See Park and Chang (2001), *Media Power and Agenda Dynamics*.

23 Kim, D. (2013), "Overpoliticization of Civil Society and Its Declining Social Significance."

24 See Chang, K. (2022a), *The Logic of Compressed Modernity*, ch. 4; Chang, K. (2022b), *Transformative Citizenship in South Korea*, ch. 6.

25 For instance, some of them have run the Korean Peninsular Seonjinhwa Foundation (https://www.hansun.org/korean/index.php).

26 See "Why Do Public Security Prosecutors Dislike 'Public Interests': The Public Security Division of the Prosecutorial Office on the Chopping Board Again" (in Korean), in *Hankyoreh*, 29 September 2018 (https://www.hani.co .kr/arti/society/society_general/863766.html). Some scholars criticize Rhee Syng-Man as the initiator of public security rule (Kim, S. 2013).

27 For instance, see Choe, K. (2018), *Power and Prosecution: The Birth and Evolution of the Monster*.

28 For this reason, after South Korea's democratic restoration, judicial independence became such a precious principle that even the court's social accountability has been seriously compromised due to its bureaucratized rigidities (as well as many individual judges' collusive orientations with the ruling interests). See Choi, S. (2015), "A Critical Analysis on the Judicial Independence in South Korea."

29 See "Public Security Prosecutor, Minister of Justice, the Key Figures in the Park Regime" (in Korean), *Kyunghyang Daily*, 9 December 2016 (https:// www.khan.co.kr/politics/politics-general/article/201612092208005); "Former Judges and Prosecutors Lead the Park Geun-Hye Government" (in Korean), *Sisa Journal*, 5 August 2015 (https://www.sisajournal.com/news/ articleView.html?idxno=142009).

30 For instance, on political and governmental career paths of former university presidents, see "What Is [University] President . . . Honor, Authority, Even 'Political Spec'" (in Korean), *Korea University Newspaper*, 5 January 2014 (https://news.unn.net/news/articleView.html?idxno=130145).

31 In recent years, many conservative (mainstream) associations of professions have undergone complicated changes in their political and regulatory rela-

NOTES TO PP. 42–47

tionship with the state due to the government's policy shifts for reforming barriers to professional services, governmental policy debacles and mishandling of critical social affairs, the rapidly changing social mixes of most professions by generation, gender, as well as educational(ized) qualification, and so forth. See "From All Conservative to Left-Click 'Professions' Rebirth: The Reasons for the Spread of Progressive Voices, Even Christian Minister, Besides Lawyers and Physicians," *Hankookilbo*, 10 January 2015 (https://www.hankookilbo.com/News/Read/201501100437361711). A highly, yet contradictorily, suggestive case is the Yoon Suk-Yeol government's attempt at medical reform (mainly by quick increases in university students majoring in medicine), which was heavily opposed by the Korean Medical Association (along with most physicians and trainees), but earnestly welcomed by the progressive Ineuihyup (the Association of Physicians for Humanism). See "Health Care Crisis Looms as Doctors Prepare for Strike over Med School Quota Expansion: Yoon's Office Says Plan is 'Irreversible,' Strike by Doctors Lacks Sufficient Rationale," *Korea Herald*, 12 February 2024. Many vocal physicians complained that they were betrayed by a state leader they had so eagerly supported and elected into national presidency.

32 See Chang, K. (2019) *Developmental Liberalism in South Korea*, ch. 7. This is quite comparable to the policy lines and performances of the Democratic administrations in the U.S. under Bill Clinton and Barack Obama, both of whom were elected to presidency after the Republican government's serious mismanagement in the economy and society.

33 Such theater presidency has frequently backfired in heavily mediatized political scandals precisely due to the state leaders' risky propensity to epistemologically manipulate social realities and government policies by winning the media's favoritism opportunistically. For a more general related account, see Thompson (2000), *Political Scandal: Power and Visibility in the Media Age*.

34 In the arguably most well-known episode in this respect, major conservative newspapers fiercely criticized and resisted the Kim Young-Sam government's comprehensive tax audit on them that was somehow unprecedented (Park and Chang, 2001). As the tax audit ended incompletely, the next government under Kim Dae-Jung also tried to rectify the news media's financial irregularities through another round of comprehensive tax audit.

2 Normal Corruption: Utilitarian Institutional Dualities and Technocratized Authoritarian (In)justice

1 "Prosecutors' Entry to the Parliament, Why Dangerous" (in Korean), *Hankyoreh 21*, 24 February 2024 (https://h21.hani.co.kr/arti/politics/poli tics_general/55143.html).

2 See Eun, J. (2016), "A Study on Gray Corruption," in which corruption as social customary exchanges and as privileged power conducts is analyzed. Gray corruption differs from what is discussed here as normal(ized) corruption under utilitarian institutional dualities, but the two lines of corruption may frequently be conflated especially when social customary exchanges clearly assume a practical problem-solving nature.

NOTES TO PP. 47–50

3 Reflexive modernization in late modern reality, as argued by Beck and Giddens (Beck, Giddens, and Lash 1994), is a structurally complicated process of social change under the uncontrollable floods of choices that expose modern society and people to more risks than opportunities. See Chang, K. (2017b) for a formal theoretical account of "reflexive modernization" in *The Wiley Blackwell Encyclopedia of Social Theory*. In global perspective, this has been an early modern reality as well.

4 The hegemonic consolidation of the (bourgeois-)liberal institutional order (and its social democratic variation) in the West cannot be meaningfully explained without thoroughly examining the concrete political economic and socio-racial conditions, relations, and activities in capitalist industrialism and external and internal colonialism.

5 See Chang, K. (2010a), *South Korea under Compressed Modernity*, ch. 7 "*Chaebol*: The Logic of Familial Capitalism"; Kang, M. (1996), *The Korean Business Conglomerate: Chaebol Then and Now*.

6 In fact, endless instances of embezzling school budgets and assets by founder/owner figures and their family members have frustrated South Korean society. For the case of Sangji University – perhaps one of the most notorious cases in modern Korean history – see Chung, D. (2017), *Sangji University Democratization Struggle 40 Years*.

7 According to *The 2001 White Book on Private Schools' Corruption* prepared by Gyosunojo (The National Trade Union of Professors), 47.7 percent of 193 universities nationwide (91 among 147 private universities and one among 46 public universities) had not received the Ministry of Education's general audit from between 1979 and 2001. Among 158 two-year colleges nationwide (16 public colleges and 142 private colleges, 97 colleges (61.4%) had not received the audit in the same period; 57 among 143 private university foundations had relatives on the boards of directors, whereas 75 among 104 private two-year college foundations had such relatives. The Union demanded, "The Ministry of Education should explicitly stipulate the regular audit intervals and prepare the measure for banning education bureaucrats' entry to private education institutions for specific periods after retirement" (*Korea University Newspaper*, 1 December 2001; https://news.unn.net/news/articleView.html?idxno=4009).

8 See The Committee on Private School Reform, the ROK Ministry of Education (2019), *The 2019 White Book on the Activities of the Committee on Private School Reform: The Recommendations for Improvement in the Private School Regulations*.

9 The Ministry of Health and Welfare indicated that, as of 2021, South Korea had 2.6 physicians per 1,000 population (including Korean medicine doctors), which was about thirty percent less than the average of all OECD countries (3.7 physicians). Only Mexico, with 2.5 physicians per 1,000 people, was behind South Korea in the OECD group. South Korea had 4.6 nurses per 1,000 people, 55 percent of the OECD average (8.4 nurses). By contrast, the number of hospital beds per 1,000 people was 12.8, which was the most among about the OECD group or three times of the OECD average (4.3 hospital beds). Interestingly, or relatedly, South Koreans' annual average number of hospital visits (including visits to private practitioners) was the highest in the OECD group at 15.7 visits (*Hankyoreh*, 25 July 2023). See

NOTES TO PP. 50–52

"the four main goals of medical reform" by the R.O.K. Ministry of Health and Welfare (https://www.mohw.go.kr/menu.es?mid=a10715020000).

10 In the United States, a country notorious for its defective conditions in popular access to medical care, a similar orientation is found among medical school students as shown in the slogan of "Road to the Happiness!" (ROAD for the four most lucrative medical fields of Radiology, Ophthalmology, Anesthesia, Dermatology (*Medi:gate News*, 12 December 2021; https://www.medigatenews.com).

11 See "Nurses Dressed in Doctor Gowns Taking Rounds ... The Illegality Caused by the Shortage of Physicians" (in Korean), *Hankyoreh*, 22 February 2023 (https://www.hani.co.kr/arti/society/rights/1080750.html).

12 Physicians' (and hiring hospitals') receiving of pharmaceutical firms' rebate for prescribing their products has been so widespread and taken-for-granted that many hospitals regard it as a hidden or informal part of the physicians' salaries. Some hospitals have been indicted of even coercing employed physicians to demand and receive such rebate while agreeing to salary freezing. See "'Rebate Instead of Monthly Salary Raise': Hospital Heads and Others Sentenced to Prison Terms" (in Korean) (*Doctors News*, 29 November 2013).

13 Another thorny issue causing international controversies and criticisms is the "export of orphans." After the Korean War, numerous children orphaned during the war, or severely impoverished due to familial hardships, were adopted internationally by families in North America and Western Europe. This process was tacitly endorsed by the South Korean government as a sort of dishonest social policy, whereas some adoption agencies (as non-profit institutions) practically profiteered by receiving sizable adoption fees from the adopting parents. To one's surprise, such business-in-practice continued into the early twenty-first century, amid innumerable young single mothers' tragic destitution and stigmatization in the patriarchally structured processes of capitalist industrialization and social change. It frontally contradicts contemporary South Korea's desperate pronatal policy under its "lowest low" fertility.

14 Hyeongjebokjiwon (the name meaning "brotherly welfare institution") was an ad hoc institution for accommodating burangja (floating persons) during the singunbu (new military) era of the 1980s (Kim, J. 2015). External investigations and victims' testaments have revealed all sorts of human rights violations, including arrestment-like institutionalization, physical attack, uncompensated forced labor, theft of personal belongings, embezzlement of public allowances, malnourishments, denied health treatment, and even summary burial of deceased inmates (Truth and Reconciliation Commission, Republic of Korea, 2022; Lee, D. 2022). For a comprehensive perspectival account of the same incident, see *Between Extinction and Rebirth: Sociology of Hyeongjebokjiwon* (in Korean), edited by The Hyeongjebokjiwon Research Team of Department of Sociology, Seoul National University (2021).

15 As pointed out earlier, this is particularly serious among private school foundations (*sahakjaedan*).

16 Most of the *chaebol* run various types of *gongikbeopin* (public interest foundations), often with mammoth sizes. Many of them have been utilized as critical components of the familial control structure of the corporate conglomerates and thus criticized as camouflaging entities for illicit private

NOTES TO PP. 52–57

interests (People's Solidarity for Participatory Democracy, 1998). See Korea Fair Trade Commission (2018) on an official appraisal on this affair.

17 Aside from legal leniency, the government has kept allowing these basic social services to be priced at such high levels as to enable the concerned social service providers to enrich themselves through virtual market transactions. When the unprecedented national economic crisis in the late 1990s led to a society-wide employment (and income) crisis, a staggering proportion of households ended up becoming heavily indebted due to their inescapable dependence on bank loans, credit cards, and even usury lending in acquiring (i.e. purchasing) basic social services, including education, housing, health care, etc. (Chang, K. 2019, ch. 5).

18 On the part of many foreign students, their enrollment at South Korean universities, despite expensive tuitions, is used as a hidden strategy of entering the local labor market illicitly and earning wages that are unthinkable in their home countries (*University Journal*, 24 December 2019; https://m.dhnews.co .kr/news/view/179520507410403).

19 This trend is apparently comparable to the situations of the U.S., the U.K., Australia, etc., where many universities' financial sustainability is increasingly dependent upon the discriminatory high tuitions paid by foreign students, in particular, from Asia. There are regular exhibitions by such universities in major Asian cities every year.

20 See "governed interdependence" as the characteristic state–business relationship in East Asia's (successful) developmental economies (Weiss 1995).

21 Among many studies and surveys on corrupt relationships between public and private sector subjects in South Korea, see Chang, J. (2010), *A Survey on the Trends of Public Sector Corruption in Korea* (in Korean); Oh, S. (2019), *Research Survey on the Level of Public Sector Corruption in Korean Society* (in Korean); Oh, S. (2020), *Survey on the Level of Public Sector Corruption in Korea* (in Korean). These are some of the thorough analytical reports based upon the annual nationwide surveys on public corruption since 1999, carried out by the Korea Institute of Public Administration, covering hundreds of civilian economic subjects.

22 Such coalescing of the key political, administrative, and prosecutorial organs used to be coordinated by the so-called *minjeongsuseok* (top presidential secretary in civil affairs), a position filled mostly by a politician, ex-prosecutor, or prosecutor-turned politician.

23 For this reason, a few prosecutors became the ex-general president Park Chung-Hee's most trusted servants, comparable to his followers from the military. Some of them were reappointed by his daughter, Park Geun-Hye, during her national presidency in the 2012–2017 period.

24 During the military's political rule, such stance of prosecutors seems to have been further intensified under the criminal justice drive for aggressively incriminating the so-called "social evils" as a sociopolitical control strategy (Choo, J. 2018).

25 Relatedly, in an article in *Hankookilbo*, 25 October 2001, entitled "Gwanseongijadeul" (https://www.hankookilbo.com/News/Read/20011025 0075223335):

It was about fifteen years ago when I covered the prosecutorial office. Then, there were not so many news media as now, so only reporters

NOTES TO PP. 58–67

from nine news media, including newspapers and broadcasting companies
... However, there were other types of reporters in reporting competition besides us. We called them *gwanseongija* (state-appointed reporters). They were intelligence agents dispatched by Agency for National Security Planning, police, Defense Security Command, etc. The organs they belonged to were by nature related to the prosecutorial office in work, but their activities were not related with it. Their work was reporting about what was going on in the prosecutorial office and whereabouts of high-rank prosecutors.

Many years have passed, but still *gwanseongija* are spotted all over. Despite in different degrees from then, as I ask a junior reporter, they are still hovering around the prosecutorial office. Also, after I became the chief of the social affairs bureau, people claiming themselves as from National Intelligence Service, police, Defense Security Command, etc. have sent "cooperation requests," saying "Let us see once." In their words, they are "in charge of *Hankookilbo* (*Korea Daily*)," but, when checked, they had nothing to do with each organ's public relations part. These are *gwanseongija* monitoring what is going on in the newspaper ...

According to the *Journal of Journalists' Association in Korea* (27 October 2001), such *gwanseongija* protested the above article and demanded, unsuccessfully, *Hankookilbo* to delete it (http://m.journalist.or.kr/m/m_article.html?no=3336).

26 For their functional efficiency under normal corruption, the prosecutors need journalists' cooperation (1) in effectively reflecting public opinion to rationalize their deliberate dealing with possibly utilitarian elite crimes and (2) in cajoling media to manipulate public opinion in favor of certain *chaebol* (future clients or employers), politicians (future political recruiters), etc.

27 See Kim, Y. (2010), *Thinking of Samsung*.

28 It is undeniable that regional rivalry (bigotry) politics originated from conservative Yeongnam (Gyeongsangdo)-origin state elites' responsibility for regional imbalances in economic development, infrastructure improvement, and public elite recruitment, besides physical afflictions by state violence. However, it is also indisputable that such politics has been utilized and reproduced by the supposedly democratic elites in the Democratic Party as a key platform for its monopolistic influence over the Honam (Jeonlado) region.

3 Class Contradictions of State Capitalist Industrialism: The "*Chaebol* Republic"

1 There is relatively abundant literature on the *chaebol* in English. See, among others, Kang, M. (1996), *The Korean Business Conglomerate*: Chaebol *Then and Now*; Chang, S. (2006), *Financial Crisis and Transformation of Korean Business Groups*; Kim, E. (1997), *Big Business, Strong State: Collusion and Conflict in South Korean Development, 1960–1990*.

2 See, among others, Eckert (1996), *Offspring of Empire: The Koch'Ang Kims and the Colonial Origins of Korean Capitalism, 1876–1945*; McNamara (1990), *The Colonial Origins of Korean Enterprise, 1910–1945*.

NOTES TO PP. 67–81

3 See a lucid explanation by Evans (1995) of predatory and developmental aspects of the state.

4 I had a personal opportunity to monitor closely the early stage of this corporate reshuffling as a journalist affiliated with *Korea Economic Daily*.

5 Theoretically, CAFs include *chaebol*-affiliated non-profit foundations because these supposedly public entities function much in a similar way to ordinary *chaebol*-affiliated firms in the control structure of the *chaebol* (PSPD Economic Democratization Committee 1998).

6 In this respect, each conglomerate head's voting right multiplier (VRM) over CAFs exactly corresponds to the potential degree of internal rent-seeking by him/her. VRM is vote-entitled stock share divided by actually owned stock share.

7 See Kang, C. (1999), *Economics of* Chaebol *Reform: Form Fleet Management to Independent Management*. Kang's position was politically endorsed by the Roh Moo-Hyun government, so that Kang was appointed as chairman of the Fair Trade Commission, a ministerial post.

8 Even among family/kin members and *gasin*, just as among any other human social groupings, trust is destined to weaken or fracture. Especially when some founders of *chaebol* fell ill or suddenly died, their children threw away such trust in order to capture the lion's share of corporate ownership ahead of other siblings. Some *gasin* themselves entered the inheritance struggle in order to establish, expand, or protect their own independent shares of corporate ownership.

9 An interesting tendency in court rulings over the *chaebol*'s financial crimes is to hold a conglomerate head, *gasin*, and, occasionally, the head's heir collectively liable for legal responsibilities without formally constituted evidence on such a collective liability. If *gasin* are penalized, it is considered that they bear part or all of the head's responsibility. If the head is penalized, it is considered that he/she bears part or all of his/her heir's responsibility. And so on. In a very revealing case, Chung Mong-Gu, head of the Hyundai/Kia Motors group, was sentenced to a prison term for embezzling corporate funds in order to assist his son's inheritance of the auto group, whereas his son, Chung Eui-Sun, was acquitted from legal breaches despite firm evidence of his wrongdoings (*Ohmynews*, 5 February 2007).

10 See Eun Mee Kim's (1997) account of slightly earlier years in which the *chaebol* gradually accumulated and showed material and political parity with state organizations.

11 See Olson (1971), *The Logic of Collective Action: Public Goods and the Theory of Groups*. In this landmark theoretical analysis of collective action, Olson presents "productive" and "distributional" coalitions as two opposing types of collective actions or entities in a modern society. Broadly speaking, a developmental coalition, if successful in bringing about developmental changes, may be considered a type of productive coalition.

12 At first, the head of the Hyundai Group, Chung Ju-Young, attempted to take over state leadership by running for national presidency himself in 1992. He was not successful but, nevertheless, turned out to be very competitive. A decade later, his sixth son once appeared one of the most popular hopefuls for national presidency but was stopped halfway by narrowly losing a controversial, survey-based determination of unified presidential candidacy of the ruling party. (The candidacy was given to Roh Moo-Hyun, who

NOTES TO PP. 82–85

was eventually elected.) The Samsung Group staged a different, much more fraudulent approach in presidential elections, such as using a major newspaper, over which it had practical control, to distort realities and manipulate public opinion, and delivering illegal political funds worth tens of millions of U.S. dollars to a conservative candidate. It became an international scandal when the South Korean ambassador to the United States, Hong Seok-Hyun (Samsung head Lee Kun-Hee's brother-in-law and former and current publisher of Samsung-related *JoongAng Daily*) had to step down after being revealed in a bugging tape to have voluntarily delivered Samsung's illegal political donations. Such political misdeeds by Samsung seem to disclose more of Samsung's political self-confidence than its strategic crudeness, as neither Hong Seok-Hyun nor Samsung head Lee Kun-Hee ended up in jail. As epitomized by a satiric description of the current state of the country as "the Republic of Samsung" (as opposed to the Republic of Korea), Samsung has spearheaded the *chaebol*'s bold social and political moves to openly control politics, administration, and the public mind (Ju, C. 1997; Cho, I. 2005).

13 Professor Chang Ha-Sung, one of the NGO's intellectual leaders, even established the Korea Corporate Governance Fund (KCGF), a sizable investment fund that would be used to warn many *chaebol* about unscrupulous elements of their corporate ownership, financing and/or managerial control (*Edaily*, 24 August 2006). KCFG once attracted many proposals for participation by mammoth global investors.

14 On 19 December 2007, South Koreans did elect Lee Myung-Bak of the conservative Grand National Party to be the next president, by giving him a wide victory. Lee, a former CEO of Hyundai Construction Co. (which used to be one of the most crucial corporate arms of Park Chung-Hee's developmentalist reign), successfully propagated his entrepreneurial career as the main rationale for his proposed national presidency (Chang, K. 2019). Congressman Chung Mong-Jun, a son of Hyundai Group's founder Chung Ju-Young, did not hesitate to terminate his political independence and join Lee's party. It is an intriguing question how much Lee, a former CEO of a CAF but not a family member of the *chaebol*'s head, represented the *chaebol*.

15 See Moore (1966), *Social Origins of Dictatorship and Democracy: Lord and Peasant in the Making of the Modern World.*

16 I have been investigating this issue in a separate ongoing study (monograph) on "Democratic Neoliberalism: The Political Paradox of Post-Development."

17 The most renowned figures in this respect included Chang Ha-Sung and Kim Sang-Jo, both of whom would later be appointed into key state positions during the Moon Jae-In presidency – namely, Chang as the Chief Presidential Secretary for Policy and Kim as Chair of the Korea Fair Trade Commission and then the Chief Presidential Secretary for Policy. Their political appointments pointed to the sustained subscription of the Democratic Party-formed governments to a sort of *situationally progressive neoliberalism.*

18 For instance, see "South Korean Activist Represents Now-Scarce Corporate Reformers" in *The Wall Street Journal* (26 February 2001).

19 See Chang, K. (2019) *Developmental Liberalism in South Korea*, ch. 4 for detailed foreigner shares of major South Korean industrial firms, public enterprises, and banks.

NOTES TO PP. 89–101

4 The Proletarian Predicament of Developmental Compression: Social Conditions of Flexibly Complex Capitalism

1 In a sense, South Korea's compressed capitalist industrialization and upgrading have been accompanied by repeatedly abrupt industrial and technological refiguration, which has also been reflected in the corresponding processes of social and spatial refiguration (cf. Knoblauch and Löw, 2017). On the international catch-up dynamics of such industrial and technological refiguration in East Asia, see Lee, K. (2019).

2 For detailed data on these matters, see Chang, K. (2019), *Developmental Liberalism in South Korea*, chs. 3 and 4.

3 I elsewhere analyzed the endemic limit of laboring South Koreans' political citizenship under the lack of their solid proletarian class identity and an infrastructurally effective political party for them, in spite of robustly organized national and industrial trade unions and their frequently impactful struggles at shop-floor and societal levels. Under a prematurely aristocratized democracy, laboring citizens and other South Koreans have been deceptively manipulated into regional rivalry (bigotry) politics that tends crucially to liquidate the sociopolitical significance of class relations and inequalities. See Chang, K. (2022b), *Transformative Citizenship in South Korea: Politics of Transformative Contributory Rights*, ch. 3, "Political Citizenship without Democratic Social Representation."

4 The analytical data used in this study are taken from the Job History Survey (2007), a retrospective survey that is part of the Korean Longitudinal Study of Ageing (Korea Labor Institute, 2007). The Korean Longitudinal Study of Aging targeted subjects aged 45 years or older from typical households nationwide, and its sample size was relatively large (i.e. 9,026 people). Its analysis of labor mobility, based on a survey of 3,070 people, was limited to married men, excluding those older than 75 and younger than 35 at marriage. It also collected data on the wives of these workers, which were combined with the husbands' personal work history data to find correlations between the working lives of the husbands and the wives.

5 For the latest authoritative observations in this respect, see Seol, D. (2024), "International Migration and Socioeconomic Linkages in East Asia" and Chang, D. (2024), "Transnational Labor Regimes and the Cambodian Case of Asianizing Capitalist Development," both in *Asianization of Asia*, edited by Chang, Kim, and Lee (2024).

6 In South Korean news media, the pervasively exploitative relationship between SMEs and (mostly *chaebol*-affiliated) big enterprises has been one of the most frequently covered and criticized economic issues. The slogan of *dongbanseongjang* (companion growth between them) has become an official policy language as embodied in Dongbanseongjangwiwonhoe (The Korean Commission for Corporate Partnership (https://www.winwingrowth.or.kr), as well as Dongbanseongjangyeonguso (The Korea Institute of Shared Growth; https://www.kisg.net/).

7 The *chaebol*'s internal trades among their affiliate firms may be seen as an (illicitly manipulated) part of such domestic value chains. See Chapter 3 in this book.

8 This has also been the case in Japan. See Heim's (2013) investigation of Toyota Group's subcontractor SMEs about their various

NOTES TO PP. 102–111

organizational and technological requirements in such hierarchical inter-firm relations.

9 *Chaebol* firms' overseas factories are much less cheap labor-oriented and sometimes much more automated than their domestic factories. Very few workers are noticed in many of such overseas factories, inducing the concerned *chaebol* to (deceitfully) complain that their Korean factories (or workers) are too unproductive. For instance, see "Hyundai Motor's Domestic Factories Far Behind Overseas Factories in Productivity" (*Yonhapnews*, 17 November 2013).

10 Some may opt to survive beyond market forces and through self-subsistence by moving to villages and islands as life-style migrants and/or running locally rare or new self-employed businesses, like cafés and even bookshops in remote places. While their financial viability may remain in question, they quite frequently attract (favorable or romantic?) media attention, which in turn induces local governments' interest and support.

11 See Chang, J. (2022) on the general condition of platform labor in South Korea. Also see Kwon, Kang, and Noh (2022) on the social organizational nature of platform workers with respect to their activism potentials.

5 Reflexive Postcoloniality: Intellectual and Cultural Contradictions of Compressed Modernity

1 Under the sequential economic rises of Japan and other sizable East Asian countries – including China in particular – such discourses, both on the regional (Asian) and the international levels, have usually been centered on East Asia. Conversely, even critical perspectives and debates on Asian development and modernization have also highlighted East Asian countries in particular. For a much heated debate on East Asian governance, see the articles in *Foreign Affairs* by Fareed Zakaria and Lee Kuan Yew (1994) and Kim Dae-Jung (1994).

2 Such philosophical–instrumental dualism was respectively expressed in *dongdoseogi* (東道西器; Eastern spirit, Western instrument) in Korea, *zhongtixiyoung* (中體西用; Chinese body, Western utility) in China, and *wakonyousai* (和魂洋才; Japanese soul, Western skill) in Japan (Yoon, S. 2017).

3 See Joseph S. Nye (2004), *Soft Power: The Means to Success in World Politics*. For a lucid account of China's stance in this regard, see Cho and Jeong (2008), "China's Soft Power: Discussions, Resources, and Prospects."

4 This may be added as part of the constitutive components of "global culture" that was once discussed among the world's foremost social theorists, including Immanuel Wallerstein, Roland Robertson, Bryan S. Turner, Alain Touraine, Zigmunt Bauman, Margaret Archer, Mike Featherstone, etc. (Featherstone 1990; Featherstone (ed.) 1990).

5 See Chang, K. (2004), "The Anti-Communitarian Family? Everyday Conditions of Authoritarian Politics in South Korea."

6 Needless to emphasize, this is reflected in South Koreans' education zeal or, as indicated by Michael Seth, even "education fever." See Seth (2002), *Education Fever: Society, Politics, and the Pursuit of Schooling in South Korea.*

NOTES TO PP. 113–116

7 In academia, while this is common in most social sciences, the discipline of economics, under the domination of neoclassical economics, has particularly detached itself from philosophical, historical, and local social foundations. In fact, even South Korea's own industrial economy – the *chaebol* system in particular – has apparently been subjected to pervasive scholarly indifference by the so-called mainstream economists at key universities. In a sense, a *positivist economics against positivism* has been responsible for the gross neglect of South Korean realities and resultant shortage of practical scientific knowledge for problem-solving. This tendency may not be unrelated to what is earlier explained in this book as *utilitarian institutional dualities* (in Chapter 2). As improvised, deformed, and/or repurposed real-world practices, relations, and institutions are summarily rejected as unworthy of serious scientific investigations, South Korea's globally famed economy has failed to provide meaningful impetuses for the scientific innovation of economics and other related disciplines.

8 See Michael D. Kennedy (2020), *Globalizing Knowledge: Intellectuals, Universities, and Publics in Transformation*, for an authoritative recent account of the global(izing) knowledge structure and its social structural ramifications. Also, see Takehiko Kariya (2012), *Education Reform and Social Class in Japan: The Emerging Incentive Divide*, on Japanese's complex situation in this regard.

9 This is interestingly analogous to what Thomas Hobbes ([1651]2017) referred to as "the war of all against all" (*bellum omnium contra omnes*). The South Korean situation – as recently manifested in the endemic clashes, albeit with occasional collusions, among politicians, media, prosecutors, even physicians (and nurses), and so forth – may be dubbed the war of all institutions against all institutions.

10 See Chang, K. (2022a), *The Logic of Compressed Modernity*, ch. 4.

11 As noted in Chapter 2, Park Geun-Hye (Park Chung-Hee's daughter) and her politico-intellectual collaborators attempted to produce and coerce a state-commissioned text book on history, which failed due to an overwhelming public opposition. Its purpose was simple and clear – to legitimate her father's (or the military's) political rule as well as all other state powers sharing common ideological and political economic stakes in history.

12 The recently impeached president, Yoon Suk-Yeol, seems to have been tactically supported by such reactionary forces, which have been opportunistically represented by the political and intellectual strategists of the so-called "New Right" (in the South Korean version).

13 As also indicated in Chapter 3, the two prominent figures in this respect were Chang Ha-Sung and Kim Sang-Jo, both of whom would later be appointed into key state positions during the Moon Jae-In presidency. Chang served as the Chief Presidential Secretary for Policy and Kim as Chair of the Korea Fair Trade Commission and then the Chief Presidential Secretary for Policy.

14 See Chang, K. (2022b), *Transformative Citizenship in South Korea*, ch. 5, "Education as Citizenship, or Citizenship by Education" and Chang, K. (2010a), *South Korea under Compressed Modernity*, ch. 3, "The Social Investment Family and Educational Politics."

15 As noted in Chapters 4 and 6 in this book and Chang, K. (2022b), ch. 5, South Korea used to be the only society in the world with such inverse relationship between women's tertiary education and employment. But the current gen-

186

NOTES TO PP. 116–118

eration of young women now all enter and stay in the labor market regardless of their marital expectation and/or status. As an interesting ramification for most women's high education and its labor market consequences, better educated women are now more likely to remain unmarried into their thirties and after, and thus should provide for themselves (*The JoongAng*, 1 June 2024).

16 Shin, S. et al. (2020), "Development of Strategies by Sector for Reducing the Gender gap in the Labor Market (III): Focusing on Gender Segregation across Fields of Study." See Light, Benson-Greenwald, and Diekman (2022), "Gender Representation Cues Labels of Hard and Soft Sciences" for a recent analysis of gendered labels on university majors, focusing on STEM (Science, Technology, Engineering, Mathematics).

17 As most women-only universities in South Korea have recently confronted serious decline in popularity due to young people's increasing avoidance of gender-divided career paths and social identities, they try to revamp their educational structure by expanding or newly establishing "hard" disciplines – in particular, the latest high-tech subject disciplines, including AI. See a related interview of the president of Ewha Women's University, perhaps the most renowned women-only university in South Korea (*Asia Economy*, 8 December 2023).

18 See Chang, K. (2022a), *The Logic of Compressed Modernity*, ch. 4.

19 See Chang, K. (2022b), *Transformative Citizenship in South Korea*, ch. 5 "Education as Citizenship, or Citizenship by Education."

20 This situation has been crucially reflected in the staggering share of (translated) foreign books – mostly Western and Japanese books – in the national book market, which reached its record highs in the 2000s (i.e. immediately after "the IMF economic crisis") between twenty and thirty percent. In this period, as noticed by the strongly impressed *New York Times* (2004), the market share of translated foreign books was highest in South Korea. If schooling tutorial books and various exam guidebooks are excluded, translated foreign books have usually outnumbered domestic books in the general monograph market. See "The Miserable Reality of 'the Heaven of Translated Books'" (in Korean) (*Chosun Daily*, 18 April 2007).

21 On South Korean academic responses to postmodernism, see Na, J. (2011), "A Study on the History of Reception of Postmodernism in Korea of the 1990s." For postmodernism's impact on mass culture in South Korea, see Kang, M. (2010), "Postmodern Consumer Culture without Postmodernity: Copying the Crisis of Signification."

22 In a sense, this trendy global inter-university competition helps to justify heavy public spending for various fields of the supposedly scientific research regardless of their practical utilities to the state and society. The government, news media, and universities seemingly collude in framing academic research competitiveness just like international competition in popular sports games, with standardized rankings praised or scolded on face value.

23 See Kim, J. (2015), *The Ruled Ruler: Studying Abroad in the United States and the Birth of South Korean Elites*, and Kim, J. (2011), "Aspiration for Global Cultural Capital in the Stratified Realm of Global Higher Education: Why Do Korean Students Go to U.S. Graduate Schools?"

24 At numerous South Korean universities, the university administration and humanities departments have recently negotiated possible mergers of the world region-segmented humanities departments in history, philosophy,

NOTES TO PP. 119–123

literature, etc. As this trend more often reflects each university administration's motivation to slim down the university for financial considerations (under the rapidly declining population of university entrants) than its fundamental scientific position, the affected faculty members (and currently enrolled students) frequently stage protests and legal disputes.

25 In recent decades, the hybridity or fusion between Western and Korean/Oriental art has become quite popular and influential, often drawing international praises and interest. This is frequently propagated, reported, and commented as a key part of the so-called "K-art." See Park, Y. (2013), *K-Art: Universal Works Reach Global Audience.*

26 *Jaeya* scholarship (*jaeyahakmun*) may include wide varieties and fields of scholarship, whose common status is defined negatively – i.e. not belonging to formal academic disciplines and departments housed in universities and colleges and/or not being practiced by university faculty and faculty candidates (and their graduate students). It has a very long tradition in Korean history as most of the Korean dynastic states for two millennia operated with quasi-scholarly orthodoxies mainly upheld by aristocratic officials as well as their kings. In the modern era, the notion of *jaeya* (or *chaeya*) is most openly or explicitly used in the discipline of history in order to differentiate empiricist formal academic history (centered on the national order and change) from local, micro-social, religious, and folk histories by ad hoc authors and authorities (Kang, D. 2000). This is not excluded from what I emphasize here as *jaeyahakmun*, but my focus is more on those extra-academia intellectual efforts that attempt to more proactively and critically address practical socio-economic, political, cultural, and historical affairs with serious bearings on society. See Yi, K. (2022) for an exemplary case of Ye Chun-ho and the Korea Social Science Institute under Ye's initiative.

27 Many of them used to correspondingly carry out educational services, called *yahak* (night-time schools), for alienated and never or little educated people. See Chun, S. (2009), *The History of Yahak Movement in South Korea: 110 Years of the Itinerary Toward Freedom.*

28 Perhaps the most noted book in this respect has been *The 880,000 Won Generation: An Economics of Hope Written at a Time of Despair*, by Woo and Park (2007).

29 There has been a subtle tendency that the South Korean government, along with its culture industry allies, has tried to reprocess or reinvent such cultural achievements into (government-sponsored) staged spectacles both globally and domestically – particularly with respect to the so-called K-Pop. See Joinau's (2023) persuasive account of this trend from a Foucauldian focus on spectacle-based governmentality. Also, see Kim, B. (2017) on the military government's effort in the aggressive Gangnam development project in conjunction with the 1988 Olympics in Seoul, as a grand urban spectacle scheme.

30 See Chang, K. (2022a), *The Logic of Compressed Modernity*, chs. 1 and 4.

31 See Chang, K. (2010), *South Korea under Compressed Modernity: Familial Political Economy in Transition*, and Chang, K. (2018), *The End of Tomorrow? Familial Liberalism and Social Reproduction Crisis* (in Korean).

32 See Chang, K. (2022a), *The Logic of Compressed Modernity*, ch.8, "Social Institutional Deficits and Infrastructural Familialism."

33 The sustained influence of these religions has been accompanied by a common side-effect of helping to sustain or reproduce gender divisions and hier-

NOTES TO PP. 123–128

archies. See "Religions' Discrimination of Women Should Be Overturned" (in Korean) in *Mindeulle*, 5 June 2024.

34 The political and legal practice of *yeonjwaje* (guilt by association) reflected and reinforced such grassroots experiences and behaviors. See Lee, G. (2023), "The Mechanism and Cracks of the Guilt by Association System from the 1960s to the 1980s."

35 It was only on 27 June 2024 that the article in criminal law on "special exception to relatives with respect to crimes of destruction and damage of property" was judged to be "unconstitutional" in the Constitutional Court (*Yonhapnews*, 27 June 2024). Property crimes to one's parents, children, and/or spouse have long been considered familial internal affairs, with which the state should not interfere. This may sound quite conservative or even irrational in spite of all such close instrumental interactions, supports, and dependencies among direct family members as explained in my theory of *familial liberalism* (Chang, K. 2018). In fact, crimes in many non-economic affairs among family members have much earlier been stipulated as strictly or duly punishable.

36 I denote and document this phenomenon as *accidental pluralism* in family ideology (Chang, K. 2010a, ch. 2).

37 In East Asia, such familial allegiance to Confucian norms and relations has often been accompanied by a sort of counter-cultural citizenship in feminist activism and other liberal reformisms in civil society. This trend diverges from many other postcolonial regions in which cultural citizenship has been addressed or promoted as an activist agenda (Hensbroek 2010). On the other hand, some East Asian states – Singapore in particular (Teo, Y. 2013) and China in the reform era (Chang, K. 1992) – have explicitly promoted a sort of technocratized Confucian familialism in their social welfare programs.

38 The notably high popularity of South Korean dramas to Chinese people, among many other Asian peoples, may be understood in this regard as they have also become familial liberal subjects in the post-socialist era (Chang, K. 2018, ch. 10; Chang, K. 1992). This possibility does not necessitate the common family structures between them. That is, familial liberalism can be manifested through varieties of family structures just as industrial liberalism can be expressed through varieties of corporate structures. See Kim, S. et al. (2007), "Variations of Family Relations: Focusing on Representations of Family Relations in Chinese and Korean Television Drama."

39 See "Can Viewers Change Drama Storylines?" in *Hankookilbo*, 6 November 2000.

6 Compressed Modernity, Gender, and Obfuscated Family Crisis: Individualization without Individualism

1 To the extent that women's individualization ramifies the weakening of family relations and functions (or the destabilization of family-dependent social reproduction), it also tends to become a policy concern.

2 Some authors use the term 'individuation' to denote similar trends (e.g. Lash 1990), but I prefer to more precisely categorize different types of individualization by adding individually discernable adjectives.

189

NOTES TO PP. 128–133

3 Beck's (Beck and Grande 2009) emphasis on individualization as a main symptom of second modernity seems to most closely correspond to reconstructive individualization.

4 While it is beyond the scope of the current chapter, nomadist individualization has been closely associated with the thundering process of informatization – in particular, with the breathtaking rise and expansion of the cyberspace. As South Korea has been spearheading informatization, its nomadist individualization trend has been critically facilitated in the cyberspace (Choi, Choi, and Bae 2007).

5 Broadly speaking, demographic individualization also comprises the trend of individualization without individualism discussed here, but it does not necessarily involve complex familial social dynamics as are observed in defamiliation and risk-aversive individualization.

6 While avoiding neologism is always desirable, I consider it a bit indispensable to use the concept of *defamiliation* in systematically delineating people's increasingly individual-based life that, however, is predicated upon their continuing subjective attachment to family.

7 I wish to thank Professor Asato Wako of Kyoto University for inducing me to think this way

8 However, it was also an instance of institutionalized familialism because people were strongly encouraged to earnestly and wisely care for their children.

9 For the latter perspective, see Kim, K. (2003), *Order and Agency in Modernity: Talcott Parsons, Erving Goffman, and Harold Garfinkel.*

10 Familism (an understanding about or position as to family) is here differentiated from familialism (a value or attitude centered on family). See Chang, K. (2010a), ch. 2, "Accidental Pluralism" for South Korean varieties of familism.

11 I characterize the social policy paradigm of the South Korean (developmental) state as *developmental liberalism,* in that its liberal social policies and programs have been tightly enmeshed with its excessive developmental orientation (Chang, K. 2019). The developmental liberal state did everything to redefine social policy – or, for that matter, social citizenship – in terms of private responsibilities for mutual support and protection. Families have been summoned in order to meet various public necessities in social reproduction (Chang, K. 1997). The developmental liberal state somewhat resembled the early modern liberal state of the West in articulating various social problems accompanying industrial capitalism as individual and familial responsibilities and in morally regimenting individuals and families to cultivate human qualities and attitudes suitable for industrial work and life (cf. Donzelot 1979). In so doing, the South Korean state was equipped with a distinct advantage of (neo-)Confucian family culture.

12 See Beck (1999), Beck and Grande (2009), etc. Beck disputes *methodological nationalism* in social theory and analysis and, instead, advocates *methodological cosmopolitanism,* in order to reflect international and global processes by which the nature of modernity in late modernizing societies is crucially determined.

13 For instance, South Korea is now the world's foremost information society as manifested in terms of its global competitiveness in ICT industry, its most effective access to internet and mobile communication, and so forth. Its

190

NOTES TO PP. 134–141

industrial restructuring and respatialization have been astonishingly swift, so that the national economy is now governed overwhelmingly by high-end technological industries, whereas job-supplying industries have been heavily relocated to China, Vietnam, and other populous Asian societies (Chang, K. 2019, ch. 8). Its exposure to experimental sciences and technologies both in industrial production and everyday personal life is seemingly unconstrained. Its world record-breaking pace of population aging has resulted in elderly people's rampant poverty and social alienation and in widespread familial conflicts concerning care provision (and sometimes wealth inheritance) (Chang, K. 2018, ch. 5). Its labor market liberalization ("flexibilization") has been incomparably radical, as measured in terms of the society-wide dominance of transitory and casual employment. Its financialization has been staggering in terms of an instant portfolio domination of major domestic industries by global capital, the snowballing debts of both the state and grassroots households, and so forth (Chang, K. 2019, ch. 5).

14 The neoliberal trend of precariatization was already pervasive by the mid 2000s. As of 2005, for instance, few non-regular employees were covered by national pension (32.8%), national health insurance (33.4%), unemployment insurance (30.7%), retirement allowance (19.6%), bonus (17.5%) extra-hour surpayment (14.6%), paid vacation (15.9 %), and so forth, whereas most regular employees enjoyed such benefits in labor and welfare (Yoon et al. 2005). Precariatization was a double-sided process in that it involved not only employment destabilization but also welfare liquidation (Chang, K. 2019; Lee and Kim 2025).

15 The so-called "candlelight protest" staged over a few months in 2008 once heightened hope for revitalized civil activism, but fell short of rekindling politically organized causes for progressive goals. See Amnesty International (2008), *Policing the Candlelight Protests in South Korea*. Also see Moon, S. (2024), *Civic Activism in South Korea: The Intertwining of Democracy and Neoliberalism* for a lucid analysis of civil society organizations and movements as wedged between democratization and neoliberalization.

16 Interestingly, according to numerous recent media reports, the American economic crisis since 2008 also led to an analogous trend – namely, many adult children, unable to find jobs after graduating from colleges, returned home to stay with their parents.

17 Such perspective on South Korean (and other Asian) women's lives will help to realistically grasp at the intergenerational perceptions and interactions between old mothers and adult daughters (cf. Jackson, 2020).

18 I am very grateful to Song Min-Young and Xu Xuehua for carrying out meticulous and effective statistical analysis of the concerned international survey data in 2006 and 2016 respectively.

19 According to our data, as of 2006, the proportions of never married women aged 30–34 and aged 35–39 were 19.8% and 3.6% for South Korea, 25.8% and 15.8% for Japan, and 25.7% and 12.0% for Taiwan. As of 2016, the corresponding figures were 35.7% and 10.0% for South Korea, 23.0% and 11.2% for Japan, and 35.9% and 19.6% for Taiwan.

20 See Yamada Masahiro (1999), *The Age of Parasite Singles*.

21 According to official data complied by the National Statistical Office, the sex ratio of third or further births was 180.2 in 1995, 143.9 in 2000, 128.2 in 2005, and 105.3 in 2022. The sex ratio of second births in the corresponding

NOTES TO PP. 141–147

years was 111.7, 107.4, 106.4, and 104.6 (https://gsis.kwdi.re.kr/statHtml/st
atHtml.do?orgId=338&tblId=DT_1AD0110R).

22 See Nietzsche ([1901]1968), *The Will to Power.*

23 According to official data compiled by the National Statistical Office, the
crude divorce rate (number of divorce cases per thousand people) increased
from 0.6 in 1980 to 1.1 in 1990, 1.5 in 1995, 2.5 in 2000, 3.5 in 2003, and
then declined to 2.6 in 2005, 2.1 in 2015, and1.8 in 2023(https://www.
index.go.kr/unity/potal/main/EachDtlPageDetail.do;jsessionid=bw47r6X8
wn51WQJ1erZ4XKoxK6R0YI-DDtwtoh_x.node11?idx_cd=1579#).

24 The relative acceptance of divorce by women in their fifties – constituting
what is popularly called *hwanghon ihon* (dusk divorce) – was crucially linked
to the observation presented above concerning the presence of young children as a deterrence to divorce. With their children now grown up, women
in their fifties seemingly had more courageously considered divorce. In this
respect, individualization is not necessarily a young generation's exclusive
cultural privilege.

25 See influential research by Emiko Ochiai (2011; also Ochiai et al. 2012), and
Pei Chia Lan (2014) in this line.

7 Complex Risk Society:
Risk Components of Compressed Modernity

1 Under the enormous social discontents and political criticisms about safety
risks, accidents, and disasters at internationally scandalous levels, the South
Korean government tries to actively build and utilize digital infrastructures
for informing and guiding citizens in key safety concerns. These include
Life Safety Information (https://www.safemap.go.kr/asds/safe.do?tab1),
National Disaster Safety Portal (https://www.safekorea.go.kr/idsiSFK/neo
/main/main.html), and so forth.

2 See Lim, Lee, and Chang (1998) for details on the causes and processes of
major accidents and disasters, particularly in the mid 1990s.

3 *Social Indicators in Korea*, the most widely publicized annual compilation of
official statistics on social, cultural and economic conditions of the country,
now carries a separate section on "Safety." In its 2004 volume, the proportions of South Koreans who felt safe were only 8.2 percent concerning traffic,
8.6 percent concerning food, and 9.1 percent concerning construction respectively (National Statistical Office, 2004: 556).

4 Taiwan appears to be quite closely comparable to South Korea in compressed modernity and its risk society properties (Chou, K. 2007; Chou and
Liou 2010).

5 See *Footsteps of South Korea Seen Through Statistics* (1995) and other statistical compilations published by the National Statistical Office. Such publications'
purpose was to celebratively display the truly compressive achievement of
material and other changes in the latter half of the twentieth century.

6 More broadly, I critically assessed South Korea's national economic crisis in
the late 1990s in conjunction with such intendedly unintended consequences
of compressed modernity (Chang, K. 1999).

7 This chapter incorporates what I argued, as an editorial writer, in editorials
of *Hankook Ilbo* (*The Korea Daily*) during the few months following the

192

NOTES TO PP. 148–153

collapse of Sampoong Department Store. An expanded, Korean version of the chapter was published in *Bigyoyeongu* (*Comparative Research*), vol. 2 (1998), under the title of "Compressed Modernity and Complex Risk Society."

8 I also think that Charles Perrow's (1984) argument on "normal accidents" is methodical and concise in configuring a high-risk social system in late-modern societies, including South Korea.

9 This has been a general tendency, albeit with diverse areas and intensities, across the postcolonial world. See Susantha Goonatilake (1984), *Aborted Discovery: Science and Technology in the Third World.*

10 However, upon his political foe, Yoon Suk-Yeol's election into national presidency, the Fourth Industrial Revolution ended up disappearing entirely from the government policy agendas.

11 See "From K-quarantine to K-bio" (*Edaily*, 20 April 2020). In this news article, Moon was quoted as saying during his cabinet meeting (14 April 2020), "As the prompt development of test kits has enabled our status to hike from K-quarantine to K-bio, we need to speed up in developing vaccines and curing medicines in order to elevate the level of our bio medicine" and, before industrial, scientific, and medical experts (9 April 2020), "The government will ensure 100 percent compensation for [industries'] developing efforts and expenses by purchasing and stocking sufficient amounts even when economic or commercial values are absent in the market." A presidential spokesman added on 12 April 2020, "The Moon Jae-In government will promptly, audaciously, and generously support [subsidize] for an early success in developing Korean curing medicines and vaccines for Covid 19."

12 South Korea was a keen subscriber to the globally influential "leading sector" theory. See Rostow (1963), "Leading Sectors and the Take-off."

13 Yee, J. (1998) points out "system failure" as the common cause of major recent accidents. Although I largely agree with him, the underdevelopment or lack of the system should be acknowledged before system failure is discussed.

14 The following summary of the uniquely South Korean types of risks is also presented in Chang, K. (1999a).

15 As noted below, due to the unprecedented national economic crisis and its radical neoliberal ramifications in social and economic conditions, South Korea's quality as risk society has been structurally transformed from the late 1990s.

16 See William F. Ogburn (1922), *Social Change with Respect to Culture and Original Nature.*

17 For instance, Kim Young-Jung (1998) cites various industrial statistics to shows that most of the industrial accidents have been caused by newly recruited workers – in particular, by those recruited within the previous six months. Such accidents are often classified as the ones caused by "educational factors."

18 Also see Chang, K. (2010c), "East Asia's Condensed Transition to Second Modernity."

19 For a critical assessment of this feature of East Asian development, see Paul Krugman (1994), "The Myth of Asia's Miracle."

20 Most of the bureaucrats, architects, and corporate managers found guilty in relation to the collapse of Seongsu Grand Bridge and of Sampoong Department Store were released from prison by mid 1997.

NOTES TO PP. 153–169

21 In another recent manifestation of this contradiction, nurses (in 2023) and doctors (in 2024) respectively declared to stage law-abiding struggle, mainly in terms of keeping legally stipulated working hours, in protesting government policies that supposedly infringe on their just and safe conditions of medical service. This implies that both South Korean nurses and doctors work normally beyond legally defined safe durations.

22 In a particularly tragic case, a recent fire incident at an electric battery factory in June 2024 claimed the lives of twenty-three workers, among whom twenty were dispatched workers and eighteen were foreign workers (*Hankyoreh*, 27 June 2024).

23 Such purposeful politico-administrative and legal stances about transformative contributory risks engender a dangerous side-effect of inducing opportunistic anti-social behaviors among virtually all subjects engaged in immediately or potentially risky activities.

8 A Beckian Metamorphosis?

1 This trend can be more broadly acknowledged across East Asia (Thurbon et al. 2023).

2 Relatedly, the lawyer profession has been quite conspicuously divided between *jeongwan* lawyers (recent retirees from high-rank court and prosecutorial positions who benefit from normalized favoritism by their successors and thus are coveted by corruption-charged top businessmen and other elites) and social advocacy lawyers (servicing civil activism, human rights, and other public causes often in volunteer-like compensation terms). The latter group's career trajectories have sometimes included running for political positions themselves as exemplified by two former presidents, Roh Moo-Hyun and Moon Jae-In.

3 Also, as explained in my earlier work (Chang, K. 2022a, ch. 4), the historical legacy of nationalist proletarianism originating from the Japanese colonial era was forcefully ingrained into the sociopolitical mindset of a critical part of laborer-cum-citizens.

4 The wide influence of *jaeya* intellectuals is often evinced in terms of their books' huge popularity in university libraries, media book reviews, social media referrals, and so forth.

5 According to Sasano Misae (2021), this is much less the case in Japan. She argues that such differences are reflected in the two countries' increasingly divergent levels of low fertility.

6 Risk-mediated class consciousness has also been reinforced by South Korean news media's frequent and intense coverage of industrial, urban, infrastructural, and natural disasters. Such coverage is conversely explained by South Koreans' endemic concern and attention in related affairs.

7 In the latest evidence in this respect, when the collective Coronavirus infection broke out in Daegu as South Korea's first such incident, so many physicians, nurses, and other citizens from other regions volunteered to serve in rescue efforts, but many of them simply could not be accommodated in rescue facilities and institutions.

REFERENCES

Alavi, Hamza. 1972. "The State in Postcolonial Societies: Pakistan and Bangladesh." *New Left Review* 74: 59–81.

Amsden, Alice. 1989. *Asia's Next Giant: South Korea and Late Industrialization.* New York: Oxford University Press.

An, Su-Chan. 2021. "Media's Instigation of Good vs. Evil Confrontation" (in Korean). *Newspaper & Broadcasting* 609: 17–24.

Ashcroft, Bill, Gareth Griffiths, and Helen Tiffin. 2002. *The Empire Writes Back: Theory and Practice in Post-Colonial Literatures,* 2nd edn. New York: Routledge.

Asia Economy (https://www.asiae.co.kr/).

Badie, Bertrand. [1992]2000. *The Imported State: The Westernization of the Political Order,* translated from French by Claudia Royal. Stanford: Stanford University Press.

Bae, Eun-Kyung. 2009. "'Economic Crisis' and Korean Women: Women's Vision-of-Life and Intersection of Class and Gender" (in Korean). *Issues in Feminism* 9(2): 39–82.

Bae, Eun-Kyung. 2010. "Are Women Responsible for the Low Fertility? For the Feminist Appropriation of the Discourses on Low Fertility" (in Korean). *Gender and Culture* 3(2): 37–75.

Baik, Jong Kook. 2001. "The Political Dynamic of Civil Society" (in Korean). *Journal of Korean Politics* 10: 163–209.

Baudrillard, Jean. [1981]1994. *Simulacra and Simulation.* Ann Arbor: University of Michigan Press.

Bauman, Zygmunt. 2000. *Liquid Modernity.* Cambridge: Polity.

Beck, Ulrich. [1984] 1992. *Risk Society: Towards a New Modernity.* London: Sage.

Beck, Ulrich. 1999. *World Risk Society.* Cambridge: Polity.

Beck, Ulrich. 2000. "The Cosmopolitan Perspective: Sociology for the Second Age of Modernity." *British Journal of Sociology* 51(1): 79–106.

Beck, Ulrich. 2011a. "We Do Not Live in an Age of Cosmopolitanism but in an Age of Cosmopolitisation: The 'Global Other' is in Our Midst." *Irish Journal of Sociology* 19(1): 16–34.

Beck, Ulrich. 2011b. "Cosmopolitan Sociology: Outline of a Paradigm Shift."

REFERENCES

Maria Rovisco and Magdalena Nowicka (eds) *The Ashgate Research Companion to Cosmopolitanism*, pp. 17–32. Burlington: Ashgate.

Beck, Ulrich. 2016. *The Metamorphosis of the World: How Climate Change is Transforming Our Concept of the World*. Cambridge: Polity.

Beck, Ulrich, and Elisabeth Beck-Gernsheim. 2002. *Individualization: Institutionalized Individualism and Its Social and Political Consequences*. London: Sage.

Beck, Ulrich, Anthony Giddens, and Scott Lash. 1994. *Reflexive Modernization: Politics, Tradition and Aesthetics in the Modern Social Order*. Stanford: Stanford University Press.

Beck, Ulrich, Wolfgang Bonss, and Christoph Lau. 2003. "The Theory of Reflexive Modernization: Problematic, Hypotheses and Research." *Theory, Culture & Society* 20(2): 1–33.

Beminor (https://www.beminor.com/).

Blossfeld, Hans-Peter, Melinda Mills, and Fabrizio Bernardi (eds) 2006. *Globalization, Uncertainty, and Men's Careers: An International Comparison*. Cheltenham: Edward Elgar.

Castel, Robert. 2000. "The Roads to Disaffiliation: Insecure Work and Vulnerable Relationships," *International Journal of Urban and Regional Research* 24(3): 519–535.

Cha, You Me. 2023. "Limitations of Franchise Regulation under the Franchise Act and Collective Autonomy in Franchising" (in Korean). *Korean Journal of Labor Studies* 29(3): 47–80.

Chakrabarty, Dipesh. 1992. *Provincializing Europe: Postcolonial Thought and Historical Difference*. Princeton: Princeton University Press.

Chang, Dae-Oup. 2024. "Transnational Labor Regimes and the Cambodian Case of Asianizing Capitalist Development." Chang Kyung-Sup, Kim Taekyoon, and Lee Joonkoo (eds) *Asianization of Asia*, pp. 50–65. London: Routledge.

Chang, Duk-Jin. 2002. "The Ruling Structure of the Corporate Group" (in Korean). Gyu-Han Bae, Joon Han, Woo-Sik Kim et al. (eds) *Changing Social Environments, Corporate Responses*, pp.125–164. Seoul: Jisikmadang.

Chang, Ha-Joon. 1994. *The Political Economy of Industrial Policy*. London: Palgrave Macmillan.

Chang, Ha-Joon. 2003. *Kicking Away the Ladder: Developmental Strategy in Historical Perspective*. London: Anthem Press.

Chang, Ji-Won. 2008. *A Survey on the Trends of Public Sector Corruption in Korea* (in Korean). KIPA Research Report 2010–14–1. Seoul: Korea Institute of Public Administration.

Chang, Jiyeun. 2022. "Work in the Age of Platform Capitalism" (in Korean). *Korean Journal of Industrial Relations* 32(4): 57–106.

Chang, Jin-Ho. 2014. "The *Chaebol* and the Economy of Irresponsibility in South Korea" (in Korean). *Critical Review of History* 108: 91–119.

Chang, Kyung-Sup. 1992. "China's Rural Reform: The State and Peasantry in Constructing a Macro-Rationality." *Economy and Society* 21(4):430–452.

Chang, Kyung-Sup. 1995. "Gender and Abortive Capitalist Social Transformation: Semi-Proletarianization of South Korean Women." *International Journal of Comparative Sociology* 36(1/2): 61–81.

Chang, Kyung-Sup. 1997. "The Neo-Confucian Right and Family Politics in

REFERENCES

South Korea: The Nuclear Family as an Ideological Construct." *Economy and Society* 26(1): 22–42.

Chang, Kyung-Sup. 1999a. "Compressed Modernity and Its Discontents: South Korean Society in Transition." *Economy and Society* 28(1): 30–55.

Chang, Kyung-Sup. 1999b. "Social Ramifications of South Korea's Economic Fall: Neo-Liberal Antidote to Compressed Capitalist Industrialization?" *Development and Society* 28(1):49–91.

Chang, Kyung-Sup. 2004. "The Anti-Communitarian Family? Everyday Conditions of Authoritarian Politics in South Korea." Chua Beng Huat (ed.) *Communitarian Politics in Asia*, pp. 57–77. London: Routledge.

Chang, Kyung-Sup. 2010a. *South Korea under Compressed Modernity: Familial Political Economy in Transition*. London: Routledge.

Chang, Kyung-Sup. 2010b. "The Second Modern Condition? Compressed Modernity as Internalized Reflexive Cosmopolitization." *British Journal of Sociology* 61(3): 444–464.

Chang, Kyung-Sup. 2010c. "East Asia's Condensed Transition to Second Modernity." *Soziale Welt* 61(3/4): 319–328.

Chang, Kyung-Sup. 2012a. "Developmental Citizenship in Perspective: The South Korean Case and Beyond." Chang Kyung-Sup and Bryan S. Turner (eds) *Contested Citizenship in East Asia: Developmental Politics, National Unity, and Globalization*, pp. 182–202. London: Routledge.

Chang, Kyung-Sup. 2012b. "Predicaments of Neoliberalism in the Post-Developmental Liberal Context." Chang Kyung-Sup, Ben Fine, and Linda Weiss (eds) *Developmental Politics in Transition: The Neoliberal Era and Beyond*, pp. 71–90. New York: Palgrave Macmillan.

Chang, Kyung-Sup. 2017a. "Compressed Modernity." Bryan S. Turner, Chang Kyung-Sup, Cynthia F. Epstein, Peter Kivisto, J. Michael Ryan, William Outhwaite (eds) *The Wiley Blackwell Encyclopedia of Social Theory*, vol. I. Hoboken: Wiley Blackwell (https://onlinelibrary.wiley.com/doi/abs/10.1002/9781118430873.est0839).

Chang, Kyung-Sup. 2017b. "Reflexive Modernization." Bryan S. Turner, Chang Kyung-Sup, Cynthia F. Epstein, Peter Kivisto, J. Michael Ryan, William Outhwaite (eds) *The Wiley Blackwell Encyclopedia of Social Theory*, vol. I. Hoboken: Wiley Blackwell (https://onlinelibrary.wiley.com/doi/10.1002/9781118430873.est0835).

Chang, Kyung-Sup. 2018. *The End of Tomorrow? Familial Liberalism and Social Reproduction Crisis* (in Korean). Seoul: Jipmundang.

Chang, Kyung-Sup. 2019. *Developmental Liberalism in South Korea: Formation, Degeneration, and Transnationalization*. New York: Palgrave Macmillan.

Chang, Kyung-Sup. 2022a. *The Logic of Compressed Modernity*. Cambridge: Polity.

Chang, Kyung-Sup. 2022b. *Transformative Citizenship in South Korea: Politics of Transformative Contributory Rights*. New York: Palgrave Macmillan.

Chang, Kyung-Sup. 2023. "Compressed Modernity and Its Life World Predicaments: Replies and Elaborations." *Korea Europe Review: An Interdisciplinary Journal of Politics, Society, and Economics*, no. 5 (December) (https://doi.org/10.48770/ker.2023.no5.32).

Chang, Kyung-Sup. 2024. "Asia in Asianization: Dimensions, Conditions, and Implications." Chang Kyung-Sup, Kim Taekyoon, and Lee Joonkoo (eds) *Asianization of Asia*, pp. 12–29. London: Routledge.

REFERENCES

Chang, Kyung-Sup and Song Min-Young. 2010. "The Stranded Individualizer under Compressed Modernity: South Korean Women in Individualization without Individualism." *British Journal of Sociology* 61(3): 540–565.

Chang, Kyung-Sup, Chin Meejung, Sung Miai, and Lee Jaerim. 2015. "Institutionalized Familialism in South Korean Society: Focusing on Income Security, Education, and Care" (in Korean). *Journal of the Korean Family Studies Association* 27(3): 1–38.

Chang, Kyung-Sup, Linda Weiss, and Ben Fine. 2012. "Introduction: Neoliberalism and Developmental Politics in Perspective." Chang Kyung-Sup, Ben Fine, and Linda Weiss (eds) *Developmental Politics in Transition: The Neoliberal Era and Beyond*, pp. 1–25. New York: Palgrave Macmillan.

Cho, Hiyeon, Lawrence Surendra, and Eunhong Park (eds) 2008. *States of Democracy: Oligarchic Democracies and Asian Democratization*. Mumbai: Earthworm Books.

Cho, Hyo-Je. 2000. "The Change in Civil Society and the Radical Restructuring of Sovereignty (in Korean). *Quarterly Changbi* 107: 40–52.

Cho, Il-Hoon. 2005. *There is no Samsung Republic* (in Korean). Seoul: Korea Economic Daily.

Cho, Seong-Jae. 2004. "Subcontracting and Marginalization of SME Workers" (in Korean). *Journal of Asiatic Studies* 118: 43–64.

Cho, Young Nam and Jong Ho Jeong. 2008. "China's Soft Power: Discussions, Resources, and Prospects." *Asian Survey* 48(3): 453–472.

Choe, Kang-Wook. 2018. *Power and Prosecution: The Birth and Evolution of the Monster* (in Korean). Seoul: Changbi.

Choi, Hangsub, Choi Youngju, and Bae Myung-hoon. 2007. *The Phenomenon of Nomadism in Digital Society and Its Policy Responses* (in Korean). Seoul: Korea Information Society Development Institute.

Choi, Hansoo, Hyung-Goo Kang, Woojin Kim, Changmin Lee, and Jongsik Park. 2016. "Too Big to Jail? Company Status and Judicial Bias in an Emerging Market." *Corporate Governance: An International Review*. 24(2): 85–104.

Choi, Jang-Jip. 2002. *Democracy After Democratization: Crisis and Conservative Origin of Korea's Democracy* (in Korean). Seoul: Humanitas.

Choi, Jungwoon. 2005. *The Gwangju Uprising: The Pivotal Democratic Movement That Changed the History of Modern Korea*. Paramus: Homa & Sekey Books.

Choi, Sun. 2015. "A Critical Analysis on the Judicial Independence in South Korea" (in Korean). *Korean Political Science Review* 49(1): 205–226.

Choo, Ji-hyun. 2018. "Ideological Interpellation of 'Folk Devil' in the Park Chung-hee Regime: Strategy for Efficiency of Criminal Justice" (in Korean). *Society and History* 117: 201–235.

Chosun Ilbo (www.chosun.com).

Chou, Kuei-Tien. 2007. "Conflicts of Technology Policy and Governance Paradigm in a Knowledge-Based Economy: A Case Analysis of the Construction of the Taiwan Biobank." *Issues & Studies* 43(3): 97–130.

Chou, Kuei-Tien, and Hwa-Meel Liou. 2010. "'System Destroys Trust?' – Regulatory Institutions and Public Perceptions of Food Risks in Taiwan." *Social Indicators Research* 96(1): 41–57.

Chun, Sung-Ho. 2009. *The History of Yahak Movement in South Korea: 110 Years of the Itinerary Toward Freedom* (in Korean). Seoul: Lifelong Learning Books.

REFERENCES

Chung, Dae-Hwa. 2017. *Sangji University Democratization Struggle 40 Years: Lively Records of the Struggle and Experimentation for the Future of South Korean Private Schools* (in Korean). Seoul: Hanul.

Chung, Ju-Yung. 2009. *There May Be Hardship, But Not Failure* (in Korean). Seoul: Jesamgihoek.

Colgan, Jeff D. and Jessica L. P. Weeks. 2015. "Revolution, Personalist Dictatorships, and International Conflict." *International Organization* 69(1): 163–194.

Crompton, Rosemary (ed.) 1999. *Restructuring Gender Relations and Employment: The Decline of the Male Breadwinner.* Oxford: Oxford University Press.

Crouch, Colin. 2004. *Post-Democracy.* Cambridge: Polity Press.

Cumings, Bruce. 1981. *The Origins of the Korean War: Liberation and Emergence of Separate Regimes, 1945–1947.* Princeton: Princeton University Press.

Cumings, Bruce. 1998. "The Korean Crisis and the End of 'Late' Development." *New Left Review* 231:43–72.

Currie, Lauchlin. 1974. "The 'Leading Sector' Model of Growth in Developing Countries." *Journal of Economic Studies* 1(1): 1–16.

Davis, Kingsley. 1984. "Wives and Work: The Sex Role Revolution and Its Consequences." *Population and Development Review* 10(3): 397–417.

Diprete, Thomas. 2002. "Life Course Risks, Mobility Regimes, and Mobility Consequences: A Comparison of Sweden, Germany, and the United States." *American Journal of Sociology* 108(2): 267–309.

Doctors News (https://www.doctorsnews.co.kr/).

Dong-A Ilbo (www.donga.com).

Donzelot, Jacques. 1979. *The Policing of Families.* New York: Pantheon.

Dore, Ronald. 1973. *British Factory, Japanese Factory: The Origins of National Diversity in Industrial Relations.* Berkeley: University of California Press.

Durkheim, Emile. 1933. *The Division of Labor in Society.* New York: Macmillan.

Durkheim, Emile. 1972. *Emile Durkheim: Selected Writings.* Cambridge: Cambridge University Press.

Durkheim, Emile. 1979. *Essays on Morals and Education.* London: Routledge & Kegan Paul.

Eckert, Carter J. 1996. *Offspring of Empire: The Koch'ang Kims and the Colonial Origins of Korean Capitalism, 1876–1945.* Seattle: University of Washington Press.

Edaily (www.edaily.co.kr).

Eun, Jonghwan. 2016. "A Study on Gray Corruption" (in Korean). PhD Dissertation in Department of Public Administration, Seoul National University.

Evans, Peter. 1995. *Embedded Autonomy: States and Industrial Transformation.* Princeton: Princeton University Press.

Featherstone, Mike. 1990. "Global Culture: An Introduction." *Theory, Culture & Society* 7(1): 1–14.

Featherstone, Mike (ed.). 1990. *Global Culture: Nationalism, Globalization and Modernity.* London: Sage.

Fine, Ben. 2012. "Neo-Liberalism in Retrospect? – It's Financialization, Stupid." Chang Kyung-Sup, Ben Fine, and Linda Weiss (eds) *Developmental Politics in Transition: The Neoliberal Era and Beyond*, pp. 51–69. Basingstoke/New York: Palgrave Macmillan.

REFERENCES

Geertz, Clifford. 1973. *The Interpretation of Cultures*. New York: Basic Books.

Giddens, Anthony. 1990. *The Consequences of Modernity*. Stanford: Stanford University Press.

Gim, Eulsik. 2012. "The Predicament of Job Creation: SMEs and Youth Running Parallel" (in Korean). *Issue and Prognosis* 75: 1–26.

Goldin, Claudia. 2006, "The Quiet Revolution That Transformed Women's Employment, Education, and Family." *American Economic Review* 96(2): 1–21.

Gong, Je-Wook. 2000. "The Korean War and the Formation of *Chaebol*" (in Korean). The Institute for Social Science, Kyungsang University (ed.), *The Korean War and Korean Capitalism*, pp. 59–99. Seoul: Hanul Academy.

Goonatilake, Susantha. 1984. *Aborted Discovery: Science and Technology in the Third World*. London: Zed Books.

Gyosunojo (The National Trade Union of Professors). 2001. *The 2001 White Book on Private Schools' Corruption* (in Korean).

Ha, Tae-Hoon. 2017. "The Candlelight Citizen Revolution That Will Last Forever in History" (in Korean). *Monthly Participatory Society*, November 2017 (www.peoplepower21.org/magazine/1534104).

Haebangjeonhusaui Insik (in Korean; *Understanding of History Before and After Liberation*), vols 1–6. Seoul: Hangilsa.

Han, Gui Young. 2021. "Discussion on the Conservatization of Men in Their 20s, Their History and Implications" (in Korean). *Politics and Public Opinion* 29: 165–202.

Han, Sang-Hee. 2017. "The Constitutional Political History of Public Security and Its Ruling Technology" (in Korean). *Hwanghaemunhwa* 95: 220–239.

Han, Sang-Jin. 2019. *Confucianism and Reflexive Modernity: Bringing Community back to Human Rights in the Age of Global Risk Society*. Leiden: Brill.

Hankook Ilbo (www.hankooki.com).

Hankyoreh (www.hani.co.kr).

Hankyoreh 21 (https://h21.hani.co.kr/).

Harvey, David. 1980. *The Condition of Postmodernity*. Oxford: Blackwell.

Heim, Stéphane. 2013. "Capability Building and Functions of SMEs in Business Groups: A Case Study of Toyota's Supply Chain." *International Journal of Automotive Technology and Management* 13(4): 338–353.

Helgesen, Geir. 2003. "Imported Democracy: The South Korean Experience." Catarina and Kinnvall and Kristina Jonsson (eds) *Globalization and Democratization in Asia*, pp. 73–91. London: Routledge.

Hensbroek, Pieter Boele van. 2010. "Cultural Citizenship as a Normative Notion for Activist Practices." *Citizenship Studies* 14(3): 317–330.

Heo, Ik-Soo. 2013. "Subcontracting of Risk, Outsourcing of Risk" (in Korean). *Federation of Korean Trade Unions Monthly* 498: 28–29.

Hirschman, Albert O. 1977. "A Generalized Linkage Approach to Development, with Special Reference to Staples." *Economic Development and Cultural Change* 25: 67–98.

Hobbes, Thomas. [1651]2017. *Leviathan*. New York: Penguin.

Hong, Chan-Sook. 2013. "Individualization and 'Gender Society'" (in Korean). *Korean Journal of Sociology* 47(1): 255–276.

Hong, Chan-Sook. 2017. "Scenarios of Female Individualization in Korea:

REFERENCES

Focused on the Context of Northeast Asian Familism" (in Korean). *Economy and Society* 113: 147–172.

Hong, Duck Ryul. 2006. "The Governance Structure of Private Universities: Problems and Tasks" (in Korean). *Democratic Society and Policy Studies* 10: 217–242.

Hong, Seong Min. 2015. "Emotional Structure and Popular Politics: Approach of Cultural Theory Toward the Nostalgia of President Park" (in Korean). *Korean Review of Political Thought* 21(1): 9–34.

Jackson, Stevi. 2020. "Interconnected Histories: Locating Women's Lives in Time and Space." Stevi Jackson and Petula Sik Ying Ho (eds) *Women Doing Intimacy: Gender, Family and Modernity in Britain and Hong Kong*, pp. 47–86. New York: Palgrave Macmillan.

Jahn, Beate. 2013. *Liberal Internationalism: Theory, History, Practice*. New York: Palgrave Macmillan

Jeong, Il Gyun. 2012. "'Modernization' and the Understandings of Tasan Chong Yag-yong in the 1950s and the 1960s in Korea" (in Korean). *Dasangwahyundae* 5: 103–153.

Jhee, Byong-kuen. 2023. "Korea 2022: Yoon's Administration and Democratic Backsliding" (in Korean). *Journal of Asiatic Studies* 191: 7–42.

Joinau, Benjamin. 2023. "Cultural Governance and New Forms of Governmentality Focus on the South Korean Case." *Journal of Arts Management, Law, and Society* 53(6): 358–374.

Journal of Journalists Association in Korea (https://www.journalist.or.kr/news/article_list_all.html).

Ju, Chi-Ho. 1997. *Samsung Republic* (in Korean). Seoul: Hangaram.

Jung, Ehwan. 1992. "The Change of Internal Labor Market and Industrial Relations in Manufacturing Industry in Korea" (in Korean). PhD Dissertation in Department of Sociology, Seoul National University.

Jung, Ehwan. 2007. "Firm Size or Work Arrangements? The Determinants of Labor Market Inequality in Korea" (in Korean). *Economy and Society* 73: 332–355.

Kang, Chul-Kyu. 1999. *Economics of* Chaebol *Reform: Form Fleet Management to Independent Management* (in Korean). Seoul: Dasanchulpansa.

Kang, Don-ku. 2000. "Making a New Myth: Another View on the Unofficial Historical School" (in Korean). *Korean Studies* 23(1): 3–26.

Kang, Myung Hun. 1996. *The Korean Business Conglomerate: Chaebol Then and Now*. Berkeley: University of California Press.

Kang, Myung Koo. 1999. "Postmodern Consumer Culture without Postmodernity: Copying the Crisis of Signification." *Cultural Studies* 13(1): 18–33.

Kariya, Takehiko. 2012. *Education Reform and Social Class in Japan: The Emerging Incentive Divide*. London: Routledge.

Kennedy, Michael D. 2020. *Globalizing Knowledge: Intellectuals, Universities, and Publics in Transformation*. Stanford: Stanford University Press.

Kim, Baek-Yung. 2017. "Gangnam Development and Olympic Effect: Focusing on the Jamsil Olympic Town Project in the 1970s and 1980s" (in Korean). *Korean Journal of Urban History* 17: 67–101.

Kim, Dae Jung. 1994. "Is Culture Destiny? The Myth of Asia's Anti-Democratic Values." *Foreign Affairs* 73(6): 189–194

Kim, Dong-No. 2013. "Overpoliticization of Civil Society and Its Declining Social Significance" (in Korean). *Phenomenon and Understanding* 120: 59–85.

REFERENCES

Kim, Eun Mee. 1997. *Big Business, Strong State: Collusion and Conflict in South Korean Development, 1960–1990.* Albany: SUNY Press.

Kim, Hee-Song. 2006. "An Examination of Ideological Elements in Criticism of Citizens' Movements: Focusing on the Criticism on 'Citizen Movements without Citizens'" (in Korean). *NGO Studies* 4(1): 191–220.

Kim, Hong-Jung. 2018. "Survivalist Modernity and the Logic of Its Governmentality." *Japanese Journal of Sociology* 27(1): 5–25.

Kim, Hyuncheol, Hyungjun Im, Seunghyun Lee, Youngbeom Ju, and Soonjo Kwon. 2023. "Establishment of Crowd Management Safety Measures Based on Crowd Density Risk Simulation." *Journal of the Korean Society of Safety* 38(2): 96–103

Kim, Il-hwan. 2022. "The Formation of Private University System and Politics of Foundation in Korea" (in Korean). PhD Dissertation in Department of Sociology, Seoul National University.

Kim, Jae Wan. 2015. "Liability, Memory and the Future of Human Rights Violation: The Case of Hyoungje Welfare Institution" (in Korean). *Democratic Legal Studies* 57: 13–53.

Kim, Jeong-In. 2010. "The Theory of Internal Development and the issue of Nationalism" (in Korean). *History and Reality* 77: 179–214.

Kim, Jongyoung. 2011. "Aspiration for Global Cultural Capital in the Stratified Realm of Global Higher Education: Why Do Korean Students Go to U.S. Graduate Schools?" *British Journal of Sociology of Education* 32(1): 109–126.

Kim, Jongyoung. 2015. *The Ruled Ruler: Studying Abroad in the United States and the Birth of South Korean Elites* (in Korean). Seoul: Dalbegae.

Kim, Kwang-Ki. 2003. *Order and Agency in Modernity: Talcott Parsons, Erving Goffman, and Harold Garfinkel.* Albany: SUNY Press.

Kim, Kyong-Dong. 2017. *Confucianism and Modernization in East Asia: Critical Reflections.* London: Palgrave Macmillan.

Kim, Sae Eun. 2017. "From Journalists to Politicians: A Socio-Historical Analysis of Korean 'Polinalists'" (in Korean). *Korean Journal of Journalism and Communication Studies* 61(3): 7–54.

Kim, Sam-Woong. 2013. "Rhee Syngman, the Origin of Public Security Rule" (in Korean). *Tomorrow-Opening History* 53: 36–51.

Kim, Soo-Ah et al. 2007. "Variations of Family Relations: Focusing on Representations of Family Relations in Chinese and Korean Television Drama" (in Korean). *Korean Journal of Broadcasting & Telecommunications Research* 65: 143–173..

Kim, Sujeong, and Hwang Jung-Mee. 2019. "Rethinking Publicness of Care amid the Kindergarten Corruption Scandal: Beyond the Transparency Issue of Accounting" (in Korean). *Issues in Feminism* 19(1): 209–245.

Kim, Taekyoon, and Kim Bo Kyung. 2024. "Asianization of the Integrated Approach for Development Cooperation." Chang Kyung-Sup, Kim Taekyoon, and Lee Joonkoo (eds) *Asianization of Asia*, pp. 154–175. London: Routledge.

Kim, Woo-Choong. 2008. *The World is Wide, and There Are Many Things to Do* (in Korean). Seoul: Gimm-Young Publishers.

Kim, Yong-Chul. 2010. *Thinking of Samsung* (in Korean). Seoul: Sapyoung.

Kim, Yong Bok. 2007. "The Party Politics and Presidential Leadership after Democratization in Korea" (in Korean). *Memory and Prospect* 17: 6–37.

Knoblauch, Hubert, and Martina Löw. 2017. "On the Spatial Re-Figuration of the Social World." *Sociologica* 11(2): 1–27.

REFERENCES

Kong, Tat Yan. 2000. *The Politics of Economic Reform in South Korea: A Fragile Miracle*. London: Routledge.

Koo, Hagen. 2001. *Korean Workers: The Culture and Politics of Class Formation*. Ithaca: Cornell University Press.

Korea Fair Trade Commission (KFTC). 2018. "The Result of Analysis of the Operation Realities of Public Interest Corporations Belonging to Large Enterprise Conglomerates" (in Korean). Press release, 29 June 2018.

Korea Herald (www.koreaherald.com).

Korea Labor Institute. 2007. *The Korean Longitudinal Study of Ageing*. Seoul: Korea Labor Institute.

Korea University Newspaper (https://news.unn.net/).

Kwon Hyun Ji, Kang Kyunghee, and Noh Gabin. 2022. "Do Institutions Still Matter? Platform Worker Activism and Its Institutional Experimentation" (in Korean). *Korean Journal of Industrial Relations* 32(4): 57–106.

Krugman, Paul. 1994. "The Myth of Asia's Miracle." *Foreign Affairs* 73(6): 62–78.

Kukinews (https://www.kukinews.com/).

Kwon, Heonik, and Byung-Ho Chung. 2012. *North Korea: Beyond Charismatic Politics*. New York: Rowman & Littlefield.

Kwon, Nae-Hyun. 2015. "Internal Development Theory and Recognition of the Later Chosŏn History" (in Korean). *History Critique* 111: 417 – 442.

Kyunghyang Shinmun (www.khan.co.kr).

Lan, Pei Chia. 2014. "Compressed Modernity and Glocal Entanglement: The Contested Transformation of Parenting Discourses in Postwar Taiwan." *Current Sociology* 62(4): 531–549.

Lash, Scott. 1990. *Sociology of Postmodernism*. London: Routledge.

Lash, Scott. 1999. *Another Modernity*. London: Sage.

Lash, Scott. 2001. "Foreword: Individualization in a Non-Linear Mode." Ulrich Beck and Elisabeth Beck-Gernsheim, *Individualization: Institutionalized Individualism and its Social and Political Consequences*, pp. vii–xiii. London: Sage.

Lee, Dae-Jin. 2022. *Surviving Brothers: 'Screaming Testimonies' of 33 Surviving Victims of Hyeongjebokjiwon* (in Korean). Seoul: Homilbat.

Lee, Doo-Won. 2007. "The Outbreak of the 1997 Financial Crisis and Its Recovery." Presented at the Conference on "A Decade After: Recovery and Adjustment since the East Asian Crisis," organized by International Development Economics Associates (IDEAs), Global Sustainability and Environmental Institute (GSEI), Action Aid, and Focus on the Global South, 12–14 July 2007, Bangkok, Thailand.

Lee, Gil Jung. 2023. "The Mechanism and Cracks of the Guilt by Association System from the 1960s to the 1980s: Focusing on the Experience of the Victims of the Guilt by Association System Who Made Their Way into Public Posts" (in Korean). *Oral History Studies* 14(1): 91–121.

Lee, Jae Eun, and Yoo Hyun-jung. 2007. "Creating the New Field of the National Crisis and Emergency Management and Its Operating Strategy: Classification and Management Plan of the National Living Safety Crises" (in Korean). *Crisisonomy* 3(2): 1 – 17.

Lee, Jeonghyun. 2013. "Issues and Realities of Employment and Labor Relations in Medium and Small Enterprises" (in Korean). *Journal of Labour Law* 47: 211–253.

REFERENCES

Lee, Joonkoo. 2024. "Asianization of Industrial Development? Global Value Chains and Asia's Evolving Regional Connections." Chang Kyung-Sup, Kim Taekyoon, and Lee Joonkoo (eds) *Asianization of Asia*, pp. 30–49. London: Routledge.

Lee, Keun. 2019. *The Art of Economic Catch-Up: Barriers, Detours and Leapfrogging in Innovation Systems*. Cambridge: Cambridge University Press.

Lee, Pyoung-Soo. 2015. "Basic Law on Service Industry Development and Medical Privatization" (in Korean). *Journal of the Korean Medical Association* 58(2): 86–88.

Lee, Seungtae. 2010. "The Corporate Control of Large Business Groups" (in Korean). *Korean Corporate Management Review* 17(2): 75–93.

Lee, Sin-Cheol. 2006. "The History of Using Korean History Textbooks as Political Means: Focusing on the Rhee Syng-Man and Park Chung Hee Dictatorship" (in Korean). *History Education* 97: 177 – 209.

Lee, Sophia Seung-yoon, and Jiwon Kim. 2025. "We All Want More Jobs: South Korean Youth's Labor Market Segmentation and Social Investment Policy Preferences in the Neoliberal Era." Chang Kyung-Sup, Kim Se-Kyun, and Lee Keun (eds) *Neoliberalization of South Korea: Economic Restructuring, Social Precarity, and Post-Developmental Democracy*. New York: Palgrave Macmillan.

Lee, Young Joo. 2023. "An Exploratory Study of Improving Migration of Risks in the Post-COVID-19 Era" (in Korean). *Safety Culture Studies* 25: 397–410.

Lew, Seok-Choon. 2013. *The Korean Economic Developmental Path: Confucian Tradition, Affective Network*. New York: Palgrave Macmillan.

Lewis, W. Arthur. 1954. "Economic Development with Unlimited Supplies of Labour." *Manchester School of Economics and Social Studies* 22(1):139–191.

Light, Alysson E., Tessa M. Benson-Greenwald, and Amanda B. Diekman. 2022. "Gender Representation Cues Labels of Hard and Soft Sciences." *Journal of Experimental Social Psychology* 98, January 2022 (https://doi.org/10.1016/j.jesp.2021.104234).

Lim, Hyun-Chin, Lee Se-Young, and Chang Kyung-Sup (eds) 1998. *The Life Quality of South Koreans: Physical and Psychological Safety* (in Korean). Seoul: Seoul National University Press.

Lim, Kyong Sok. 2009. "A Viewpoint about Park Chung-Hee Era" (in Korean). *History and Reality* 74: 3–12

MacKinnon, Malcolm H. 1993. "The Longevity of the Thesis: A Critique of the Critics." Hartmut Lehmann and Guenther Roth (eds) *Weber's Protestant Ethic: Origins, Evidence, and Contexts*, pp. 211–244. Cambridge: Cambridge University Press.

Maeil Business Newspaper (https://www.mk.co.kr/).

Marx, Karl, and Frederick Engels. [1945–46] 1970. *The German Ideology*. New York: International Publishers.

Marx, Karl, and Frederick Engels. 1978. *The Marx–Engels Reader*, 2nd edn. New York: W. W. Norton.

Masahiro, Yamada. 1999. *The Age of Parasite Singles* (in Japanese). Tokyo: Chikumashobo.

McNamara, Dennis. 1990. *The Colonial Origins of Korean Enterprise, 1910–1945*. Cambridge: Cambridge University Press.

Medi:gate News (https://m.medigatenews.com/).

REFERENCES

Mobrand, Erik. 2019. *Top-Down Democracy in South Korea*. Seattle: University of Washington Press.

Moon, Seungsook. 2024. *Civic Activism in South Korea: The Intertwining of Democracy and Neoliberalism*. New York: Columbia University Press.

Moore, Barrington, Jr. 1966. *Social Origins of Dictatorship and Democracy: Lord and Peasant in the Making of the Modern World*. Boston: Beacon Press.

Moore, Mick. 1984. "Mobilization and Disillusion in Rural Korea: The Saemaul Movement in Retrospect." *Pacific Affairs* 57(4): 577–598.

Na, Jong-seok. 2011. "A Study on the History of Reception of Postmodernism in Korea of the 1990s" (in Korean). *Philosophical Studies* 120: 83–108.

National Statistical Office (NSO), Republic of Korea. 1996. *Changes in Social and Economic Indicators since Liberation* (in Korean).

National Statistical Office (NSO), Republic of Korea. 1997. *Social Indicators in Korea*.

National Statistical Office, Republic of Korea. 2002–2006. *Annual Report on Live Births and Death Statistics (Based on Vital Registration)*.

New York Times (www.nytimes.com).

Newsis (https://www.newsis.com/).

Nietzsche, Friedrich. [1901]1968. *The Will to Power*, edited by Walter Kaufman. New York: Vintage Books.

Nye, Joseph S. 2004. *Soft Power: The Means to Success in World Politics*. New York: Hachette.

Ochia, Emiko. 2011. "Unsustainable Societies: The Failure of Familialism in East Asia's Compressed Modernity." *Historical Social Research* 36(2): 219–245.

Ochiai, Emiko, Aya Abe, Takafumi Uzuhashi, Tamiya Yuko, and Shikata Masato. 2012. "The Struggle Against Familialism: Reconfiguring the Care Diamond in Japan." Shahra Razavi and Silke Staab (eds) *Global Variations in the Political and Social Economy of Care: Worlds Apart*, pp. 61–79. London: Routledge.

Ogburn, William F. 1922. *Social Change with Respect to Culture and Original Nature*. New York: Viking.

Oh, Moon-Wan. 1997. "The Legal Logic of Law-Keeping Struggle" (in Korean). *Law Labor Studies* 6: 248–295.

Oh, Seyoung. 2019. *Research Survey on the Level of Public Sector Corruption in Korean Society* (in Korean). KIPA Research Report 2019–2011. Seoul: Korea Institute of Public Administration.

Oh, Seyoung. 2020. *Survey on the Level of Public Sector Corruption in Korea* (in Korean). KIPA Research Report 2020–2010. Seoul: Korea Institute of Public Administration.

Ohmynews (www.ohmynews.com).

Olson, Mancur. 1971. *The Logic of Collective Action: Public Goods and the Theory of Groups*. Cambridge: Harvard University Press.

Olson, Mancur. 1982. *The Rise and Decline of Nations*. New Haven: Yale University Press.

Part, Myoung-Kyu. 2014. *National, People, Citizen* (in Korean). Seoul: Sohwa.

Park, Sang-In. 2020. "Too Big to Jail: How Powerful Korean Executives Escape Indictment or Conviction." *Promarket: Insights Shaping the Future of Capitalism*, 15 April 2020 (https://www.promarket.org/2020/04/15/too-big-to-jail-how-powerful-korean-executives-escape-indictment-or-conviction/).

REFERENCES

Park, Seong-Je. 2017. *Power and Media: The Era of Giregi Journalism* (in Korean). Seoul: Changbi.

Park, Seung-Gwan, and Chang Kyung-Sup. 2001. *Media Power and Agenda Dynamics* (in Korean). Seoul: Communication Books.

Park, Yong Sang. 2012. "National Security and the Freedom of Expression: Especially in Enforcing Korean National Security Act" (in Korean). *Justice* 128: 87–131.

Park, Young Taek. 2013. *K-Art: Universal Works Reach Global Audience.* Seoul: Korean Culture and Information Service.

Peng, Ito. 2009. "The Good, The Bad, and the Weird: Political and Social Economy of Care in South Korea." Paper presented at the Global COE Symposium on "Family and Intimacy in Asia," Kyoto University, 23 November 2009.

People's Solidarity for Participatory Democracy (PSPD), Economic Democratization Committee. 1998. *White Book on Public Interest Foundations: Indicting Public Interest Foundations That Are* Chaebol's *Camouflaged Affiliate Firms* (in Korean). Seoul: Jijeong.

Perrow, Charles. 1984. *Normal Accidents: Living with High-Risk Technologies.* New York: Basic Books.

Pressian (www.pressian.com).

Rezrazi, El Mostafa, and Nouha Benjelloun Andaloussi. 2020. "The Evolution of South Korea's ODA Strategy: The Moroccan Case." Policy Paper at Policy Center for Global South, Rabat, Morocco.

Rostow, W. W. 1959. "The Stages of Economic Growth." *Economic History Review* 12(1): 1–16.

Rostow, W. W. 1963. "Leading Sectors and the Take-off." W. W. Rostow (ed.) *The Economics of Take-Off into Sustained Growth*, pp. 1–21. London: Palgrave Macmillan.

Rueschemeyer, Dietrich, Evelyne Stephens, and John Stephens. 1992. *Capitalist Development and Democracy.* Chicago: University of Chicago Press.

Sasano, Misae. 2021. "Family Values in Korea and Japan: Focusing on Gender and Cohort." PhD Dissertation, Department of Sociology, Seoul National University.

Seol, Dong-Hoon. 2024. "International Migration and Socioeconomic Linkages in East Asia." Chang Kyung-Sup, Kim Taekyoon, and Lee Joonkoo (eds) *Asianization of Asia*, pp. 66–90. London: Routledge.

Seoul Economic Daily (https://www.sedaily.com/)

Seth, Michael. 2002. *Education Fever: Society, Politics, and the Pursuit of Schooling in South Korea.* Honolulu: University of Hawaii Press.

Shin, Kyung-Ah. 2014. "The Changes in Male Breadwinner Consciousness and Its Implications for Gender Relations in Korean Family" (in Korean). *Korean Journal of Women's Studies* 30(4): 153–187.

Shin, Seon-Mee et al. 2020. "Development of Strategies by Sector for Reducing the Gender gap in the Labor Market (III): Focusing on Gender Segregation across Fields of Study" (in Korean). Research Report, 2020–2029. Seoul: Korea Women's Development Institute.

Shin, Yong-Ha. 1997. *A Study of Social Thoughts of the Silhakpa in the Late Chosun Era* (in Korean). Seoul: Jisiksaneopsa.

Simon, Herbert A. 1947. *Administrative Behavior: A Study of Decision-Making Processes in Administrative Organization.* New York: Macmillan

Sisa Journal (https://www.sisajournal.com/).

REFERENCES

Song, Ho-Geun. 1991. *Labor Politics and the Market in South Korea* (in Korean). Seoul: Nanam.

Song, Won-Guen, and Sang-Ho Lee. 2005. *The Business Structure of Korean Chaebols and Concentration of Economic Power* (in Korean). Seoul: Nanam.

Song, Won Keun, Shin Hak-rim, Lee Won-jae, and Lee Il-young. 2016. "*Chaebol* (Conglomerates) in Korea, *Chaebol's* Korea?" (in Korean). *Quarterly Changbi* 44(4): 449–476.

Streeten, Paul. 1959. "Unbalanced Growth." *Oxford Economic Papers* 11(2): 167–190.

Teo, Youyenn. 2013. "Support for Deserving Families: Inventing the Anti-welfare Familialist State in Singapore." *Social Politics* 20(3): 387–406.

The Committee on Private School Reform, the ROK Ministry of Education. 2019. *The 2019 White Book on the Activities of the Committee on Private School Reform: The Recommendations for Improvement in the Private School Regulations* (in Korean).

The Hyeongjebokjiwon Research Team of Department of Sociology, Seoul National University (ed.). 2021. *Between Extinction and Rebirth: Sociology of Hyeongjebokjiwon* (in Korean). Seoul: Seoul National University Press.

The Institute for Democratic Policy. 2015. "An Analysis of the Controlling Power of the Four Largest *Chaebol* over News Media's Advertisements (in Korean)."

The JoongAng (www.joins.com).

The Wall Street Journal (www.wsj.com).

Therborn, Göran. 2020. *Inequality and the Labyrinths of Democracy*. London: Verso.

Thompson, John B. 1995. *The Media and Modernity: A Social Theory of the Media*. Stanford: Stanford University Press.

Thompson, John B. 2000. *Political Scandal: Power and Visibility in the Media Age*. Cambridge: Polity.

Thurbon, Elizabeth, Sung-Young Kim, Hao Tan, and John Mathews. 2023. *Developmental Environmentalism: State Ambition and Creative Destruction in East Asia's Green Energy Transition*. Oxford: Oxford University Press.

Tilly, Louise, and Joan Wallach Scott. 1987. *Women, Work, and Family*. New York: Routledge.

Truth and Reconciliation Commission, Republic of Korea. 2022. "Reference Materials in Respect to the Truth Revelation Decision on the Human Rights Violation Incident of Hyeongjebokjiwon" (in Korean).

University Journal (https://dhnews.co.kr/).

Vogel, Ezra. 1979. *Japan as Number One: Lessons for America*. Cambridge: Harvard University Press.

Wade, Robert. 1990. *Governing the Market: Economic Theory and the Role of Government in East Asian Industrialization*. Princeton: Princeton University Press.

Weber, Max. 1948. *From Max Weber: Essays in Sociology*, edited by H. H. Gerth and C. Wright Mills. London: Routledge.

Weber, Max. 1968. *Economy and Society: An Outline of Interpretive Sociology*. Totowa: Bedminster.

Weiss, Linda. 1995. "Governed Interdependence: Rethinking the Government–Business Relationship in East Asia." *Pacific Affairs* 8(4): 589–616.

REFERENCES

Whittaker, D. Hugh, Timothy Sturgeon, Toshie Okita, and Tianbiao Zhu. 2020. *Compressed Development: Time and Timing in Economic and Social Development*. Oxford: Oxford University Press.

Woo, Seok-Hoon, and Park Kwon-Il. 2007. *The 880,000 Won Generation: An Economics of Hope Written at a Time of Despair* (in Korean). Seoul: Redian.

Yang, Gi-Ho. 2000. "An Analysis of South Korean Civic Groups' Political Functions: Focusing on the People's Solidarity for Participatory Democracy" (in Korean). *Journal of the 21ˢᵗ Century Political Science* 10(2): 61–77.

Yecies, Brian, and Ae-Gyung Shim. 2011. "Contemporary Korean Cinema: Challenges and the Transformation of 'Planet Hallyuwood'." *Acta Koreana* 14(1): 1–15.

Yee, Jaeyeol. 1998. "Risk Society as a System Failure: Sociological Analysis of Accidents in Korea." *Korea Journal* 38(1): 83–101.

Yi, Ki Ho. 2022. "Politics of 'Chaeya' and Ye Chun-ho" (in Korean). *Trend and Prospect* 115: 73–108.

Yonhapnews (www.yonhapnews.co.kr).

Yoon, Jin-Ho. 1994. *Precarious Laborers in Korea* (in Korean). Incheon: Inha University Press.

Yoon, Jin-Ho, Yu-Sun Kim, Jang-Ho Kim, Dae-Myung Roh, and Jae-Eun Seok. 2005. "The Direction of Labor and Welfare Policies for Allied Growth and Bipolarization Annulment" (in Korean). Report submitted to the Presidential Commission on Policy and Planning, November 2005.

Yoon, Sang-Chul. 1997. *The Democratic Transition Process of South Korea in the 1980s* (in Korean). Seoul: Seoul National University Press.

Yoon, Sang Woo. 2018. *The Sociology of Neoliberalism and Capitalism* (in Korean). Seoul: Hanul.

Yoon, Seungjoo. 2017. "Eastern Spirit, Western Instrument." Bryan S. Turner, Chang Kyung-Sup, Cynthia F. Epstein, Peter Kivisto, J. Michael Ryan, William Outhwaite (eds) *The Wiley-Blackwell Encyclopedia of Social Theory*, vol. II. Hoboken: Wiley-Blackwell (https://doi.org/10.1002/9781118430873.est 0849).

Zakaria, Fareed, and Lee Kuan Yew. 1994. "Culture is Destiny: A Conversation with Lee Kuan Yew." *Foreign Affairs* 73(2): 109–126.

INDEX

Page numbers in *italic* refer to a figure in the text

"1987 system" (1987–*nyeon cheje*) 30
3D jobs (dirty, difficult, dangerous)
    100, 157

abortion 141
abuse, physical, mental, and spiritual
    51
academia/academics 24, 32–34,
    38–39. *see also* universities
"accident republic" 148
accidents 18–19, 145–149, 151–152,
    162, 169, 192n1, 193n13,
    193n17
  and foreign workers 154, 194n22
  industrial accidents 146, 150, 151,
    154, 162
accountability 39, 71
activism 162. *see also* social
    movements
  and corruption 44, 60–61
  and democracy 37, 44, 81–82,
    165–166, 174n5
  and labor 134, 191n15
  and neoliberal reformism 84, 85
  and political parties 61, 165–166
  and reform movements 60–61,
    81–82
  and risk society 153, 165–166,
    169–170, 194n21

and safety 153, 194n21
and state-projective politics 37, 38,
    44
and working class 90, 125, 153,
    169, 184n3
"advanced nations" (*seonjinguk*) 14,
    38, 48
aggrandizement 72, 74, 79
American influences 49, 112. *see also*
    Western influences
  and democracy 13, 25, 29, 31, 32
Amsden, Alice 67, 77
appropriation, sociopolitical 117, 119
arts, pure 119, 188n25
Asian culture 17, 109, 110, 111, 112,
    185n4. *see also* traditional/
    indigenous culture
"Asian era" 6
Association of Physicians for
    Humanism (Ineuihyup) 40, 61,
    177n31
Atlantic Council, Global Citizen
    Award 174n5
authoritarianism
  and *chaebol* system 15–16, 80,
    82–83, 85–86
  and corruption 54–58, 59, 180n22,
    180n23, 180n24, 181n25,
    181n26

209

INDEX

authoritarianism (*cont.*)
  and democracy 13, 29, 32–33, 42,
    59, 82–83
  and familialism 111, 124
  and postcolonialism 11, 27, 29
authoritarianism, developmental statist
  82
authoritarianism, moral 111, 124
automobiles 151

Badie, Bertrand 27
bads, production of 35, 164
Basic Law for Past History
    Examination for Truth and
    Reconciliation 174n6
Beck, Bonss and Lau, Christoph 8,
  173n7
Beck, Ulrich
  and compressed modernity 7–8, 20,
    161–163
  and second modernity 8, 18, 126,
    132–133, 173n7
  and globalization 173n7
  Metamorphosis of the World viii,
    20, 163
  and reflexivity 8, 9, 173n7
  and risk society vi, 3, 9, 19,
    147–148, 155, 163–165,
    172n2
  and compressed modernity 7–8,
    20
Beck, Ulrich and Beck-Gernsheim,
  Elizabeth 128, 129–130
behavior, corporate 71
birth-cohort 91, 92–93
births 141, 191n21
Bong Joon-Ho 121
bourgeoisie 15, 17, 64, 65, 67. *see
  also chaebol* system (industrial
  conglomerates)
bugukgangbyeong (rich nation, strong
  army) ideology 32
Busan, South Korea 51

"candlelight uprising" (2016–2017)
  25, 28, 61, 174n5, 191n15

capitalism 5, 6. *see also* neoliberalism;
  risk society
  and *chaebol* system 15–16, 48–50,
    64–87
  and corruption 48–49, 65
  and democracy 15–16, 65–66, 68,
    69, 80–82, 83–84, 85–87
  and social class 15–16, 64, 65,
    67
  and workers' rights 65, 66
and corruption 48–50, 166
  and *chaebol* system 48–49, 65
  and universities 49–50, 178n6,
    178n7
  and welfare 49, 50, 52
and democracy 82–87, 183n14
  and *chaebol* system 15–16,
    65–66, 68, 69, 80–82, 83–84,
    85–87
  and neoliberalism 34, 35, 41,
    85–87, 115
and developmental compression
  88–93, 103–104
and developmental state 66, 99
and economic development 32–33,
  65, 113–114
  and *chaebol* system 66, 70
  and democracy 32–33, 34, 41,
    86–87, 99, 115
  and neoliberalism 34, 41, 86–87,
    115
and factories 102, 185n9
and family life 131, 190n11
and fertility rates 98, 105
and gender 89–90, 125–126
and individualism 126, 131
and inequalities 66, 166
and labor 16, 98–103, 125,
  133–134, 191n13
  and "IMF conditionalities" 89,
    104
  and neoliberalism 89, 104,
    191n14
and Lee Myung-Bak 35, 41–42, 84,
  183n14
and Park Chung-Hee 64, 68–69

INDEX

and risk society 146, 148, 149, 157, 164, 166–167
  and neoliberalism 7, 19, 147, 154, 167
and Roh Moo-Hyun 34, 86
and social class 5, 15–16, 64, 65, 67
  and neoliberalism 66, 123–124, 168
  and social conditions 16–17, 88–93, 98–103
  and working life courses 88–90, 103–104, 133
  and neoliberalism 17, 89, 104, 167–168
capitalism, Confucian 109, 117
capitalism, consumer 131
capitalism, developmental 89–90
capitalism, familial. *see chaebol* system (industrial conglomerates)
capitalism, flexibly complex 16–17, 98–103
capitalism, industrial. *see* capitalism
capitalism, market 166
care giving institutions 51, 52
career opportunities/political and government appointments 38, 39, 40
carers, women as 131, 137
cartels/cartelization 43, 44, 61, 63
catastrophism, emancipatory 163–165
censorship 33–34, 121, 175n18, 186n11
chaebol-affiliated firms (CAFs) 71–80, 182n6, 182n7, 182n8, 182n9. *see also chaebol* system (industrial conglomerates)
chaebol system (industrial conglomerates) 64–87
  and aggrandizement 72, 74, 79
  and authoritarianism 15–16, 80, 82–83, 85–86
  and capitalism 15–16, 48–50, 64–87
    and corruption 48–49, 65

and democracy 15–16, 65–66, 68, 69, 80–82, 83–84, 85–87
  and neoliberalism 66, 69–70, 82–87
  and social class 15–16, 64, 65, 67
  and workers' rights 65, 66
and collusion 49, 65, 66, 68, 81
and competition 65, 71, 77
conglomerate heads 71–74
  and corruption 45, 73, 74, 79–80, 182n9
  and hierarchy 77–78, 79–80, 182n9
  and judicial institutions 79–80, 182n9
  and rents/rent-seeking 72, 74–76, 182n6
  and stock ownership 72, 73, 74, 182n6
and conservatism 80–81, 82, 83, 183n14
and corporate debt 69, 73, 74, 86
and corruption 45–46, 68, 75, 162, 183n13
  and capitalism 48–49, 65
  and conglomerate heads 45, 73, 74, 79–80, 182n9
  and embezzlement 48, 54, 55, 74, 75
  and welfare 52, 179n16
and democracy 166–167
  and capitalism 15–16, 65–66, 68, 69, 80–82, 83–84, 85–87
  and *chaebol* system reform 80–82, 182n11, 182n12, 183n14
  liberal democracy 16, 61, 82
development and organization of 67–70, 71–80, 182n5
and developmental state 64, 65, 71, 76, 82
and economic development 65, 66, 68, 70, 76
  and "IMF conditionalities"/ financial crisis 66, 70, 81, 84–85

211

INDEX

chaebol system (industrial
conglomerates) (*cont.*)
and education 49–50, 53
and entrepreneurship 67, 82
and exploitation 101, 184n6
and exports 68, 72, 76, 86
and familial control of management
70, 73, 76, 77
and corruption 52, 54, 179n16
and hierarchy 78, 182n8
and familial servants 78, 182n8,
182n9
and foreign students 53, 180n18
and hierarchy 77–78, 79–80, 101,
182n8, 182n9
and industrial policy 53, 70, 76
and journalism 80, 81, 82–83,
182n12
and judicial institutions 54, 55,
79–80, 81, 86
and justice 79–80, 83–84, 101,
182n9
and Kim Dae-Jung 81, 86
and Kim Young-Sam 70, 81
and labor 66, 69, 100, 185n9
and Park Chung-Hee 42, 68–69, 80
and profitability 52, 72, 180n17
and property rights 64, 71
and reform 80–85, 182n11,
182n12, 183n13, 183n14
and rent-seeking 74–76, 77, 86–87,
182n6
and Rhee Syng-Man 67, 68
and shareholders 65, 71, 72
and SMEs (small and medium-sized
enterprises) 100, 101, 184n6
and social class 15–16, 17, 64, 65,
67
and elite class 66, 82–83,
166–167
and stock ownership 71–72, 73, 74,
78–79, 182n6, 182n8
and subsidization 72, 77
and trust 78, 182n8
and welfare 49–50, 52, 53, 179n16,
180n17

and workers' rights 65, 66, 71
and working life courses 16–17, 103
Chang Ha-Joon 76
Chang Ha-Sung 183, n.13, 184n17,
186n13
change, social
and compressed modernity 10, 133
and individualization 129, 132, 133
and reflexive modernity 7, 8, 9, 47
chemical industry 69
cheomdangisul (state-of-the-art
technology) 148
children, number and sex of 140–141,
169
China 11, 111, 112, 157, 165, 170
Chinese social survey 135–136,
191n19
chongsu. see conglomerate heads
Chosun era 117, 130
Chun Doo-Hwan 23, 27, 29–30,
174n8
Chung Eui-Sun 182n9
Chung Ju-Young 182n12
Chung Mong-Gu 75, 182n9
citizen professionals 40–41, 60–61
Citizens' Alliance for Welfare
(Wooribokjisiminyeonhap) 61
Citizens' Coalition for Democratic
Media (Mineonlyeon) 60
Citizens' Coalition for Economic
Justice (Gyeongsilyeon) 60
citizenship, cosmopolitan cultural 117
citizenship, risk 155–156, 157,
194n23
civil society 13, 28–29, 40, 44, 114
civilism, political 25
class relations 17, 184n3. *see also*
social class
climate crisis, global 164–165
coalitions 80, 81, 82, 83, 182n11,
183n14
coalition of political, administrative
and judicial organs of state 56,
180n22
coercion, public physical 35, 38, 39,
114

212

INDEX

cohabitation 161
Cold War 114
collusion
  and *chaebol* system 49, 65, 66, 68, 81
  and corruption 44, 56, 58, 62–63
  and democracy 43, 44, 46, 62–63, 166
  and elite class 56, 66
  and journalism 43, 44, 46
  and justice 56, 58
colonialism 5
colonialism, Japanese 25, 67–68
Commercial Law 75
compartmentalization, institutional 113, 119
competition 65, 71, 77
  global 118, 187n22
complicity 55
compression, developmental 16–17, 19, 88–105. *see also* social conditions; working life courses
  and capitalism 88–93, 103–104
  and working life courses 90–98, 103–105
    and birth-cohort 91, 92–93
    and labor 93, 103–104, 184n4
    and men 90, 91, 105, 184n4
    and women 90, 92–93, 105
Confucianism
  and capitalism 109, 117
  and culture 17–18, 111, 116
  and family life 123, 124, 130, 131, 189n37
  and women 125, 126, 131
conglomerate heads 71–74
  and corruption 45, 73, 74, 79–80, 182n9
  and hierarchy 77–78, 79–80, 182n9
  and judicial action 79–80, 182n9
  and rents/rent-seeking 72, 74–75, 182n6
  and stock ownership 72, 73, 74, 182n6
conservatism 135, 149
  and *chaebol* system 80–81, 82, 83

and conservative coalitions 81, 82, 183n14
and corruption 46, 58, 60, 61, 62
and culture 112, 121
and democracy 13, 24, 31, 38, 81, 174n10, 175n11
  conservative party 25, 35, 39
  conservative presidents 23, 28, 29, 39, 41, 42
  and corruption 46, 60
  and journalism 37, 43, 46
and journalism 37, 43, 46, 58, 62, 82, 83
conservative party 25, 35, 39, 80–81, 82
constituentization 24, 33, 43–44, 48
construction sites 146
consumption 156, 157
  cultural consumption 117, 118, 119
Coronavirus pandemic 149, 193n11
corruption 14–15, 45–63
  and activism 44, 60–1
  and authoritarianism 54–8, 59, 180n22, 180n23, 180n24, 181n25, 181n26
  and capitalism 48–50, 166
    and *chaebol* system 48–9, 65
    and industrialization 53, 62
    and universities 49–50, 178n6, 178n7
    and welfare 49, 50, 52
  and cartels/cartelization 61, 63
  and *chaebol* system 45–6, 68, 75, 162, 183n13
    and capitalism 48–9, 65
    and conglomerate heads 45, 73, 74, 79–80, 182n9
    and embezzlement 48, 54, 55, 74, 75
    and welfare 52, 179n16
  and collusion 44, 56, 58, 62–3
  and conservatism 46, 58, 60, 61, 62
  and democracy 62–3, 162
    and conservatism 46, 60
    and liberal democracy 61, 63, 68
    and reform movements 28, 61

213

INDEX

corruption (*cont.*)
  and democracy (*cont.*)
    and state-projective politics 24,
      36, 41–4, 57, 177n32, 177n34
    and dualism 11–12, 47–54, 55, 59
    and economic development 35, 59
    and entrepreneurship 46, 50, 52,
      170
    and exploitation 51
    and familial control of management
      in *chaebol* system 52, 54,
      179n16
    and favoritism 35, 45, 55, 68,
      194n2
    and human rights 51
    and industrial development 53, 62
    and institutions 14–15, 45–63, 166,
      170, 177n2
    and intelligence agencies 57, 173n1
    and journalism 46, 58, 62
    and judicial institutions 15, 53, 54,
      55–7, 58, 60, 62
    and justice 54–8, 162, 166, 180n22
      and democracy 44, 162
    and loyalty 39, 55, 113
    and manipulation of public opinion
      80, 181n26
    and medical services 50–1, 53,
      178n9, 179n12
    and patronage 55, 59
    and political parties 59–60, 61
    and presidents of South Korea
      and impeachment of presidents
      28, 36, 42, 45, 61
      and Lee Myung-Bak 42, 68, 166
      and Park Chung-Hee 173n1,
      180n23
      and Park Geun-Hye 28, 30, 35,
      36, 42, 61, 166, 180n23
    and private schools 46, 54–5
    and problem-solving 15, 47, 55, 62
    and reform movements 28, 59, 60–1
    and social class 46, 50, 58, 166,
      181n26
      and elite class 46, 58, 60, 162,
      181n26, 181n28

    and state prosecutors 24, 46, 56–7,
      180n23, 180n24, 181n25,
      181n26
    and subsidization 50, 51, 52
    and welfare 46, 55, 60–1
      and capitalism 49, 50, 52
      and care giving institutions 51,
      52
      and *chaebol* system 52, 179n16
      and human rights 51, 179n14
      and inmate exploitation 51
      and Western influences 14, 47–8
corruption, gray 177n2
corruption, mutually embedded
  54–58, 180n22
corruption, normal 14–15, 45–63,
  166, 170, 177n2. *see also*
  corruption
corruption, systematized 45–47, 166
cosmopolitanism 3, 117, 122, 132,
  133
cosmopolitanism, methodological
  173n7, 190n12
cosmopolitanism, reflexive 9, 133,
  173n7
Crouch, Colin 7
cultural influences 17–18, 109–124.
  see also Western influences
  and conservatism 112, 121
  and cosmopolitanism 117, 122, 132
  and cultural consumption 117, 118,
    119
  and education 121–122, 168,
    188n29
  and elite class 111, 120–121
  and family life 110–111, 124, 134,
    189n38
    and Confucianism 123, 124, 130,
    131, 189n37
  and institutionalization 116, 119
  and instrumentalism 17, 110, 111,
    168
  and modernization 110, 117, 118,
    119
  and popular culture 110, 121–122,
    124, 188n29, 189n38

214

INDEX

and postcolonialism 109–124
  and Asian culture 17–18, 109, 111, 112
  and indigenous societies 11, 17–18, 112
  and knowledge 109–111, 115–119
  and Western influences 17–18, 109, 112, 117–118, 120
and social sciences 118, 120, 122
and traditional/indigenous culture
  Asian culture 17, 109, 110, 111, 112, 185n4
  and China 111, 112
  and Confucian capitalism 109, 117
  and Confucianism 17–18, 109, 111, 116, 117
  and *dongdoseogi* (Eastern spirit, Western instrument) 109, 110, 111, 112
  and universities 116–117, 118, 119, 187n24, 188n25
  and Western influences 11, 12, 118–119, 187n24, 188n25
and universities
  and humanities and arts 115–119, 188n25
  traditional/indigenous culture 116–117, 118, 119, 187n24, 188n25
  and Western influences 118–119, 168, 187n24
cuttage, institutional 26, 27

daughters 138, 140, 141
debt, corporate 69, 73, 74, 86
debt, personal 180n17
defamiliation 128–132, 143–144, 190n6, 190n8. *see also* family life
  and gender 126, 127, 129–132, 135, 143, 169
  and individualization 127–129, 143, 190n4, 190n5
  and women 126, 127, 135, 143

defamiliation, institutionalized 129, 131, 132, 190n8
defamiliation, reconstructive 129
defamiliation, risk-aversive 129
democracy 12–13, 23–44. *see also* state-projective politics
  and academia/academics 24, 32–34, 38–39
  and activism 37, 44, 81–82, 165–166, 174n5
  and American influences 13, 25, 29, 31, 32
  and authoritarianism 13, 29, 32–33, 42, 59, 82–83
  and capitalism
    and *chaebol* system 15–16, 65–66, 68, 69, 80–82, 83–84, 85–87
    and Lee Myung-Bak 35, 84, 183n14
    and neoliberalism 34, 35, 41, 82–87, 115
    and Park Geun-Hye 35, 84
  and cartels/cartelization 43, 44, 63
  and censorship 34, 175n18
  and *chaebol* system 61, 166–167
    and capitalism 15–16, 65–66, 68, 69, 80–82, 83–84, 85–87
    and *chaebol* system reform 80–82, 182n11, 182n12, 183n14
  and civil and political rights 27, 29, 32, 175n11, 175n13
  and civil society 13, 28–29, 40, 44, 114
  and collusion 43, 44, 46, 62–63, 166
  and conservatism 13, 24, 31, 38, 81, 174n10, 175n11
    conservative party 25, 35, 39
    conservative presidents 23, 28, 29, 39, 41, 42
  and corruption 46, 60
  and journalism 37, 43
  and constituentization 24, 33, 43–44, 48

215

INDEX

democracy (*cont.*)
and corruption 62–63, 68, 162
and conservatism 46, 60
and justice 44, 162
and reform movements 28, 61
and state-projective politics 24,
36, 41–44, 177n32, 177n34
and economic development 59, 104,
115
and capitalism 32–33, 34, 41,
86–87, 99, 115
and "IMF conditionalities"/
financial crisis 35, 41, 104,
177n34
and Kim Dae-Jung 115, 186n13
and Kim Young-Sam 41, 104,
177n34
and education 33–34, 186n11
and elite class 23, 29, 33, 166–167,
175n11
and institutional cuttage 26, 27
and institutional functional
conflations 26, 36–41
and institutions, judicial 24, 39, 62,
80, 176n28
and institutions, state 23–24, 42–43
and journalism
and collusion 43, 44, 46
and conservatism 37, 43
and reform of *chaebol* system 80,
81, 182n12
and state-projective politics
23–24, 37–38, 43–44, 177n34
and Kim Dae-Jung 42, 115,
177n34, 186n13
and military takeovers 13, 27, 29,
32–33, 34, 42, 114
and monopolization of power 27,
29, 33–34
and Moon Jae-In 25, 28, 42
and Park Geun-Hye 24–25, 28, 30,
186n11
and capitalism 35, 84
and state-projective politics 35,
36, 39, 42
and parliament 13, 23, 32, 174n6

and elections 33, 36, 37, 44
and political parties 26, 29, 33,
43–44, 59–60, 166–167
conservative party 25, 35, 39
and Democratic Party 24, 25, 29,
181n28
and postcolonialism 11, 23, 25–31,
174n3, 174n6, 174n8
and Rhee Syng-Man 23, 27, 29
and Roh Moo-Hyun 28, 34, 42,
174n8
and security of the state 32–33, 34,
175n13
and self-representation 13, 31, 37,
175n11
and social representation 13, 31,
166
and welfare 44, 99
and Western influences 13, 25, 29,
31, 32, 38
and Yoon 23, Suk-Yeol 175n13,
186n12
democracy, free 28, 34, 114
democracy, liberal
and *chaebol* system 16, 61, 82
and corruption 61, 63, 68
and postcolonialism 23, 25, 27, 28
democracy, society-representative 23,
31–36
Democratic Party 24, 25, 29, 59–60,
181n28, 183n17
democratization, institutional 28, 29,
104
democratization, social 131
dephilosophicalization, social-
institutional 111–115
deregulation 70
developmental state 35, 104, 156,
168, 190n11. *see also*
liberalism, developmental
and capitalism 66, 99
and *chaebol* system 64, 65, 71, 76,
82
developmentalism, mercantilist 84
dictatorship 29, 31, 83. *see also* Park
Chung-Hee

216

INDEX

disasters 41–42, 145, 146, 150, 157, 169, 170
diversification 77, 152
divorce 136–137, 142, 143–144, 161, 192n23, 192n24
doctors 50, 51, 178n9, 194n21
domestic labor displacement 16–17. *see also* working life courses
dongdoseogi (Eastern spirit, Western instrument) 17, 109, 110, 111, 112
dualism, utilitarian institutional 11–12, 47–54, 55, 59
Durkheim, Emile 4–5, 28

East Asia 6. *see also* China; cultural influences; Japan; South Korea; Taiwan
  and cultural influences 109, 112, 117, 118
  and economic development 109, 185n1
  and family life 127, 142–144, 191n19
  and individualism/individualization 127, 136, 142–144
  and risk society 157, 170–171
  and working life courses 90, 103
ecological/environmental issues 41–42, 145, 146, 169
economic development 98–99, 161, 175n15
  and capitalism 65, 113–114
    and *chaebol* system 66, 70
    and democracy 32–33, 34, 41, 86–87, 90, 115
    and neoliberalism 34, 41, 86–87, 115
  and *chaebol* system 68, 76, 81
    and capitalism 65, 70
    and neoliberalism 66, 70
  and corruption 35, 59
  and democracy 59, 104, 115
    and capitalism 32–33, 34, 41, 86–87, 99, 115
    and "IMF conditionalities"/

financial crisis 35, 41, 104, 177n34
  and Kim Dae-Jung 115, 186n13
  and Kim Young-Sam 41, 104, 177n34
East Asia 109, 185n1
  and gender 94, 95, 125
  and inequalities 157, 191n13
  and Kim Young-Sam 27–28, 32, 35, 81, 104
  and democracy 41, 104, 177n34
  and Park Chung-Hee 68, 113, 155
  and risk society 146, 147, 149–150, 155–156, 157, 194n23
  and safety 151–152, 169–170
  and working life courses 89, 90, 94, 95, 103–104, 133, 191n13
Economic Reform Alliance 75
economics, study of 186n7
education 92, 120–122. *see also* universities
  and *chaebol* system 49–50, 53
  and cultural influences 121–122, 168, 188n29
  and democracy 33–34, 186n11
  and labor 105, 116, 134, 186n15
  and women 116, 187n17
education, extra-curricular 121–122, 124, 188n26, 188n29
educational attainment
  and women 162
  and employment 105, 116, 169, 186n15
  and family life 105, 139, 169
  and younger people 105, 162, 169
educational institutions 51–52, 54–55. *see also* academia/academics; universities
educational learning, rigid 118, 120
efficiency 148, 152–153
elderly people 162, 191n13
elections, parliamentary 33, 36, 37, 44
elite class
  and *chaebol* system 66, 82–83, 166–167
  and collusion 56, 66

217

INDEX

elite class (*cont.*)
  and corruption 46, 58, 60, 162,
    181n26, 181n28
  and culture 111, 120–121
  and democracy 23, 29, 33,
    166–167, 175n11
  and journalism 58, 181n26
  and judicial system 58, 181n26
elites, Chosun 111
elites, cultural 120–121
elitism 29
embezzlement 42
  and *chaebol* system 48, 54, 55, 74,
    75
emergency services 150
"emperor presidency" (*jewangjeok
    daetongryeongje*) 57–58
employment, continuous/lifetime
    90–93, 96. *see also* working life
    courses
employment stability 94, 97, 100,
    103–104, 105, 133, 162
employment system, lifetime. *see*
    labor; working life courses
England 79
entrepreneurial class 67
entrepreneurship 102
  and *chaebol* system (industrial
    conglomerates) 67, 82
  and corruption 46, 50, 52, 170
exclusion, political 24
experimentation, reflexively simulative
    10
exploitation 98, 170
  and *chaebol* system 101, 184n6
  and corruption 51
  and self-employment 102, 185n10
  and SMEs (small and medium-sized
    enterprises) 101, 184n6,
    185n10
exports 68, 72, 76, 86

factions, political 60
factories 102, 151, 185n9
factory girls (*yeogong*) 89
Fair Trade Commission 78

familial control of management in
  chaebol system 70, 73, 76, 77
  and corruption 52, 54, 179n16
  and hierarchy 78, 182n8
familialism 123–124, 130, 136,
    189n35, 189n38, 190n10. *see
    also chaebol* system (industrial
    conglomerates); family life
  and authoritarianism 111, 124
  and religion 123, 188n33
  and Western influences 124, 131,
    189n37
  and women 132, 135, 136, 168,
    169
familialism, institutional 130, 131,
    132
familialism, liberal 123–124, 189n35,
    189n38
familialization 105, 168–169
familism 124, 130–132, 190n10
family-centeredness 123–124, 126,
    129–132, 143, 144
family crisis. *see* family life
family life 125–144, 162. *see also*
    defamiliation; familialism;
    marriage; patriarchy; women
  and capitalism 131, 190n11
  and cultural influences 110–111,
    134
  and Confucianism 123, 124, 130,
    131, 189n37
  and popular culture 124,
    189n38
  and defamiliation 128, 129–132,
    169, 190n6
  and women 129, 132, 143
  and divorce 136–137, 142,
    143–144, 161, 192n23, 192n24
  and East Asia 127, 142–144
  and educational attainment 105,
    139, 169
  and family support 134, 138,
    191n16
  and individualism/individualization
    18, 125–129, 130, 131,
    134–135, 136, 143

218

INDEX

and institutionalization 128, 129, 130, 132
and labor 131, 139
and men 93–98, 140, 142
and parenthood 111, 140–141, 169
and social class 123–124, 125
and social institutions 126, 129
and social reproduction 125–126, 128
and women as carers 131, 137
and working life courses 93–98, 105
and younger people 140, 169
  and marriage 129, 137–138, 139
  and men 140, 142
  and patriarchy 129, 169
  and young women 137, 138, 168, 169
family policies 105
family values 123, 130
farming, subsistence 98
favoritism 35, 45, 55, 68, 194n2
fertility rates 125–126, 140–141, 161, 169
  and capitalism 98, 105
  and defamiliation 132, 143
financial crises 180n17
financial crisis, South Korea 1997 120, 125
  and *chaebol* system 66, 70, 81
  and democracy 27–28, 35, 41, 104
  and state-projective politics 35, 41
  and working life courses 89, 95
financialization, South Korea 191n13
Fine, Ben 7
foreign books 187n20
"foreign loan-based enterprises" 69
foreign students 53, 180n18
foreign workers 100, 154, 194n22
"four grand rivers-saving project" 35, 41–42
"Fourth Industrial Revolution" 149, 193n10
France 79
franchises, standardized service 102
Fukushima nuclear disaster 157
funds, secret 45, 74

gas explosions 145, 146
Geerts, Clifford 116–117
gender 18, 125–144, 188n33. *see also* family life; individualism; individualization; labor; men; women; working life courses
and capitalism 89–90, 125–126
and defamiliation 126, 127, 129–132, 135, 143, 168–169
and economic development 94, 95, 125
"gender-bashing" 135
gender preferences 140–141, 191n21
Germany 79, 103
"ghost doctors" 51
Giddens, Anthony vi, 7, 8
Global Citizen Award, Atlantic Council 174n5
globalization 9, 53, 86, 100, 173n7
Grand Canal System, Korean 35, 41–42
Greece 151

Hangukminjudang party 29
Harvey, David 7
hierarchy, nested 77–78, 79–80, 101, 182n8, 182n9
hierarchy, social 116, 188n33
historico-social conditions 11, 12
history education 33–34, 186n11
hospitals 50–51, 53, 178n9, 179n12
housing 123, 162
humanities 115–119
Hwang Gyo-An 39
Hyeongjebokjiwon, Busan 51, 179n14
Hyundai 58, 75, 182n9, 182n12, 183n14

ICT industry 190n13
"IMF conditionalities" 28, 35, 41
and *chaebol* system 66, 70, 84–85
and labor 89, 104
impeachment of presidents 28, 36, 42, 45, 61
imprisonment of presidents 42, 45

219

INDEX

Imsijeongbu (Provisional Government) group 174n3
incentives 76
independence, financial 138, 142
indigenization, political institutional 27
indigenous societies 27, 67. *see also* traditional/indigenous culture
individual-family relations 129
individualism 25, 125–144
  and capitalism 126, 131
  and East Asia 136, 142–144
  and family life 125–127, 129, 130, 131, 136, 137
  and individualization 18, 127, 136, 142–144
  and women 125–127, 136
individualism, cultural 130
individualism, institutional 129, 130
individualism, liberal 25
individualization 125–144
  and East Asia 127, 136, 142–144
  and family life 18, 127–129, 134–135
    and defamiliation 126, 127, 128, 135, 143, 190n4, 190n5
  and individualism 18, 127, 136, 142–144
  and social change 129, 132, 133
  and women 18, 125–135, 137, 143, 189n1
    and defamiliation 126, 127, 135, 143
    and family life 18, 125–127
    and labor 126, 189n1
individualization, demographic 128, 137, 190n5
individualization, institutionalized 128, 129
individualization, nomadist 128, 190n4
individualization, positive 128
individualization, reconstructive 128, 190n3
individualization, risk-aversive 127, 128, 134–135, 143–144, 190n5

individualization without individualism 18, 127, 136, 142–144
induction, analytic 3
industrial economy, South Korea 90, 133, 186n7. *see also chaebol* system (industrial conglomerates)
industrial policy 53, 70, 76, 149, 156, 157
industrial safety 146, 150, 151, 153, 154, 162
  industrial accidents 146, 150, 151, 154, 162
industrial workers 88, 98, 99, 100, 101–102
industrialization 161, 193n10. *see also* capitalism
  and Coronavirus pandemic 149, 193n11
  and corruption 53, 62
  and risk society 19, 149, 151, 170, 193n11
  and safety 149, 170
  and Western influences 131, 149
  and working life courses 16–17, 89, 90, 91, 94, 96
industry, heavy 69
inequalities, economic 66, 162
inequalities, gender 169
inequalities, social 146, 154–157, 162, 166
inequalities, socioeconomic 162, 169
  and capitalism 66, 166
  and economic development 157, 191n13
  and justice 134, 166
  and labor 133–134, 162
  and risk society 146, 154–157
inertia 26, 47
inexperience, repeated 152, 193n17
informal sector 96
injustice, risk. *see* risk injustice
inmate exploitation 51
innovation 118, 164
insolvency, readjustment of 69

220

INDEX

instability, political 25–31
institutional functional conflations 26,
    36–41, 173n1, 176n31, 177n31
institutional order, liberal 48, 178n4
institutional simulation,
    compartmentalized 113
institutionalization 40
  and culture 116, 119
  and family life 128, 129, 130, 132
  and institutionalized rentier
    consciousness 113, 186n9
  and postcolonialism 14, 47–48
institutions, judicial
  and *chaebol* system 54, 55, 80, 81,
    86
  and corruption 15, 53, 54, 55–57,
    58, 60, 62
  and democracy 24, 39, 62, 80,
    176n28
institutions, social 14, 88, 132
  and corruption 47, 48, 62
  and family life 126, 129
institutions, state 23–24, 42–43,
    113–114
instrumentalism 17, 110, 111, 168
Insurance for the Elderly, National
    Long-Term Care (LTC) 52
intelligence agencies 57, 173n1
Itaewon stampede disaster 145, 150,
    170
Italy 79

jaeya scholarship 120, 188n26
janghaksaeng (scholarship awardee)
    58
Japan 25, 67–68, 103, 111, 112, 157,
    170
Japanese social survey 135–136, 138,
    143–144, 191n19
jayuminjujuui (free democracy) 114
"Job History Survey", Korean
    Longitudinal Study of Aging
    91, 92, 184n4
journalism
  and *chaebol* system 80, 81, 82–83,
    182n12

and conservatism 37, 43, 46, 58,
    62, 82, 83
and corruption 46, 62
  and elite class 58, 181n26
  and intelligence agencies 57–58,
    180n25
and democracy 13–14, 26
  and collusion 43, 44, 46
  and conservatism 37, 43, 46
  and reform of *chaebol* system 80,
    81, 182n12
  and state-projective politics
    23–24, 37–38, 43–44, 177n34
judicial institutions. *see* institutions,
    judicial
"June uprising" 29
justice 189n35
  and *chaebol* system 79–80, 83–84,
    101, 182n9
  and corruption 54–58, 60, 62, 166,
    180n22
    and collusion 56, 58
    and democracy 44, 162
  and inequalities 134, 166
justice, social 134
justice system. *see* institutions,
    judicial
justice, technocratized authoritarian
    54–58, 180n22

Kang Chul-Kyu 76, 182n7
killings/murder 162
Kim Dae-Jung
  and *chaebol* system 81, 86
  and compressed neoliberalism 28,
    84–85, 86
  and democracy 42, 115, 177n34,
    186n13
  and economic development 115,
    186n13
Kim Sang-Jo 184n17, 186n13
Kim Young-Sam
  and *chaebol* system 70, 81
  and economic development 27–28,
    32, 35, 81, 104
  and democracy 41, 104, 177n34

221

INDEX

kindergartens 51–52
knowledge, intentionality of 8
Korea Corporate Governance Fund
    (KCGF) 183n13
Korea General Social Survey (KGSS)
    135–136
Korean Confederation of Trade
    Unions (Minjunochong) 61
Korean Longitudinal Study of Aging,
    "Job History Survey" 91, 92,
    184n4
Korean Medical Association 50,
    177n31
Korean Teachers and Educational
    Workers Union (Jeongyojo)
    54, 61
"Korean wave" (*hallyu*) 121–122

labor
    and activism 134, 191n15
    and capitalism 16, 98–99, 100,
        125, 133–134, 191n13
    and "IMF conditionalities" 89,
        104
    and neoliberalism 17, 34, 89,
        104, 191n14
    and *chaebol* system 66, 69, 100,
        185n9
    and education 105, 116, 134,
        186n15
    and family life 131, 139
    and inequalities 133–134, 162
    and welfare 133–134, 191n14
    and women 125–126
        and education 105, 116,
            186n15
        and individualism/
            individualization 126, 189n1
        and marriage 105, 125–126
        working wives 97–98, 105, 139,
            184n4, 187n15
        young women 90, 105, 187n15
    and working life courses 88–89,
        94–96, 102, 184n4
    and developmental compression
        93, 103–104, 184n4

and women 93, 97
and younger people 90, 105, 169,
    187n15
labor, division of 93, 97, 131, 139
labor, formal wage 94–96
labor mobility 97, 184n4
labor, platform 102
labor relations 66, 69
labor shortages 98, 100
labor, skilled 16, 103–104
labor, transitional 98–99
Lash, Scott 7, 8
law-making 36–37
Lawyers for a Democratic Society
    (Minbyeon) 40, 60
Lee Myung-Bak
    and capitalism 35, 41–42, 84,
        183n14
    and corruption 42, 68, 166
    and democracy 24, 25, 28, 30, 35,
        84, 183n14
    and state-projective politics 24, 25,
        28, 30
Lewis, Arthur 98
liberalism, developmental 190n11. *see
    also* developmental state
liberalism, familial 123–124, 189n35,
    189n38
life choices 18, 126, 127, 132, 136,
    137
life, quality of 19, 146
lifetime employment. *see* working life
    courses
loss-making operations 72
loyalty 39, 55, 113

"M-curve" 105
manipulation. *see* corruption
"marginal work" 94–95, 96
marriage 136–139, 141, 161
    and defamiliation 132, 169
    and East Asia 143–144, 191n19
    and individualism 125–126, 137
    and labor 105, 125–126
    and women 105, 125–126, 132,
        136–139, 191n19

INDEX

married women 97–98, 105, 129,
137, 139
never married women 138, 139,
191n19
and younger people 129, 137–138,
139
marriage, arranged 138–139
marriage, childless 141
marriage, patriarchal 138–139
Marx, Karl/Marxism 5, 172n3
massacres 28, 174n6
medical services 177n31, 178n9,
194n21. *see also* welfare, social
and corruption 50–51, 53, 178n9,
179n12
men
and family life 93–98, 136–137,
139, 169
young men 140, 142
and working life courses 16, 90, 91,
93–98, 184n4
and capitalism 89, 103, 105
and self-employment 95, 96
mental health 162
metamorphosis, Beckian viii, 20,
163–171
Mexico 178n9
military institutions 26, 39
military service 92
military takeovers 13, 27, 29, 32–33,
34, 42, 114
Park Chung-Hee 27, 29, 114
Ministry of Justice 75
mobility, labor 97, 184n4
modernity, antinomic liberal 47–54,
178n4
modernity, compressed. *see also* Beck,
Ulrich; capitalism; *chaebol*
system (industrial
conglomerates); corruption;
cultural influences; democracy;
family life; individualization;
risk society; Western influences;
women; working life courses
first compressed modernity 132,
134, 135–142

second compressed modernity
126–135, 143, 191n16
and Beck 8, 18, 126, 132–133,
173n7
modernity, cuttage 26
modernity, economic 15, 48, 65
modernity, innovative/(re)inventive
11
modernity, late 7–9, 129
modernity, Western 7, 10, 11, 19,
111, 113
modernization and Beck 164
modernization, economic 6, 117
modernization, institutional 48, 113,
117, 118, 119, 186n9
modernization, liberal 98, 110, 169
modernization, reflexive vi, 7–9, 14,
47–48, 178n3
modernization, social 6, 117, 131,
161
monopolization of power 27, 29,
33–34
Moon Jae-In 115, 149, 174n8
"candlelight revolution"
(2016–2017) 25, 28, 61–62,
174n5
and democracy 25, 28, 42
Moore, Barrington Jr. 82
morbidity 162
movies 121, 124
mudoseogi (no spirit, Western
instrument) 112

National Assembly, South Korea
36–37
National Council of Professors and
Researchers for Democratic and
Equal Society (Mingyohyeop)
40, 61
national-cum-cosmopolitan
developmental initiatives
164–165
National Intelligence Service (NIS),
South Korea 173n1
National Long-Term Care (LTC),
Insurance for the Elderly 52

223

INDEX

National Movement Headquarter for
 Reform and Corruption
 Expulsion in Private Schools 54
"national revival" (*minjokjungheung*)
 69–70
National Security Law
 (*Gukgaboanbeop*) 34, 175n11
National Union of Media Workers
 (Eonlonnojo) 61
neoliberalism 132
 and activism 84, 85
 and *chaebol* system 66, 69–70,
  82–87
 and civil and political rights 167,
  192n3
 and democracy 34, 35, 41, 85–87,
  115
 and "IMF conditionalities" 28, 35,
  41
  and *chaebol* system 66, 70, 84–85
  and labor 89, 104
 and Kim Dae-Jung 28, 84–85, 86
 and labor 17, 34, 89, 104, 191n14
 and neoliberal reformism 82–87,
  115
 and precariatization 17, 90,
  98–103, 104, 167–168, 191n14
 and risk society 7, 19, 145–157
 and social class 66, 123–124, 168
 and working life courses 17, 89,
  104, 167–168
neoliberalism, compressed 82–85
news media. *see* journalism
NGOs (non-governmental
 organizations) 37, 38, 81–82
non-profit foundations 52, 182n5
nuclear power 145, 154
nurses 51, 153, 178n9, 194n21
nurturing 131

offshoring/outsourcing 100, 102, 133,
 185n9
oil tankers 145

"Parasite" movie 121
parenthood 111, 140–141, 169

Park Chung-Hee
 and capitalism 64, 68–69
 and *chaebol* system 42, 68–69, 80
 and corruption 173n1, 180n23
 and democracy 23, 39, 42, 173n1
 military takeover 27, 29, 114
 and economic development 68, 113,
  155
"Park Chung-Hee nostalgia" 34
Park Geun-Hye 33–35
 and censorship 33–34, 121, 186n11
 and corruption 30, 35, 36, 166,
  180n23
 and impeachment 28, 36, 42, 61
 and democracy 24–25, 28, 30,
  186n11
 and capitalism 35, 84
 and state-projective politics 35,
  36, 39, 42
parliament 13, 23, 32, 174n6
 and elections 33, 36, 37, 44
Parsons, Talcott 129
party politics 23, 24. *see also* political
 parties
patriarchy 93–98, 104–105, 144. *see
 also* family life; working life
 courses
 and daughters 138, 140, 141
 and familialization 168, 169
 and marriage 129, 138–139
 and men/sons 139, 140, 169
 and parenthood 140, 141
 and women 129, 134–135,
  138–139, 168
 and younger people 129, 139
patronage 55, 59, 69
People Power Party 25, 39
People's Solidarity for Participatory
 Democracy (Chamyeoyeondae)
 37, 60, 81–82, 183n13
pharmaceutical industry 51, 179n12
physicians. *see* doctors
poisoning, chemical and heavy metal
 146
political parties
 and activism 61, 165–166

224

INDEX

and corruption 59–60, 61
and democracy 26, 29, 33, 59–60,
 166–167
 and state-projective politics 24,
  25, 43–44
politics, democratic 80–82, 182n11,
 182n12, 183n14. *see also*
 democracy
pollution 146
popular culture 110, 121–122, 124,
 188n29, 189n38
postcolonialism 7–8, 10–12, 45–63,
 67–68, 165–171
 and cultural influences 109–124
 and Asian culture 17–18, 109,
  111, 112
 and indigenous societies 11,
  17–18, 112
 and knowledge 109–111,
  115–119
 and Western influences 17–18,
  109, 112, 117–118, 120
 and democracy 25–31
 and authoritarianism 11, 27, 29
 and civil and political rights 27,
  29
 and human rights 29, 174n6,
  174n8
 liberal democracy 23, 25, 27,
  28
 and modernization 31, 174n3
 and institutionalization 14, 47–48
 and risk society 5–6, 7, 173n4
 and Western influences 6, 10–12,
  14, 17–18, 109–124
postcolonialism, reflexive 10, 17–18,
 109–124, 165–171
postmodernism 7
poverty 162, 191n13
precariat 99
precariatization 98–103, 104, 140
 and labor 90, 167–168, 191n14
 and industrial workers 98, 99,
  100, 101–102
precariatization, developmental 99,
 104

precariatization, neoliberal 90,
 98–103, 104, 167–168, 191n14
presidents of South Korea
 conservative presidents 23, 28, 29,
  39, 41, 42
 and corruption
 and impeachment of presidents
  28, 36, 42, 45, 61
 and imprisonment ot presidents
  42, 45
 and Lee Myung-Bak 42, 68, 166
 and Park Chung-Hee 173n1,
  180n23
 and Park Geun-Hye 28, 30, 35,
  36, 42, 61, 166, 180n23
prison sentences 54
problem-solving 15, 47, 55, 62
professional associations 40–41,
 176n31
professions/professionals 39–40, 50,
 60–61
profitability 50, 52, 72, 180n17
progress 20, 122, 164, 165
progressivism, situational 83–84
proletarianization 130, 167
proletariat 88–89, 90–93, 103–105
prosecutions 153, 193n20
public opinion, manipulation of 80,
 181n26
public service 13, 36–37, 82, 150

"quality" mass production (QMP)
 103

rationality, postcolonial reflexive
 165–171
rationalization, social 4
"rebate" payments 51, 179n12
refamiliation 128–129
reflexivity vi, 6, 8, 9, 47, 173n7. *see
 also* cosmopolitanism, reflexive;
 modernization, reflexive;
 postcolonialism, reflexive
reform movements, civil-liberalist 28,
 40–41, 58–62, 81–82, 181n28.
 see also activism

INDEX

reform of *chaebol* system 80–85, 182n11, 182n12, 183n13, 183n14
reformism, neoliberal 82–87, 115
reification 115–119
reinstitutionalization 25
religion 123, 172n2, 188n33
rent-seeking 68, 74–75, 77, 86–87, 182n6
rentier consciousness, institutionalized 113, 186n9
representation, social 13, 31, 166. *see also* self-representation
reproduction, social 125–126, 128
retirement allowance 96, 191n14
Rhee Syng-Man 23, 27, 29, 67, 68, 174n3
rights, civil and political 56, 157
  and democracy 27, 29, 32, 165–166, 175n11, 175n13
  and neoliberalism 167, 192n3
  and postcolonialism 27, 29
rights, human 29, 51, 174n6, 174n8, 179n14
rights, property 65, 71, 189n35
rights, welfare 69
rights, workers' 65, 66, 71, 98–99, 153, 194n21
risk components 145–148. *see also* risk society
risk, democracy as 23–25
risk generation 170
risk injustice 147
risk, modernity as 4–8
risk society 18–19, 145–157, 165–171. *see also* accidents; safety
  and activism 153, 165–166, 169–170, 194n21
  and Beck vi, 3, 7–8, 19, 147–148, 155, 163–165, 172n2
  and compressed modernity 9, 20
  and capitalism 146, 147, 148, 149, 157, 164, 166–167
  and neoliberalism 7, 19, 147, 154, 167

and consumption 156, 157
and disasters 145, 146, 150, 157, 169, 170
and East Asia 157, 170–171
and ecological/environmental issues 145, 146, 169
and economic development 146, 147, 149–150, 151–152, 155–156, 157, 169–170, 194n23
and efficiency 148, 152–153
and industrialization 19, 149, 151, 170, 193n11
and inequalities 146, 154–157
and postcolonialism 5–6, 7, 173n4
and quality of life 19, 146
and repeated inexperience 152, 193n17
and social class 169, 170
and Western influences 149, 151
risk society, complex 18–19, 145–157
risk society, condensive 147, 150–152, 193n17
risk society, developed 147, 148–149
risk society, slapdash 147, 152–154, 155
risk society, un(der)developed 147, 149–150, 193n13
risk society, utilitarian 153
risk, structural 1–20
risks, transformative contributory 154–157, 194n23
rivalry politics 60, 181n28
Roh Moo-Hyun 28, 34, 42, 86, 174n8
Roh Tae-Woo 27, 45
Rueschemeyer, Dietrich 3
rural population 89

safety 151–153, 192n3. *see also* accidents
  and activism 153, 194n21
  and disasters 145, 146, 150, 157, 169, 170
  and economic development 149–150, 151–152, 169–170

226

INDEX

industrial safety 146, 150, 151, 153, 154, 162
  industrial accidents 146, 150, 151, 154, 162
  and industrialization 149, 170
  and nurses 153, 194n21
  and prosecutions 153, 193n20
  and repeated inexperience 152, 193n17
  and workers' rights/working conditions 153, 194n21
Sampoong Department Store, Seoul 145, 150, 193n20
Samsung Group 58, 75, 182n12
schools, private 46, 54–55
security of the state 32–33, 34, 175n13
security, public (*gongan*) 39
segregation, gender 118–119
self-employment 17, 95, 96, 102, 167–168, 185n10
self-representation 13, 31, 37, 175n11
Sentencing Commission, Supreme Court 54
Seongsu Grand Bridge 18, 145, 193n20
servants, familial (*gasin*) 78, 182n8, 182n9
Sewol Ferry sinking 145, 150, 170
shareholders, ordinary 65, 71, 72
silhak (practical scholarship), Chosun 116–117
SK conglomerate 75
SMEs (small and medium-sized enterprises) 100–102, 184n6, 185n10
social class 162. *see also* elite class; precariatization; proletariat; working class
  and capitalism 5, 15–16, 64, 65, 67
  and neoliberalism 66, 123–124, 168
  and *chaebol* system 15–16, 17, 64, 65, 67
  and bourgeoisie 15, 17, 64, 65, 67

  and elite class 66, 82–83, 166–167
  and class relations 17, 184n3
  and collusion 56, 66
  and corruption 46, 50, 58, 60, 162, 166, 181n26, 181n28
  and cultural influences 111, 120–121
  and democracy 23, 29, 33, 166–167, 175n11
  and family life 123–124, 125
  and journalism 58, 181n26
  and risk society 169, 170
  and working life courses 17, 90, 184n3
social concession policy 69–70
social conditions 11, 12, 16–17, 98–103. *see also* family life; working life courses
Social Indicators in Korea 192n3
social movements 13, 37, 117, 162, 165
social relations 6, 88, 129, 173n7
"social safety net" 83, 96
social sciences
  and cultural influences 111–115, 118, 120, 122, 186n7, 187n22
  and democracy 32, 34, 38
social security programs 69–70, 156
socioeconomic order, liberal 4
solidarity, class 90
solidarity, organic 4
sons 139, 140
South Korea. *see* capitalism; compression, developmental; corruption; cultural influences; family life; risk society; working life courses
"standard working life" 96
state policy 69, 155
state-projective politics 13, 23, 31–44
  and activism 37, 38, 44
  and cartels/cartelization 43, 44
  and civil society 40, 44
  and coercion 35, 38, 39, 114

227

INDEX

state-projective politics (*cont.*)
and corruption 24, 36, 41–44, 57,
177n32, 177n34
and financial crisis, South Korea
1997 35, 41
and institutional conflations 26,
36–41, 173n1, 177n31
and career opportunities/political
and government appointments
38, 39, 40
and NGOs (non-governmental
organizations) 37, 38
and professional associations
40–41, 176n31
and journalism 23–24, 37–38,
43–44, 177n34
and Kim Dae-Jung 42, 177n34
and Kim Young-Sam 41, 177n34
and Lee Myung-Bak 24, 25, 28, 30
and military takeovers 13, 27, 29,
32–33, 34, 42
and Park Geun-Hye 35, 36, 39, 42
and parliamentary elections 33, 36,
37, 44
and political parties 24, 25, 43–44
and society-representative
democracy 23, 31–36
and state institutions 23–24, 42–43
and statist representation 32–33,
34–36, 175n12, 175n13
state prosecutors 24, 46, 56–57,
180n23, 180n24, 181n25,
181n26
stock ownership 71–72, 73, 74,
78–79, 182n6, 182n8
subsidization, state 50, 51, 52, 72, 77
success, socioeconomic 111
suicide of presidents 45
suicide rates 162
support, familial 134, 138, 191n16
suppression 29, 56
Supreme Court, Sentencing
Commission 54
survival strategies 123, 155
sweatshops 89, 100
Sweden 79

Taiwan 127, 143, 144, 192n4
Taiwanese social survey 135–136,
143, 144, 191n19
technologies, "advanced" 148–149
textbooks 33, 186n11
theatre presidency 43, 177n33
Therborn, Göran 7
"three-five rule" 54
tourists, medical 53
trade unions 61, 134, 184n3
traditional/indigenous culture
Asian culture 17, 109, 110, 111,
112, 185n4
and China 111, 112
and Confucian capitalism 109,
117
and Confucianism 17–18, 109,
111, 116, 117
and *dongdoseogi* (Eastern spirit,
Western instrument) 109, 110,
111, 112
and universities 116–117, 118, 119,
187n24, 188n25
and Western influences 11, 12,
118–119, 187n24, 188n25
traffic accidents 151
train derailments 145
triangulation 4
trust 78, 182n8
Truth and Reconciliation Commission
174n6
Turner, Bryan S. 7

unemployment 95–96
unintendedness 8, 165–171, 172n2
universities 187n17
and capitalism 49–50, 178n6,
178n7
chaebol system 53, 180n18
and corruption 49–50, 178n6,
178n7
and cultural influences
and humanities and arts 115–119,
188n25
and social sciences 111–115, 120,
186n7, 187n22

228

INDEX

traditional/indigenous culture 116–117, 118, 119, 187n24, 188n25
and Western influences 115, 118–119, 168, 187n24
and foreign students 53, 180n19
unknowns, known 8

value chains 101–102
voting right multiplier (VRM) 78–79, 182n6

wages 69, 98
wakonyosai (Japanese soul and Western skill) 111
waste dumping 146
wealth accumulation 123–124
Weber, Max 4, 172n2
welfare pluralism 50
welfare rights 69
welfare, social 96, 157
 and *chaebol* system 49–50, 52, 53, 179n16, 180n17
 and corruption 46, 55, 60–61
  and capitalism 49, 50, 52
  and care giving institutions 51, 52
  and *chaebol* system 52, 179n16
  and human rights 51, 179n14
  and inmate exploitation 51
 and democracy 44, 99
 and labor 133–134, 191n14
 and profitability 52, 180n17
Western influences 17–18, 45–63, 109–124
 American influences 13, 25, 29, 31, 32, 49, 112
 and corruption 14, 47–48
 and cultural influences 17–18, 109–124
  and cultural consumption 117, 118, 119
  and *dongdoseogi* (Eastern spirit, Western instrument) 109, 110, 111, 112
  and modernization 110, 117, 118, 119

and postcolonialism 17–18, 109, 112, 117–118, 120
and traditional/indigenous culture 11, 12, 118–119, 187n24, 188n25
and universities 115, 118–119, 122, 168, 187n24
and democracy 13, 25, 29, 31, 32, 38
and familialism 124, 131, 189n37
and industrialization 131, 149
and postcolonialism 6, 10–12, 14
 and Asian culture 17–18, 109–124
and risk society 149, 151
Williams, Raymond 7
wives, working 97–98, 105, 139, 184n4, 187n15
women 135–142. *see also* divorce; fertility rates; parenthood
 and education 162
  and family life 105, 139, 169
  and labor 105, 116, 169, 186n15
  and universities 116, 187n17
 and family life 18, 125–144
  as carers 131, 137
  and Confucianism 125, 126, 131
  and daughters 138, 140, 141
  and defamiliation 126, 127, 129, 132, 135, 143
  and East Asia 143–144, 191n19
  and educational attainment 105, 139, 169
  and familism/familialism 131–132, 135, 136, 168, 169
  and individualization/ individualism 18, 125–127, 136
  and patriarchy 129, 134–135, 138–139, 168
  and young women 138, 168, 169
 and financial independence 138, 142
 and individualism 125–127, 136
 and individualization 18, 125–135, 137, 143, 189n1

229

INDEX

women (*cont.*)
and individualization (*cont.*)
and defamiliation 126, 127, 135, 143
and family life 18, 125–127
and labor 126, 189n1
and labor 92–93
and capitalism 125–126
and education 105, 116, 169, 186n15
and individualism/
individualization 126, 189n1
and marriage 105, 125–126
working wives 97–98, 105, 139, 184n4, 187n15
and young women 90, 105, 187n15
and liberal modernization 98, 169
and marriage 105, 125–126, 132, 136–139, 191n19
married women 97–98, 105, 129, 137, 139
never married women 138, 139, 191n19
working class 168, 170
and activism 90, 125, 153, 169, 184n3
working conditions 69, 153, 155–156, 162, 194n21
working life courses 88–105. *see also* labor; patriarchy
and birth-cohort 91, 92–93
and capitalism 88–90, 103–104, 133
and neoliberalism 17, 89, 104, 167–168
and *chaebol* system (industrial conglomerates) 16–17, 103
and East Asia 90, 103
and economic development 89, 90, 94, 95, 103–104, 133, 191n13
and employment stability 94, 97, 100, 103–104, 105, 133, 162

and family life 93–98, 105
and gender 89–93, 105, 184n4
and industrialization 16–17, 89, 90, 91, 94, 96
and "marginal work" 94–95, 96
and men 16, 90, 91, 92, 93–98, 184n4
and capitalism 89, 103, 105
and "marginal work" 94–95, 96
and self-employment 95, 96
and mobility, labor 97, 184n4
and retirement allowance 96, 191n14
and self-employment 17, 95, 96, 102
and social class 17, 90, 184n3
and trade unions 61, 184n3
and women 90, 92–93
and working wives 97–98, 105, 139, 184n4, 187n15
world risk society 9

yahak (night-time schools) 188n27
yeonjwaje (guilt by association) 189n34
Yoon Bo-Sun 27
Yoon Suk-Yeol 25, 46, 154, 175n13, 177n31, 186n12, 193n10
younger people 170
and educational attainment 105, 162, 169
and family life 140, 169
and marriage 129, 137–138, 139
and men 140, 142
and patriarchy 129, 169
and young women 137, 138, 168, 169
and labor 90, 105, 169, 187n15
and young men 140, 142, 169
and young women 90, 105, 137, 138, 168, 169, 187n15